RURAL SOCIOLOGISTS AT WORK

CANDID ACCOUNTS OF THEORY, METHOD, AND PRACTICE

Edited by
Johannes I. ("Hans") Bakker

Routledge
Taylor & Francis Group
NEW YORK AND LONDON

First published 2016
by Routledge
711 Third Avenue, New York, NY 10017

and by Routledge
2 Park Square, Milton Park, Abingdon, Oxon, OX14 4RN

Routledge is an imprint of the Taylor & Francis Group, an informa business

© 2016 Taylor & Francis

The right of the editor to be identified as the author of the editorial material, and of the authors for their individual chapters, has been asserted in accordance with sections 77 and 78 of the Copyright, Designs and Patents Act 1988.

All rights reserved. No part of this book may be reprinted or reproduced or utilized in any form or by any electronic, mechanical, or other means, now known or hereafter invented, including photocopying and recording, or in any information storage or retrieval system, without permission in writing from the publishers.

Trademark notice: Product or corporate names may be trademarks or registered trademarks, and are used only for identification and explanation without intent to infringe.

Library of Congress Cataloging in Publication Data
Rural sociologists at work: candid accounts of theory,
　　method, and practice/Johannes I. ("Hans") Bakker, editor.
　　pages cm
　　Includes bibliographical references and index.
　　1. Sociology, Rural—Study and teaching. 2. Sociology,
　　Rural—Methodology. 3. Sociologists. I. Bakker, J. I.
　　HT411.R866 2016
　　307.72071—dc23
　　2015013084

ISBN: 978-1-61205-867-2 (hbk)
ISBN: 978-1-61205-868-9 (pbk)
ISBN: 978-1-315-67576-3 (ebk)

Typeset in A Caslon and Copperplate
by Florence Production Ltd, Stoodleigh, Devon, UK

Printed and bound in Great Britain by
TJ International Ltd, Padstow, Cornwall

RURAL SOCIOLOGISTS AT WORK

This collection of original chapters, written by prominent social scientists, elucidates the theory and practice of contemporary rural sociology. The book applies lessons from the careers of sociologists and their field research endeavors, covering a wide range of topics: agricultural production, processing, and marketing; international food security and rural development; degradation of the biophysical environment across borders; and the study of community, family, health, and many other issues in an increasingly globalized world. The authors' candid accounts provide insight into possibilities for enhancing opportunity and equality and serving basic human needs.

Johannes I. ("Hans") Bakker is the Stanley Knowles Distinguished Visiting Professor at Brandon University, Manitoba, Canada Emeritus lifetime member of the Rural Sociological Society, and Chair of the Senior Rural Sociologists Research Interest Group.

This book is dedicated to the memories of two rural sociologists, William (Bill) Freudenberg (1951–2010) and Ralph B. Brown (1960–2014), both of whom have made important contributions to the discipline and inspired many others not only in rural sociology but in many other ways. Of particular relevance to the chapters in this book are the following quotations: "The most that any of us can hope for is to make a difference with others and possibly leave the world a bit better than we found it" (William Freudenberg). "What is important is the search for truth—not the defense of it. . . . What draws people to academia and research is a love of learning. . . . Our job is to search for truth not defend it" (Ralph B. Brown).

Table of Contents

ACKNOWLEDGMENTS   IX

CANDID ACCOUNTS BY RURAL SOCIOLOGISTS: EDITOR'S
INTRODUCTION   XI
JOHANNES I. ("HANS") BAKKER

PART I: BACKGROUND ACCOUNTS   1

CHAPTER 1   GENERAL INTRODUCTION   3
LAWRENCE BUSCH

CHAPTER 2   RURAL SOCIOLOGY: A SLIGHTLY PERSONAL
HISTORY   9
STEPHEN TURNER

CHAPTER 3   "I COULD TELL STORIES 'TIL THE COWS
COME HOME": PERSONAL BIOGRAPHY
MEETS COLLECTIVE BIOGRAPHY   35
JULIE N. ZIMMERMAN

Part II: Candid Accounts 63

Chapter 4 An Accidental Rural Sociologist 65
Michael D. Schulman

Chapter 5 From Estate Agriculture to the Industrial Diet: The Trajectory of a Canadian Rural Sociologist 81
Anthony Winson

Chapter 6 The Intersection of Biography and Work as a Rural Sociologist 105
Linda Lobao

Chapter 7 Rural Sociologists at Work: Dual Careers, Single Focus 117
Cornelia Butler Flora and Jan L. Flora

Part III: Theory and Method 141

Chapter 8 Rural Sociology: An Intellectual Crescent Wrench 143
Ralph B. Brown

Chapter 9 Avoiding Burnout: All Who Wander Are Not Lost 155
Conner Bailey

Chapter 10 The Accidental Rural Sociologist 171
Bill Reimer

List of Contributors 193
Index 197

Acknowledgments

The Editor would like to acknowledge the Rural Sociological Society (RSS), especially William (Bill) Lacy. This book has benefited from the support of the Senior Rural Sociologists' Research Interest Group (RIG) of the RSS and from the RSS executive. The Rural Development Institute (RDI) at Brandon University, Brandon, Manitoba, Canada also has provided direct financial and artistic assistance with many drafts of the book cover. This includes its Director, William (Bill) Ashton and freelance designer Alida Grelowski. Special thanks are also extended to the President, and Faculty Senate of Brandon University whose support of the Editor as the Stanley Knowles Distinguished Visiting Professor provided the academic context in which to complete this work. Professor Scott Grills has been a valuable colleague at Brandon. In turn, personal help and capable academic leadership of Professor Wayne Thompson, when he was Chair of Sociology and Anthropology at the University of Guelph, played a significant role in the Editor's entry into the field of rural sociology. Professor J. Heidi Gralinski-Bakker provided significant assistance during the final stage of the editing process.

Candid Accounts by Rural Sociologists

Editor's Introduction

Johannes I. ('Hans") Bakker, *Brandon University*

Why this Book?

Imagine you had the chance to interview a highly productive scholar. Then imagine that the person you were speaking with really opened up about her or his career. Think how beneficial it would be to know some of the background story and to hear the unvarnished truth. That is the inspiration for this book. In this book you will find candid accounts. The authors were asked to write in the same way as they might talk to people in general, particularly students. As far as possible they have avoided the stilted academic prose that is sometimes required by journal editors and university press reviewers. This is a highly personal book. For the most part the authors reveal a great deal about themselves. Some of the authors are a little bit less candid than others, of course, but by and large you will find information in this book that you will not find anywhere else. I myself have learned things about colleagues

I have known for forty years. As a member of the Rural Sociological Society (RSS) I have had numerous opportunities to speak with colleagues. Yet some of the details reported here were never mentioned in countless conversations. I had never known the social class background of some of my colleagues and had no idea of some of the difficulties they faced early in their careers. When someone is highly successful it is easy to assume that it was smooth sailing all the way.

The key idea for this book—*candid accounts*—was motivated by my reading of an edited book by Alan Sica and Stephen Turner (2005): *The Disobedient Generation*. (I will say more about that below.) The title, however, is an intertextual reference to a book many of us read in graduate school: *Sociologists at Work* (Hammond 1964). Another important book that tells us a great deal about sociologists is entitled *Sociological Lives* (Riley 1988), but I learned about that book much later. I realized that there was nothing similar to those three books that focused specifically on the discipline of rural sociology. Hence, we have here: *Rural Sociologists at Work: Candid Accounts of Theory, Methods, and Practice*.

When thinking about ways to succinctly describe the goal of this book, I decided to limit my focus to a brief Introduction. The General Introduction by Professor Lawrence Busch says many of the things I might have said in a longer Editor's Introduction.[1] The significance of the background stories about rural sociology as a discipline, and the personal stories about people's lives, consists of the focus on the interplay between person and context, between the personal and the sociological or "structural." In addition, the accounts clearly bring out the role of experience and serendipity in contributions to the progress of scientific knowledge. In general, the narratives highlight the personal journeys of scholars in rural sociology. How did each person come to be a rural sociologist? Was it somewhat accidental? Moreover, how did their life paths lead to some of their specific contributions to the discipline? How did they get involved in the broader field of rural studies? In some cases, how did rural studies also lead to even broader social science contributions, especially to the political economy and economic sociology traditions (Swedberg 1996:173–206).[2]

On its own, such material adds to the history of rural sociology described clearly by Stephen Turner in his introductory chapter.

We learn about early key figures such as Charles Josiah Galpin (Nelson 1969: 34–44, 181–185) and Carl C. Taylor (1940, Nelson 1969:42–43) as well as more contemporary scholars. At one time, a key figure was Everett M. Rogers (1962), who developed a theory of the diffusion of innovations.[3] However, the chapters of this book concern a new generation that was influenced by the political changes of the later 1960s. Many of us were influenced by the work of Fred Buttel (Buttel and Newby 1980), who was a leader of the new generation, but who unfortunately died far too young (Wikipedia editors 2014).

By focusing (for the most part) on personal accounts, these chapters also provide a picture of ways in which context (at diverse levels of influence) may have made a difference in the paths taken and roads traveled by these scholars during their careers. In some cases, the narratives describe how early experiences contributed to career choices (e.g. Zimmerman, Winson, Schulman); to the meaning(s) attributed to rural sociology (e.g. Brown, Bailey); and to the purpose of the work undertaken (e.g. Lobao; Flora and Flora; Reimer). The personal melds with the interpersonal and professional. In other cases, the narratives describe the ongoing contributions to career of an interplay among diverse (and complex) aspects of people's lives—including those that might be characterized as interactional or social psychological (e.g. Flora and Flora; Lobao) as well as those that might be characterized as more clearly sociological or "structural" (e.g. Reimer). In all of the chapters, the social, cultural, political and economic are linked to the personal.

Indeed, it is clear in these narratives that the interplay between context and career is both bidirectional and ongoing. Consistent with Turner's explication of the earlier context in which these scholars are partially embedded, most describe interests that are oriented toward social justice. Motivated by these interests (and others), the scholars' contributions to rural sociology include efforts aimed at improving the agro-food system and biophysical environment in North America and globally. The authors discuss explicit and implicit research theories they have constructed to help them to explain the phenomena they have experienced. For example, they discuss the environment (e.g. Reimer), obesity and food (e.g. Winson), social class in different regions (e.g. Lobao), and many other specific topics.

Ideas and feelings are discussed in this book about rural sociologists that are not even revealed when having a coffee or tea, a late-night glass of wine or a Saturday afternoon beer (Standage 2005).[4] This book is about people's lives. It is about the authors' lives and about the lives of the people they have attempted to understand and often help. The setting for some of the work has been in areas of the world that are more rural than urban. At the same time, however, the whole notion of the rural has been interpreted not just to mean small towns in the Prairies or family farms in New England. The focus here is the whole world, not just North America. Many of the authors have done extensive research outside North America. Moreover, the stereotypes that many people have of rural places are shattered. This is not a book about the Hallmark card versions of small towns in Vermont, with white Congregational church steeples.

Overview of the Chapters

Each of the chapters is important. The main theme concerns rural sociology as a "discipline" and rural studies as an "interdisciplinary field". Many of the authors have also done multidisciplinary and interdisciplinary work. This book is representative of a few senior rural sociologists from one generation. Many other excellent rural sociologists contributed to this book in various ways and indeed, there is such an abundance of excellent insightful material that Bakker is already planning a second book that will continue along similar lines but will emphasize the linkages between methodology and theory even more.

It should be said that the discipline of rural sociology, although established in the 1930s as a separate discipline, has many intellectual roots in an amalgam of disciplines and fields, as well as political movements. One example is the work of the Marxist writer Chayanov (1966). He had a theory of the "self exploitation" of the labor of family members on the family farm. Another key thinker in the Marxist tradition was (and is, intellectually) Karl Kautsky ([1899] 1988). The significance of Kautsky's work has not always been recognized, in part due to cleavages within Marxist circles (Blackledge 2006). It was only after selections from his famous book on *The Agrarian Question* were translated (Banaji 1976) that my generation of graduate students became aware of his work and its more general relevance. In an early essay (Bakker 1981) I also argue in favor of "Bringing Weber Back In" to theoretical discussions in rural sociology, so I was gratified when reading the complete translation of Kautsky's seminal work to see that he cited early work by Weber on migrant labor in Prussia (Weber [1892] 1984). Weber's importance for rural sociology and *Agrarsoziologie* has been emphasized by Honigsheim (1946, 2000) and by Munters (1972).[5] The work of the famous Canadian student of political economy, Harold Adams Innis ([1930] 1962) cannot be fully understood apart from the ways in which both the Marxist and non-Marxist "Liberal" "political economy" traditions evolved in different paths in England, Germany, Austro-Hungary and Europe generally.

I will not attempt to elaborate on my own Neo-Weberian views here, except to say that my own experience in rural sociology has taught me a great deal about the complex ways in which "rurality" still remains extremely important. Misinterpretations of Weber continue to haunt rural sociology and sociology (Joosse 2014). It should not be assumed that only the insights of Karl Marx are important, of course, and I myself have argued that Mohandas Karamchand ("Mahatma") Gandhi is also an important "Critical Theorist" (Bakker 1983a). Weber's Methodological emphasis on value relevance (*Wertbeziehung*) and value freedom (*Wertfreiheit Werturteilsfreiheit, Wertneutralität*, Eliaeson 1990) sets him apart from both Marx and Gandhi to some extent (Bakker 1983). There is a great deal more that could be said. An excellent starting point is a set of essays that appeared under the capable leadership of Alessandro Bonanno after the International Rural Sociological Association (IRSA) conference in Seoul, South Korea (Bonnano, Bakker, Kawamura, Jussaime, and Shucksmith 2010). In those essays a variety of theoretical and methodological approaches are applied to several different countries and regions of the world.[6]

Chapter 1 General Introduction

In this General Introduction to the book, the eminent rural sociologist, Lawrence Busch, points out that the last four decades have brought significant changes in the discipline of rural sociology and that the biographical information in the personal sketches and background stories in this volume reflect those changes. They also point to the profound changes in rurality around the world. Small producers in the global "South" now compete with large-scale producers in the global "North" in ways that were not possible before World War II. Today, in North America, he points out, there is a "technology treadmill" and "farms" are even more dependent on "cities" than ever before. It can also be said that globally "farms" are dependent on international trade and the world capitalist system. Professor Busch feels that Rural Sociology has come to "a fork in the road."

Chapter 2 Rural Sociology: A Slightly Personal History

As mentioned, Stephen Turner's essay in his co-edited book *The Disobedient Generation* was a key factor in the motivation to assemble a set of candid accounts by rural sociologists. Therefore, it is enormously gratifying that Professor Turner not only agreed to write something for this book, but also chose to write a very solid intellectual contribution to the history of American rural sociology rather than just a superficial Preface. His background story provides a very important context. He details the societal forces that had an important impact on how Rural Sociology was initially framed as a separate discipline rather than just a branch or "section" of general sociology and the association then called the American Sociological Society. He elaborates on ways in which the discipline has continued to retain a commitment to political engagement and solid empirical research. (His own very candid and personal story can be found in Sica and Turner 2005.)

Chapter 3 "I Could Tell Stories 'Til the Cows Come Home": Personal Biography Meets Collective Biography

Julie N. Zimmerman, she did not set out to be specifically a rural sociologist; but, in her case, she did not originally set out to become a historian specialized in the history of a discipline either. Her title reflects her ability to integrate her deeply personal experiences with the historical background of rural sociology as a discipline and rurality as a topic. She has a better understanding of the history of rural sociology than any other sociologist except her mentor, Olaf Larson.

Chapter 4 An Accidental Rural Sociologist

Michael D. Schulman, a former President of the Rural Sociological Society (RSS), did not start out wanting to become a rural sociologist but during his long career he has definitely established himself as a respected member of the Rural Sociological Association, even becoming President. His narrative account may be very helpful to those just setting out either as undergraduates or graduate students. One does not necessarily have to know in advance what one will wind up doing in order to have a very successful career.

Chapter 5 From Estate Agriculture to the Industrial Diet: The Trajectory of a Canadian Rural Sociologist

Tony Winson, like Zimmerman and Schulman, also provides an autobiographical perspective on the ways in which his experiences shaped his theoretical and methodological outlook. Professor Winson has an excellent grasp of many aspects of Marxist and Marxian theory and did an early article on Max Weber's empirical work on rural migration that remains a classic (Winson 1982). Winson is a Canadian academic and his work helps us to remember that North America includes Canada as well as the United States and Mexico (Blake and Nurse 2003). His recent work on what he calls "the industrial diet" is not limited to Canada, however. It is provocative and solidly based in detailed analysis of the facts globally (www.industrialdiet.com). An introduction to rural sociology for undergraduate students can be found in a chapter by Bakker and Winson (1993). We look at the ways in which heuristic ideas put forward by Ferdinand Tönnies (Tönnies [1887] 1940) concerning *Gemeinschaft* & *Gesellschaft* have sometimes been misinterpreted to simply imply a contrast between small, rural communities and large, urban metropolitan places.

Chapter 6 The Intersection of Biography and Work as a Rural Sociologist

Professor Lobao, another former President of the Rural Sociological Society (RSS), provides an overview of her own life story. She is quite forthcoming about her working-class background and some of her early work experiences. Like Michael D. Schulman and Tony Winson, Linda Lobao is quite candid about her life and work. She does not hesitate to reveal some difficulties she has encountered along the way to a sterling career. In a manner similar to other authors she tackles the kinds of problems that Freire (1972) has discussed. Her work has involved true interdisciplinarity, with an empirical focus on large regions rather than just a few counties, and a keen awareness of theoretical and methodological trends in the discipline of human (social) geography, including a rethinking of political economy as broader than just "economics."

Chapter 7 Rural Sociologists at Work: Dual Careers, Single Focus

Both Cornelia and Jan Flora were former Presidents of the Rural Sociological Society. Like other authors, the Floras attempt in their work as rural sociologists to move from problem solving to solution seeking. They believe that engaging people appreciatively in analyzing resources and assets across the capitals often brings new insights. In addition, the story-telling aspect of the discovery stage creates narrative that can be "deconstructed" to identify resources related to each of the capitals.

The Floras view the interaction of three types of "actors" (or agents) as important: the *Market* (consisting of the collectivity of for-profit firms and proprietors), the *State* and the *Common Good* (as articulated through the values that play out through civil society). They cite Karl Polanyi's work, *The Great Transformation* (1944) as part of their focus on the need *not* to separate the factors of production or to reify the notion of an unregulated market. The Floras conclude:

> We were privileged to be a part of several social movements, in both their national and international aspects—feminist, anti-war, ethnic, class, and sovereignty struggles. The movement for

inclusion continues. The importance of informal connections, e.g., social capital in feminist communities of interest, continues to be critical for building toward a feminist and inclusive future. The impact on us as a family, as well as the continued activities of the connections formed in Latin America, Africa, and Asia and between Latin American and North American scholars and activists, can hopefully continue to contribute to the process of changing the world—which is what we set out to do.

Chapter 8 Rural Sociology: An Intellectual Crescent Wrench

Due to his serious illness, Ralph B. Brown was only able to finish a draft of his chapter, but Conner Bailey was in constant communication with Ralph during his last weeks of life. Conner graciously accepted responsibility for going over the manuscript with Ralph and making a few improvements (Hans Bakker also made a few changes.) Ralph then signed off on those changes. If he had lived longer he might have written a longer and more detailed piece. However, as it stands it is not only readable, but also highly stimulating. Ralph had the ability to focus in on what is truly important when discussing any issue. So this chapter is a very welcome addition and the book as a whole is dedicated to Ralph and to another colleague, Bill Freudenberg, who also died way too soon. (Unlike Ralph, Bill did not have time to write even a draft, but like Ralph, he actively encouraged this endeavor.) Blumberg (2004) presents an overview of the importance of a theory-based approach to the study of agrarian civilizations. I believe that if Professor Brown had had more time his very deep knowledge of Southeast Asia and the Middle East would have allowed him to develop his ideas along a comparative historical dimension.

Chapter 9 Avoiding Burnout: All Who Wander Are Not Lost

This chapter by Conner Bailey is also candid and autobiographical, but he emphasizes theory and methods in a way that supplements the views expressed by Brown. They are on the same wavelength when it comes to using the right methodological tools and at the same time remaining committed to social justice. He allows us to see his world and he develops an overview of his career. The specific case study material he discusses helps to illuminate his overall point. Like Ralph Brown, Conner Bailey is highly expert concerning Southeast Asia, but nevertheless very well grounded in the realities of everyday life in rural parts of North America as well. Like several other authors, he is also a former President of the Rural Sociological Society and has been an active participant in the RSS for a long time.

Chapter 10 The Accidental Rural Sociologist

Like Tony Winson, Professor William (Bill) Reimer is also a Canadian. He has been highly successful in helping to organize large-scale projects that have provided an overview of major trends in Canada and the U.S. He contributed to an edited collection on *Rural Sociology in Canada* (Hay and Basran 1992) that deserves to be better known. Many of the statements made by Lawrence Busch in the General Introduction have been extensively researched by Reimer. A fascinating coincidence is that he used essentially the same title for his chapter as Michael Schuman. Both consider themselves to be rural sociologists in part due to accidental factors. Bill's parents were avid explorers and he has definitely continued to follow in their footsteps. His organizational skills have stood him in good stead. He has carried out statistical analysis of macro-level data that is highly sophisticated and not just "abstracted empiricism." He outlines lessons he has learned in his work with the New Rural Economy Project (the NRE). He stresses the importance of rural and urban relations for the revitalization of rurality and the continued adaptation of rural sociology as a discipline.

Relevance and Future Directions

There is a good deal of continuity among all the chapters in terms of an emphasis not only on theory and methods but also on practice. Unfortunately, we do not have space in this relatively short book to fully develop the practice dimension. It would also be nice to move beyond stories by North American rural sociologists to other locations and other disciplinary backgrounds in rural studies. The very notion of "political economy" requires more discussion. As Swedberg (1998) points out, the use of the term "political economy" in English somewhat masks the complexity of the struggle over methods (*Methodenstreit*) and values (*Werturteilstreit*) that marked European debates carried out in the German language, especially before World War I. Those were not just "German" or even "Austro-Hungarian" debates but were widely read outside Central Europe as well. The idea of "economic sociology" is an outgrowth of those debates. Harold Innis (1930, 1962) is a sociologist and rural sociologist precisely because he was also an "institutional economist" and historian. Part of what makes Max Weber a "rural sociologist" (Honigsheim 1946) is the fact that he was also, at the same time, wearing many other hats. He was a historian of agriculture and rural life, an applied anthropologist, a political economist and an astute student of cutting-edge research on the study of comparative religions (Hongisheim 2000). The term "economic sociology" could easily be considered "sociological economics" with the "sociological" being a broadening of the original meaning of the term "political economics." Part of the continuity in the brilliant insights of Karl Marx (1971, 1976) and Max Weber (1968) is precisely due to the fact they were not sociologists in any narrow sense of the word. They did not conform to Durkheimian views (1982). All of that is implicit in many of the chapters of this book, but the intellectual history of the methodology will require further development elsewhere.

There has to be a great deal of selectivity when discussing a topic as complex and wide-ranging as rural sociology, especially when we add rural studies. For example, there is no room here to include excellent work on rural mental health that has been done in Norway by Tom Sorensen, Ralph Klein, and Andreas Sorensen. Sorensen is a medical doctor and he has done a longitudinal project in the Lofoten Islands that is a model of careful investigation and social action.[7] Indeed, there is still much more to say about all three major topics mentioned in the subtitle: theory, methods and practice. Therefore, a second book (by a different publisher) will supplement this one with articles by such prominent rural sociologists as Douglas Constance, Archibald Haller, Alex McIntosh, Tony Fuller, Ken Bessant, Sonya Salamon, and

Alessandro Bonanno among others. Moreover, there are many rural sociologists who will not be represented in either book, even though their ideas have made significant contributions and their life stories are likely of great interest (e.g. Heffernan 1972, 1982; Geisler 2014).[8] Rural sociology is a rich discipline, a fact greatly under-appreciated in social science generally.

Given the unique perspectives presented in this volume, I believe that the work generated by these authors can be helpful to junior colleagues who wonder about the trajectories of their own lives and careers. This work can supplement rural sociology texts; it can also stimulate student (and other) interest in traditional texts about contributions to rural sociology in the RSS "decennial volume series" (e.g. Dillman and Hobbs 1982; Flora, CB and Christenson 1991; Brown and Swanson 2003; Bailey, Jensen, and Ransom 2014). Along similar lines, it is also likely to provide a way to approach the four decades of back issues of *The Rural Sociologist* (up to December 2012) that are now available through the RSS website (http://ruralsociology.org) thanks to Ralph Brown and Jared Friesen.

Graduate students serious about a dissertation in Rural Sociology could start with this book and then work their way through a great deal of the relevant literature much more easily. New undergraduate students can use this book to help them to appreciate the fact that rural sociology is not just a minor off-shoot of general sociology but a vibrant, stimulating and exciting discipline worth pursuing for its intellectual content and its practical value in solving many of the problems facing the world today. The great advantage of this book is that it brings rural sociology alive. Once the spark has been ignited it will become more relevant to go into more depth concerning the past and the future of the discipline and the study of rurality and urbanity in general.

If this set of essays can help inspire a new generation of graduate students, and young academics and professionals, then it will serve an important function. I have frequently mentioned to undergraduate students that they should not ignore the exciting possibilities that a career based in the study of rural sociology and its cousin disciplines, such as agricultural economics and crop science, can offer. It should not always merely be a matter of stumbling into the discipline and becoming an "accidental rural sociologist" (Schuman, Reimer).

Notes

1. In a second volume to be published by Brandon University and the Rural Development Institute at Brandon, I will describe my own background and my specific interest in linking sociological theory to the Logic of Method. A few hints are presented here.
2. We will not always capitalize rural sociology in the chapters that follow, but the capitalization here and there is meant to emphasize the distinction between the *discipline* of "Rural Sociology" per se and the broader multidisciplinary (and occasionally interdisciplinary) *field* of rural studies. All the authors contributing to this book (other than Stephen Turner) are rural sociologists even though they may also have contributed to other disciplines, like sociology and geography as well as multidisciplinary teams of researchers.
3. Rogers carried out many empirical research studies and he suggested a research theory that was widely used around the world for the study of diverse cases. Extension agents used the theory to study diffusion of hybrid corn, fertilizers and other innovations in agriculture. Today, some of the assumptions made in the 1950s and early 1960s have been severely criticized.
4. Standage is not a rural sociologist, but his popular book about the consumption of beverages touches on the political economy of agricultural commodities and "staples" in many ways.
5. A full comprehension of any thinker requires reading her or his work in the original language. The journal *Sociologia Ruralis* translates Munters's Abstract into three languages. The German version of Munters's thesis statement uses "agrarian sociology" (*Agrarsociologie*). "Rural sociology is not innocent of a certain 'professional blindness.'" *La sociologie rurale n'est pas à l'abri d'un certain 'aveuflement perofessionanel.'*" "*Die Agrarsociologie ist an dieser 'Betriebsblindheit' nicht schuldlos*" (Munters 1972: Abstract).
6. The International Rural Sociological Association (IRSA) conference will next be held in Toronto, Canada, in August, 2016. The IRSA conferences draw scholars from around the world, not only from rural sociology.
7. Sorensen, Kleiner and Sornsen 2014. "Psychiatry on the Same Path as Rural Sociology: Research on the Lofoten Islands, Norway." Unpublished paper presented at the RSS conference in New Orleans, August 2, 2014.
8. Professor Heffernan feels that he is too busy running his farm and experimenting with using new methods of production to publish more at this time. His work is central to the Missouri School discussed by Stephen Turner.

Bibliography

Bailey, C., L. Jensen, and E, Ransom (Eds.). 2014. *Rural America in a Globalizing World: Problems and Prospects for the 2010s*. Morgantown, WV: West Virginia University Press.

Bakker, J. I. (Hans). 1981. "Bringing Weber Back In: Rural Values, Social Class, and Rural Sociology." *The Rural Sociologist* 1:221–230 (see http://ruralsociology.org).

Bakker, J. I. (Hans). 1983. *Toward A Just Civilization*. Toronto: Canadian Scholars' Press.

Bakker, J. I. (Hans) and Anthony Winson. 1993. "Rural Sociology," pp. 500–517 in *Contemporary Sociology: Critical Perspectives*, edited by P. S. Li and B. S. Bolaria. Toronto: Copp Clark Pitman, Longman.

Banaji, Jarius. 1976. "Summary of Selected Parts of Kautsky's *The Agrarian Question.*" *Economy and Society.* 5 (1):1–49.

Blackledge, Paul. 2006. "Karl Kautsky and Marxist Historiography." *Science & Society.* 70 (3):337–359.

Blake, Raymond, and Andrew Nurse (Eds.) 2003. *The Trajectories of Rural Life: New Perspectives on Rural Canada.* Regina, Saskatchewan: Canadian Plains Research Center.

Blumberg, Rae Less. 2004. "Extending Lenski's Schema to Hold Up Both Halves of the Sky—a Theory-Guided Way of conceptualizing Agrarian Socieities that Illuminates a Puzzle about Gender Stratification." *Sociological Theory* 22 (2):278–291.

Bonnano, A., J. I. (Hans) Bakker, Y. Kawamura, R. Jussaime, and M. Shucksmith (Eds.) 2010. *From Community to Consumption: New and Classical Themes in Rural Sociological Research.* Bingley, UK: Emerald Publishing Company.

Brown, David, and Louise E. Swanson (Eds.) 2003. *Challenges for Rural America in the Twenty-First Century.* University Park, PA: Pennsylvania State University Press.

Brown, David, and Kai Schafft. 2011. *Rural People and Communities in the 21st Century: Resilience and Transformation.* New York: Polity.

Buttel, Frederick H. and Howard Newby (Eds.) 1980. *The Rural Sociology of the Advanced Societies: Critical Perspectives.* Monclair, NJ and London: Allanheld, Osmon/Croom Helm.

Chayanov, A. V. 1966. *Theory of Peasant Economy*, edited by D. Thorner and R. Smith. Homewood, IL: Richard D. Irwin.

Constance, Douglas H. 2008. "The Emancipatory Question: The Next Step in the Sociology of Agrifood Studies." *Agriculture and Human Values* 25:151–155.

Constance, Douglas H. 2014. "Rural Sociology," pp. 62–74 in *Encyclopedia of Agricultural and Food Systems, Vol. 5,* edited by Neal K. Van Alfen. San Diego, CA: Elsevier.

Constance, Douglas H., and William D. Heffernan. 1991. "The Global Poultry Agrifood Complex," *International Journal of Sociology of Agriculture and Food* 1:126–141.

Dillman, Don, and Daryl J. Hobbs (Eds.) (1982) *Rural Society in the U.S.: Issues for the 1980s.* Boulder, CO: Westview Press.

Durkheim, Emile [1895] 1982. *The Rules of Sociological Method*, translated by W.D. Halls. New York: Free Press.

Eliaeson, Sven. 1990. "Influences on Max Weber's Methodology." *Acta Sociologica* 33 (1): 15–30.

Flora, Cornelia B. (Ed.) 2001. *Interactions Between Agroecosystems and Rural Communities.* Boca Raton: CRC Press.

Flora, Cornelia B., and James A. Christenson (Eds.) 1991. *Rural Policies for the 1990s.* Boulder, CO: Westview Press.

Flora, Jan L., and Cornelia B. Flora. 1991. "Local Economic Development Projects: Key Factors." pp. 141–156 in *Rural Community Economic Development,* edited by N. Walzer. New York: Praeger Publishers.

Freire, Paulo (1972). *Pedagogy of the Oppressed.* New York: Herder & Herder.

Geisler, Charles. 2014. "Disowned by the Ownership Society: How Native Americans Lost Their Land." *Rural Sociology* 79 (1):56–78.

Hammond, Phillip E. (Ed.) 1964. *Sociologists at Work.* New York: Basic Books.

Hay, David A., and Gurcharan S. Basran (Eds.) 1992. *Rural Sociology in Canada.* Toronto: Oxford University Press.

Heffernan, William D. 1972. "Sociological Dimensions of Agricultural Structures in the United States." *Sociologia Ruralis* 12:481–499.
Heffernan, William D. 1982. "Structure of Agriculture and Quality of Life in Rural Communities," pp. 337–346 in *Rural Society in the U.S.: Issues for the 1980s*, edited by D. A. Dillman and D. J. Hobbs. Boulder, CO: Westview Press.
Honigsheim, Paul. 1946. "Max Weber as Rural Sociologist." *Rural Sociology* 11 (3):207–218.
Honigsheim, Paul. 2000. *The Unknown Max Weber*, edited by Alan Sica. New Brunswick, NJ and London: Transaction Publishers.
Innis, Harold Adams. 1930. *The Fur Trade in Canada*. New Haven, CT: Yale University Press.
Innis, Harold Adams. 1962. *The Fur Trade in Canada*. Revised edition prepared by S. D. Clark and W. T. Easterbrook. Toronto: University of Toronto Press.
Joosse, Paul. 2014. "Becoming a God: Max Weber and the Social Construction of Charisma." *Journal of Classical Sociology*. 14 (3):266–283.
Kautsky, Karl. [1899] 1988. *The Agrarian Question*. London: Zwan.
Kearney, Richard. 2003. *Strangers, Gods and Monsters: Interpreting Otherness*. London and New York: Routledge.
Marx, Karl. [1863] 1971. Capital, Vol. 4, *Theories of Surplus Value*. Moscow: Progress.
Mark, Karl [1867] 1976. Capital, Vol. 1, *Critique of Political Economy*. London: Penguin.
Merschrod, K. (2008). *A Sociology: The Dynamics of Collectivities and Their Application to Social Change and Development*. Ithaca, NY: lulu.com
Munters, Q. J. 1972. "Max Weber as Rural Sociologist." *Sociologia Ruralis*. 12 (1):129–146.
Nelson, Lowry. 1969. *Rural Sociology: Its Origin and Growth in the United States*. Minneapolis, MN: University of Minnesota Press.
Polanyi, Karl. [1944] 1957, 2001. *The Great Transformation: The Political and Economic Origins of Our Time*. Boston, MA: Beacon Press.
Riley, Matilda White (Ed.) 1988. *Sociological Lives*. Newbury Park, CA: Sage.
Rodefeld, Richard D., Jan L. Flora, Donald Voth, Isao Fujimoto, and James Converse (Eds.) 1978. *Change in Rural America: Causes, Consequences, and Alternatives*. St. Louis: C.V. Mosby.
Rogers, Everett M. 1962. *Diffusion of Innovations*. New York: Free Press of Glencoe.
Sica, Alan, and Stephen Turner (Eds.). 2005. *The Disobedient Generation: '68ers and the Transformation of Social Theory*. Chicago: The University of Chicago Press.
Standage, Tom. 2005. *A History of the World in 6 Glasses*. New York: Walker & Company.
Swanson, L. E. (Ed.) *Agricultural and Community Change in the U.S.: The Congressional Research Reports*. Boulder, CO: Westview Press.
Swedberg, Richard. 1998. *Max Weber and the Idea of Economic Sociology*. Princeton, NJ: Princeton University Press.
Taylor, Carl C. 1940. "The Contribution of Sociology to Agriculture," pp. 1042–1055 in U.S. Department of Agriculture. *Farmers in a Changing World: The Yearbook of Agriculture 1940*. Washington, DC: U.S. Government Printing Office. With a Foreword by Claude R. Wickard and Henry A. Wallace.
Tönnies, Ferdinand. [1887] 1940. *Fundamental Concepts of Sociology (Gemeinschaft und Gesellschaft)*, translated by C. P. Loomis. New York: American Book Company.

Weber, Max. [1922] 1968. *Economy and Society*, translated and edited by G. Roth and C. Wittich. Berkeley, CA: University of California Press.

Weber, Max. [1892] 1984."Die verhältnisse der Landarbeiter im ostelbischen Deutschland." Gesamtausgabe Section I, volume. III. Frankfurt: Mohr Siebeck.

Wikipedia contributors, "Frederick H. Buttel," *Wikipedia, The Free Encyclopedia*, http://en.wikipedia.org/w/index.php?title=Frederick_H._Buttel&oldid=*527291578* (accessed October 30, 2014).

Wimberley, Ronald C. 2009. North Carolina State University's Rural Sociology Program in the College of Agriculture and Life Sciences and in the Department of Sociology and Anthropology." Unpublished paper presented at NCSU on March 9, 2009.

Winson, Anthony. 1982. "The 'Prussian Road' of Agrarian Development: a Reconsideration." *Economy and Society* 11 (4):381–408.

Young, Frank W. 1970. "Reactive subsystems." *American Sociological Review* 35:297–307.

Young, Frank W. 1999. *Small Town in Multilevel Society*. New York: University Press of America.

Young, Ruth C. 1968. "A Structural Approach to Development." *Journal of Developing Areas* 2:363–375.

PART I
BACKGROUND ACCOUNTS

1
GENERAL INTRODUCTION

LAWRENCE BUSCH, *MICHIGAN STATE UNIVERSITY*

The past forty years have brought profound changes in both rural societies and Rural Sociology, many of which are reflected in the biographical sketches contained in this volume. Whereas even as late as the 1970s an argument could be made that US cities were dependent on farms, there is little doubt today that farms are dependent on cities. Put differently, virtually no US farms produce their own food. Nearly all farm products are inputs into either food manufacturing (despite growing interest in farmers' markets and community-supported agriculture), and the vast majority of farmers are now dependent on the agricultural input industry for seeds, pesticides, fertilizers and machinery. Indeed, led by the poultry industry in the 1940s (Sawyer 1971), farm practices are more and more delimited by the demands of input producers and output purchasers. Input producers determine who can plant what seed and what can(not) be done with the harvest. If Monsanto is successful, it will even determine planting, harvesting, irrigation and other aspects of farm production (Bennett 2014) for many farmers. And output processors increasingly demand particular seed varieties, cosmetic qualities, harvest dates, packaging and delivery times so as to serve the food-processing and supermarket sectors. The situation is hardly different in Canada, and in much of Europe, Japan, Australia, and New Zealand.

Of course, there are still far too many poor farmers in the world, each trying to eke out a living—often on very small farms. As a result of improved transportation and better communications, as well as declining trade barriers, they are often in direct competition with small producers in other nations and/or with far better capitalized and subsidized farmers in the rich world. Hence, in many instances, those remaining in rural areas are those who, for one reason or another, could not make it in the city. And it was noted recently that the world has reached the tipping point in terms of settlement: more than half of all people now live in cities.

Moreover, environmental concerns, hardly discussed in terms other than of conservation a century ago, were only on the horizon for many people in the 1970s. There was certainly concern about overuse of pesticides and of "the limits to growth" (Meadows, Meadows, Randers, and Behrens, 1972), but the contemporary environmental issues with respect to agriculture—methane from cows, fertilizer runoff, energy consumption in production and distribution, declining biodiversity in crop plants and farm animals, among others—were rarely noticed or discussed by rural sociologists. Today, environmental issues are front and center; entirely rural issues are perhaps too rapidly becoming a residual category.

Similarly, while forty years ago there were still many vibrant though often declining rural communities, today there are fewer of them and they are far less isolated and different from larger urban areas. Readers of this volume will already be aware that the technology treadmill (Cochrane 1993) has led to ever-larger farms. With the decline of the farm population, the rural communities that serviced those farmers and their families have declined as well. Similarly, in mining and fishing communities, new technologies have displaced thousands of workers. In addition, the Wal-Mart-ization of the countryside, combined with the aging of the rural and farm populations, has played a considerable role in hollowing out the downtowns of hundreds of rural communities.

But of arguably greater consequence is how the Internet has begun to dissolve the rural/urban differences that were once the central concerns of Rural Sociology. By this I mean not the superficial differences, such as those rightly derided by Howard Newby (1980) as analogous to the difference between Sunday morning and Tuesday afternoon behavior, but the profound differences in outlook and behavior that once made for sharp distinctions. As the British essayist, G. K. Chesterton (1919, 180), put it nearly a century ago:

> The man who lives in a small community lives in a much larger world. He knows much more of the fierce varieties and uncompromising divergences of men. The reason is obvious. In a large community we can choose our companions. In a small community our companions are chosen for us. Thus in all extensive and highly civilized societies groups come into existence founded upon what is called sympathy, and shut out the real world more sharply than the gates of a monastery.

Today, this distinction between small communities and large urban agglomerations is evaporating. It is not merely that the transport and communications systems are far better than they were in the past. Nor is it that cities, especially in the United States, now sprawl over vast suburbs. It is that, largely because of the embrace of personal computers, the Internet and the cell phone, even many of the residents of small rural villages can *choose* their companions. The interests for a small town banker or grocery store owner are such that he (and it is still mostly he) can be in touch instantly with other like-thinking persons. Even farmers, especially those with large operations, once seen as the quintessential example of rural life, are far more likely to be in contact with those with similar views in farm organizations, agricultural supply chains and like-minded friends located some distance from their respective farms. As Davis and Hinshaw (1957) foresaw, many farmers now wear a business suit; they are as much at home with commodities brokers and input suppliers as they once were with their neighboring farms.

It appears to me that, as a result of these transformations, Rural Sociology has come to the proverbial fork in the road. It is nearly impossible to go forward since much of the subject matter no longer exists, but it is possible to pursue other roads not yet taken. Many of those other roads involve interdisciplinary activities with other social sciences such as geography, as well as with various branches of the biological sciences.

The goal of the book is to allow the background story to become a bit clearer. Some of the chapters are fairly candid about the trajectories that rural sociologists have had in their careers. Several authors came to rural sociology somewhat by chance. Indeed, I was one of those persons, coming to rural sociology largely as a result of the cancelation of a Peace Corps program for junior high school social studies teachers in Nigeria and reassignment to an agricultural program in Guinea. After three and a half years in Guinea and Togo as a beekeeper, I was hooked.

However, after obtaining my Ph.D. at Cornell, I was somewhat frustrated by the directions in which the field was going at that time, both in terms of theory and methods. After several years of largely fruitless attempts to use county-level data to examine rural industrialization and healthcare delivery, I realized that the agricultural scientists across the hall offered a more interesting and more important topic—at least to me. Study of the organization of agricultural research in partnership with Bill Lacy (Busch and Lacy 1983) led to further studies of specific issues in plant biology—the (then) new biotechnologies and crop biodiversity, among others. As I entered these fields previously unknown to me, I also began to realize the limitations of sociology; by participating in meetings, as well as engaging in discussions and joint research with biological scientists, philosophers and economists, among others, I began to realize that rural sociology need not stop at the narrowly defined social, that material culture mattered as well.

Then, again fortuitously, I was confronted with endless talk about standards—for seeds, grain, meal, oil, and margarine—while wandering around in canola fields in Saskatchewan. I began to realize that standards were not merely technical rules, but also the means by which social life was organized (Busch 2011). Moreover, I learned that when standards became taken for granted they took on a life of their own.

As I approach the end of my career, I realize that students interested in the discipline of rural sociology or the broader field of rural studies will find this a helpful way to be introduced to topics that cannot be covered in quite the same way in textbooks. I myself learned a few things about colleagues who I have known for years. Also, some of the authors in this collection have pursued topics with which I am less familiar. I recommend this book to anyone interested in the "candid accounts" and the cogent comments on theory, methods and practice found in separate chapters. Moreover, the various contributions to this volume should help to provide some options by re-examining the past so as to orient the future.

Bibliography

Bennett, Drake. 2014. "What are They Doing at Monsanto?" *BusinessWeek*, July 7–13, pp. 52–59.
Busch, Lawrence. 2011. *Standards: Recipes for Reality*. Cambridge, MA: MIT Press.
Busch, Lawrence and William B. Lacy. 1983. *Science, Agriculture, and the Politics of Research*. Boulder, CO: Westview Press.
Chesterton, Gilbert K. 1919. *Heretics*. London: John Lane.
Cochrane, Willard. 1993. *The Development of American Agriculture*. Minneapolis, MN: University of Minnesota Press.
Davis, John H. and Kenneth Hinshaw. 1957. *Farmer in a Business Suit*. New York: Simon & Schuster.
Meadows, Donella H., Dennis L. Meadows, Jørgen Randers, and William W. Behrens III. 1972. *The Limits to Growth*. New York: Universe Books.
Newby, Howard. 1980. "Trend Report: Rural Sociology." *Current Sociology* 28:3–109.
Sawyer, Gordon. 1971. *The Agribusiness Poultry Industry*. New York: Exposition Press.

2

Rural Sociology

A Slightly Personal History

Stephen Turner, *University of South Florida*

This chapter presents a brief history of American Rural Sociology. It discusses the key early figures, such as C.J. Galpin, Kenyon Butterfield, Dwight Sanderson, and Thomas Carver Nixon. But the focus is on the next generation, and the distinctive institutional character of rural sociology as it developed in the twenties and thirties, and evolved in relation to events in the postwar period. Rural sociology shared many features with the "Social Survey" movement, including its commitment to community development, and to some extent its methods. The "Survey Movement" petered out, for reasons having to do with the willingness of communities to subject themselves to the kind of scrutiny needed for reform. The community studies of Rural Sociology were caught between similar forces, and were also politically vulnerable. Postwar rural sociology responded to these vulnerabilities, but faced changes in agriculture that undermined the original purpose of improving rural life. The field nevertheless retained its commitment to engagement, and found new ways of doing so. In this respect, it deviated significantly from general, which had an acrimonious split from the survey movement. Ironically, however, general sociology has returned to engagement, at a time that rural sociology has lost its original subject matter and raison d'être.

Introduction

American rural sociology has a distinctive history, deeply rooted in the tradition of land grant universities, with its arrangement of three institutions, the college of agriculture, the agricultural experiment station, and the cooperative extension service, but also rooted in the campaigns to improve Rural Life of the Country Life Commission, and beyond that the social reform movements of the late nineteenth century. The interest in rural sociology was not simply American, however. There are international analogues to all of these institutions, as well as to the early efforts to survey rural life: both Germany and Sweden had large-scale surveys around the turn of the twentieth century. The German one was done by the *Verein für Sozialpolitik*, the Social Policy association, contributed to by a youthful Max Weber, who also produced a dissertation on agrarian history ([1909] 1976).[1] Yet these studies did not lead directly to institutionalization in universities and to an academic discipline operating alongside and in relation to general sociology, as they did in America, though a variant form, of folk studies, became important in central Europe and Romania.

The Country Life Commission, and the extensive, fretful, discussion of the decline of the Rural Church that accompanied and followed it, were both part of the vast movement for social reform of the late nineteenth and early twentieth century. Rural sociology, as a discipline and institution, in ways that contrast to parallel developments in "General Sociology," retained features of these origins in reformism. The passage from reform movement to academic discipline was complex and fraught. But the history repays study. Rural sociology is one of the most elaborate and sustained cases of the institutionalization of engaged scholarship, that is to say scholarship that has simultaneously attempted to speak to, for, and about its audience, and to do so within complex larger structures with which it was necessary to conform and creatively adapt: universities and schools of agriculture and the ever-changing structure of governmental agricultural work, including extension, federal research and policy, and the political structures that support this system.

This volume of autobiographies is significant because it records a significant new phase in the history of the field, during which there was the need to adapt to radical changes, indeed, the disappearance, of its original subject matter, a disappearance in which this same set of institutions played a role. In this introduction, I will give a history, though a personal history, of rural sociology. It will reflect my own point of view, as a historian of general sociology who has always taken account of rural sociology (Turner 1990, 2014), and as a participant of sorts, during my time as a graduate student in a joint department of sociology and rural sociology.

The Social Movement Background

American rural sociology, like American sociology itself, grew directly out of the movements for social reform that developed after the American Civil War. "Education" and publicity, as well as claims to expertise, were central to these movements. The rural population was exposed to them through Chautauquas, camp meetings with an educational program that, as Merle Curti put it, "provided an outlet for pent-up emotions, a balm for frustrated hopes, and a source of uplift and recreation for isolated rural populations" (1938:761). But they were more than this: such causes as prison reform were promoted by speakers who were adept at combining stories, personal experience, and reform ideas in a satisfying, edifying, package. The scale of reform activity was astonishing. Dozens of organizations, from missionary societies and the Women's Christian Temperance Union to anti-poverty organizations, the Home Efficiency movement, the American Purity Alliance, the Antipoverty League, the Anti-Saloon League, the Postal Progress League (which worked for rural free delivery), Arts and Crafts Societies, and so forth—a seemingly endless list of causes. These movements and organizations took up special aspects of the cause of reform, but also supported one another. Sociology was a tiny offshoot of these movements, their academic arm. And in the beginning the relations between sociology and these movements and their charitable organizations, such as the Charity Organization Society and the Settlement Houses, was close. Most of the early graduate degrees in sociology went to people who were employed in charities and the shift to a preponderance of academic careers only took place after World War I.

Progressivism as a movement, which dates from around 1910, grew out of these social reform movements, brought them together, and imposed a degree of intellectual order and consistency on the project of reform. Central to the Progressive movement was the idea of science, and the belief in experts speaking directly to and energizing the people in the cause of reform. The Country Life Commission was established by Theodore Roosevelt, who was to become the standard-bearer of the Progressive Party in the 1914 elections, and much of the thinking of early rural sociology not only shared the basic outlook of "Progressivism," but also shared sources. As with other areas of reform, there were both public and private efforts. Where the urban efforts had the support of the Russell Sage Foundation and the state and national bureaus of labor statistics, much of the work on the rural church was sponsored by such institutions as the Presbyterian board of home missions, or the Rockefeller funded Institute for Social and Religious Research, as well as such official bodies as the Country Life Commission. Schools of agriculture participated in the commission, and were expected to play a major role in implementing its recommendations. The rural version of progressivism did not go by this name, but there was a distinctive ideological flavor to its activities and passions, just as with progressivism generally. But the rural version, because it was institutionalized within the system of agricultural education, extension, and research, survived even as the urban version faded.

The Social Survey movement institutionalized the practice of reform in a particular way, by attempting to bring the forces of reform together, in one community after another. These surveys were very different from what we now think of as surveys. They were designed to feed knowledge back to the community in order to spur and inform the forces of community regeneration. The great urban surveys of

Pittsburgh and Springfield stressed publicity. These surveys produced exhibit halls with many displays, especially maps with pins in them representing facts, such as the location of diseases, and opened the halls to citizens and schoolchildren, who were brought there in droves. The technique was to combine the knowledge of community leaders who were involved in different phases of aid—charities, health workers, and the directors of charitable institutions, such as orphanages—together to share information and seek common solutions. But the key was education or publicity: to show the citizens what needed to be done and, incidentally, to show them who needed to lead them.

C. J. Galpin pioneered a rural version of these surveys at the same time, but with different methods, methods that were even more participatory than the urban surveys. He recruited school systems into projects that illustrated social facts in an easily comprehensible form. He employed spot maps, "a simple form of graph easily comprehended by the child and well within his ability to make" (1918:333). Almost any statistical fact could be represented on these maps, such as "the number of any significant class of machines or appliances for use in the home or on the farm" (1918:333). They were "well-adapted for making an impression as exhibits at school fairs, community fairs, and even county and state fairs" (1918:334). They also contained a lesson, directed at the isolated hoe farmer and especially at his children: prosperity and social connectedness went hand in hand.

Readings in Rural Sociology edited by John Phelan and published in 1920, with 600 pages of short articles, some from academic sources, some from the country press, gives a clear idea of what the sources were. Paul Kellogg, editor of *The Survey*, the main organ of "social work" and the social survey, is represented by an article on the aims of the survey ([1912] 1920), followed by C. J. Galpin with examples of surveys in rural communities ([1912] 1920). Lewis Hine, a participant in the Pittsburgh Survey, was represented with an article on "Children or Cotton" ([1913–1914] 1920). Like the "social workers" around the survey movement, the topics ranged across problem areas and institutions, but with some distinctive foci: regional differences were important, with each region represented by several chapters. Policy, especially the need for a farm policy, was explicitly discussed. Co-operativism, tenant farming, immigrant farmers, child labor and farm labor generally, machinery, and economics were examined. But the bulk of the book was about institutional facts: rural health, both physical and mental, recreation and the arts, communication and transportation, policing and corrections (including prison agriculture), the home, the schools, extension, and of course the country church, the village, and what would now be called "development": how to organize a community, leadership, and an examination of the organizations representing rural interests.

The tone of these essays was generally constructive and optimistic: "progress" was both a goal and a focus. However, "progress" meant something quite specific. All across the world in the late nineteenth century and after, rural people were migrating to the cities in large numbers, leaving small towns and villages in decline. E. A. Ross called this "folk depletion" (1916): under different names this topic, especially questions about who left the farm and how they differed from those who did not, became a major theme of rural sociological research. It is an important feature of this research and the thinking that went along with it that farm-leaving was part of the personal experience of not only virtually all the early rural sociologists, but of many "general" sociologists as well. E. A. Ross was a farm boy himself. And the experience was part of the family history of many of those who were not farmers. My own grandfather, who became a YMCA worker and thus part of the institutional machinery of social service that grew out of the reform movements, grew up on an Indiana farm. I was with him in 1962 when he returned to the farm for the last time. It was, of course, long since sold, consolidated with other farms. We went to the overgrown country graveyard where his parents and his siblings who had died in childhood were buried. When we drove through one nearby (much depleted) village he commented, "ten lived and eleven starved to death." Most, in fact, had simply left.

Those who abandoned these small towns, villages, and farms left behind threatened institutions, such as the rural church, and pockets of impoverished and socially disconnected farm families, notably, in America, the "poor hoe farmers" who resisted schooling for his children, agricultural innovation, and modern amenities. The transformation of rural life and its unequal consequences, and especially the problem of preserving and improving rural life and rural institutions, led to the great themes of early rural sociology: the diffusion of innovation, the study of the rural church and of rural education, and studies of migration as social mobility, and especially the study and conceptualization of "community" and the relation between town and country.

The First and Second Generations

The founders of Rural Sociology were committed to rural sociology not so much as a career, but as a cause. But they were also intellectually serious. C. J. Galpin was the son of a minister, and arrived at the University of Wisconsin to serve as a student pastor, after having taught zoology as a professor. He had no Ph.D., but he had an M.A. from Harvard, where he had taken several courses each from Hugo Munsterberg, the psychologist of work who served Harvard as a connection to German social science, including Weber, and metaphysics from Josiah Royce and William James, the leading philosophers of their era. Kenyon Butterfield also had no Ph.D., but he had served as a college president before becoming a commissioner on the Commission on Country Life. He was the primary mover behind the Smith-Lever Act, which created the Co-operative Extension Service. Dwight Sanderson had been a state entomologist, Professor of Zoology, and head of a society for economic entomology before going to the University of Chicago for a Ph.D. in Sociology. Harvard Professor Thomas Nixon Carver was an economist who taught the only course in Sociology at Harvard before the establishment of a sociology department in the 1930s. Carver, who grew up on a farm, was prolific, writing twenty-five books, including an introduction to Sociology and several works on the rural church, in addition to his theoretical writings in economics and work in agricultural economics.

The emergence of the field of Rural Sociology under the influence of these men has been well described. The field has had excellent chroniclers, notably Lowry Nelson, whose *Rural Sociology* ([1948] 1969) is a model of disciplinary history and sociological analysis, Edmund de Brunner (1935, 1955), Frederick Buttel and Howard Newby's *The Rural Sociology of the Advanced Societies* (1980), and, more recently, the volumes by Julie Zimmerman and colleagues dealing with rural sociology in the USDA (Larson et al. 1992, 2003; Zimmerman et al. 2010). Nelson's book is about the period in which rural sociology secured its place in colleges of agriculture, created its own society and journal, and defined its relation to sociology generally.

When Rural Sociology became institutionalized, sociology was becoming institutionalized as well, but the paths of the two fields diverged. Sociology, especially after encouraging the separation of social work into a professional field, became and strived to be a conventional academic discipline, with a bounded topic among the social sciences, with a defined set of methods, a set of disciplinary journals, and a base in undergraduate instruction. Rural sociology had a different structure: its research was supported within the framework of the agricultural research complex, and developed in relation to its other functions, notably the extension service. The USDA had a Farm Research arm that employed sociologists and was directed by sociologists. Until the National Science Foundation began to support sociology in the fifties, there was nowhere else in the federal government that provided a stable place for sociology.

Dwight Sanderson's department at Cornell was a leader in producing Ph.D.s in rural sociology, at a time when the depression had cut demand for general sociology Ph.D.s to almost nothing. At the time of his death in 1944, a tribute explained his achievement:

> That the department which he directed became recognized as a leading one in the United States is evidenced by the large number of graduate students who come to Cornell to study in this field. In the last quarter century, 40 students have taken the doctor's degree in rural sociology, in addition to the large number who received the master's degree. Practically all of these men now hold responsible positions in the field of rural sociology in colleges of agriculture, experiment stations, and in the United States Department of Agriculture, as well as in several foreign countries.
>
> (http://ecommons.library.cornell.edu/handle/1813/17813)

These students and their peers elsewhere were the second generation. This was a distinctive and quite different group from the first generation. From this time into the 1970s, Rural Sociology departments were composed, especially at the senior ranks, of people who were from rural or small town backgrounds. They were not necessarily from farms directly, but often came from the institutional world of rural life—churches, the extension service, schools, and so forth. Their engagement with the subject was personal—they cared about country folk, about their well-being, and about improving their lives. And this permeated their work.

What was the work? Cornell was a leading department, perhaps the best. Rural sociology as a field, however, had only a few Ph.D. programs. The subject was taught in many general sociology departments, but many states had no program in the land grant college of agriculture. Missouri had a more typical Ph.D. program, and one that is well documented. A review of what it did during the 1930s and 40s can tell us a great deal about how the field worked and what it did.

Missouri had one of the earliest general sociology departments, dating from 1900, with the arrival of Charles Ellwood, himself from a small farming community in upstate New York, and a graduate of Cornell and the University of Chicago. Ellwood included rural sociology in the department. He was the teacher and also friend of Carl C. Taylor, who received a Ph.D. in sociology in 1920 for a study of a nearby village, and went on to a distinguished career in Rural Sociology, both at universities, such as North Carolina State and the USDA, finishing it as President of the American Sociological Society itself. He was also the teacher of Edgar T. Thompson, who went on to Chicago after his Missouri M.A. on "The Effect of the Introduction of a Special Interest Factor on the Social Control of a Small Community" and became the acknowledged expert on the sociology of the plantation system. What was to become a long departmental tradition of identifying and distinguishing different population groups was begun by E. L. Morgan and O. Howells in 1925 ("The Rural Population Groups of Boone County," based on Howells's M.A. thesis of 1923).

A formally distinct department of rural sociology came in 1926, with the division of the Department of Farm Life into departments of rural sociology and agricultural economics, with Morgan, a contributor to the Phelan volume, who had worked on Galpin's maps, as Chair. The programs were physically separated, with the rural department housed in the agricultural side of campus. In 1929 it was given a specific mission: training rural social workers. Growth in the program was explosive, and increased further as the depression set in and additional funds were made available. Appointments were made with the extension arm of the university, especially in support of development, rural organization, and leadership. But the department had a reputation in the state as a "welfare department."

The direction of the department changed with Morgan's death in 1937, the transfer of the social work training to the general sociology department, and the arrival in 1938 of Charles E. Lively as Chair, a position he would hold for decades. Lively brought a new research-oriented direction to the department, beginning with a study of social areas in the state using WPA funds and an allocation for research from the Dean. His assistant, Cecil Gregory, stayed with the department as a faculty member until his death in 1970, and continued this work, of which more will be said shortly: it was emblematic of the contribution the department made to the state and to the university. At the same time it was an emblem of the difference between the aims of rural sociology and those of general sociology. The departmental history notes that "C. E. Lively's perception of fundamental research was that of fact finding to facilitate rational action among rural people and others concerned with agriculture and rural life." As he put it, "The Department of Rural Sociology is the fact finder behind the policy maker."[2] This was a vision that differed from the new model of sociology as a "behavioral science" that emerged in the postwar period. And it encapsulated and reflected the differences between general sociology and rural sociology.

We can think of there being two kinds of sociology: the kind that cumulates, adding to the stock of established theory or making previous forms of knowledge obsolete, and the kind that describes facts in the world, usually facts that change, but in ways that are usable to public audiences and clients, or merely interesting to them. The latter is a staple of rural sociology. The kinds of sociological life histories that Clifford

Shaw produced in the 1930s can and are produced today. Similarly for other descriptions of social worlds and social experiences. They do not depend on theoretical or methodological novelty. The novelty is in the world being described. The same goes for basic statistical facts, such as facts about church survival, attendance, and type: the same percentage methods that sufficed for Robert and Helen Merrill Lynd in *Middletown* (1929), a book that, despite the large number of statistical tables, reached a mass audience, suffice for this purpose for the intended audience of religious professionals and concerned members of the public. Here again, what changes are the facts, not the methods. Much of rural sociology falls, and has always fallen, into this second category.

> The long investment in the delineation of distinct social and cultural areas in rural Missouri was a success, but of the second kind. As the department history notes:
>
>> The social areas reflect the great diversity of the economic and social characteristics of Missouri and have been used, not only by sociologists, but by scientists in other disciplines in the university for drawing random samples for the study of health, aging, rural churches, diffusion of agricultural practices and other research projects.

The work needed to be updated with new census results, and applied to new topics, such as consumer preferences, in response to new clients, including those in the College of Agriculture itself. It was valued by the relevant audiences. But it was not a contribution to the first kind of sociology, except in the sense that it could be imitated by others and applied elsewhere: it was descriptive sociology. And much of it was descriptive sociology that was done for an audience of people, policymakers, and officials—for example, health officials, and workers in the agricultural complex of extension workers, researchers, and so forth.

This was a distinction that the rural sociologists themselves were well aware of. Lowry Nelson says:

> In historical perspective, it would be difficult to show that any basic principles or generalizations resulted from the vast outpouring of funds for research in the sociology of rural life during

the 1930s and early 1940s. Nor could such an outcome have been expected. All the research was devoted to the solution of problems, with the possible exception of the studies of stability—instability of communities and of the county social organization reports. It was research born of crisis and oriented to practical matters of policy formation. Nevertheless there were certain noteworthy achievements.

([1948] 1969:99)

The achievements were the destruction of "the myth that farming and economic security went hand in hand" and the recognition of social strata in rural communities, as well as the recognition of the importance of migration.

Even descriptive sociology, however, relies on ideas. And rural sociology had, from the start, some guiding ideas. The common focus of much of rural sociological thinking was the idea of social connection, especially in the form of the idea of community. Galpin took the definition of "community" to be his important achievement. His study *The Social Anatomy of an Agricultural Community* of 1915 inaugurated a long series of community studies. Community was an integrative, overarching idea, which took in many aspects of concern: leadership and organizations, churches, schools, communication, and trade relations. It was also the key to a certain kind of descriptive sociology: one could describe the community at a given time in a way that enabled it to be compared to other communities, and in a way that both the community and outsiders could learn something about what needed to change or what could be emulated.

These themes, and the practice of studying communities, recur in the theses and dissertations of the Rural Sociology Department. Titles from the 1920s include "Survey of a Negro Rural Community in Pike County, Missouri" in 1923; "Some Determinants of Boys and Girls 4-H Club leadership" in 1928; and "Community Relations of Young People," also in 1928. M.A. theses in the 1930s included "The Role of Women in a Rural Community in Central Missouri" in 1938 and "Studies of Levels of Living in Three Southeast Missouri Counties" in 1937. Later theses became more specialized, and more likely to be statistical studies based on surveys. But the basic themes remained: "The Community Orientation of Physicians in Twenty Rural Counties in Missouri" in 1962, and studies of communication, leadership, and so on. Rural health, which appears in Phelan (1920), became a particular concern of the department.

There is an impressive degree of continuity in these themes. There were church-related surveys from the 1920s on to the late 1980s. The subject turned into one of the department's most successful research efforts. Lawrence Hepple received foundation money for a large study of the rural church in Missouri, which ran from 1952 to 1961. It enabled him to survey churches and distinguish church characteristics, which provided a data base that could be, and was, returned to, for comparative purposes, in later years, twice, in 1967 and 1982 (Hassinger et al. 1988). The studies were descriptive, but they described changes that were poorly understood, and came to an important result that contradicted the original impetus for church studies in the 1910s and 20s: they showed that the churches were healthy, and in the last study, showed that the non-farmer newcomers to rural areas who were part of the new migration to rural areas (especially by retirees) were pillars of the churches.

Communications remained an interest, especially since it overlapped with extension. This was not simply descriptive. The basic ideas had deep roots in the rural reform movement (Sealander 1997:43–57). But the empirical elaboration of these ideas did produce cumulation. Herbert F. Lionberger, a department Ph.D. who joined the department as a faculty member in 1946, made a reputation with his studies of diffusion. His early research showed that low-income farmers in four north and west central Missouri counties, representing the better farming regions in the state, profited less than their more affluent neighbors from the dissemination of scientific farming information through agricultural extension programs. This was familiar territory: these were the analogues to the poor hoe farmers that concerned Galpin, and concerned extension workers from the beginnings of extension work (1918:333–334).

Despite all this continuity, there was a great deal of change, and the reasons are revealing. The golden era for the second generation of rural sociology ended, or was decisively transformed, in 1946, when the USDA was prohibited from doing rural sociology. The problem was the tradition of community studies. In retrospect, there were two flaws in the tradition of community studies. One was expressed by a surveyor, who made the point that taking a community survey was not unlike taking a photograph—and that like the photograph, the subject might not be happy with the result. The second was that the idea of community carried a great deal of ideological or valuative baggage. Community was a goal as well as a descriptive fact, and improving community life was understood as part of the larger project of the improvement of life for country people.

There were many problems with this model. The urban version of the survey proved to be unsustainable. In part, it failed because of money—the Russell Sage Foundation lost its money in the stock market crash. But it also failed because of a lack of interest on the part of the communities themselves in this kind of reform exercise. When these became official studies, sponsored by the USDA or the state university or experiment station, they also came to be open to political threats. Agricultural policy was already a viper's nest of competing bureaucracies and constantly subject to congressional intervention. Economic policy had long been an issue: the USDA economists were often at odds with the extension service linked Farm Bureaus, and many congressmen simply believed that the role of the agricultural economists and statisticians should be to advocate for more income for farmers. Charles Hardin, who provided a contemporary account of the demise of the Bureau of Agricultural Economics in the USDA, interpreted some of these conflicts in terms of value issues. One was over the nature of farm subsidies or price supports. It was not so much over policy, on which the two sides agreed, but on how to characterize what was occurring. The Farm Bureaus preferred the idea that the supports enabled farmers to get a fair price in the free market. The economists understood the policy as a form of relief from the vagaries of the market. The Farm Bureaus wanted an advocate for more support. The economists were concerned with the statistics that showed that the levels of support were equitable already. Rural sociology was on one side of another value conflict: rural sociology stressed "socialization," community, cooperative endeavor, communication, and so forth. But much of the focus of the agricultural research system was market- and competition-oriented, and concerned with making the individual farmer succeed and not merely survive. The use of 4-H clubs to generate competitions in growing vegetables, and the stress on prizes for stock and for grain production per acre reflected that orientation.

There were other value conflicts, however. The problem of walking a fine line between offending powerful interests with strong value commitments and "providing facts" came to a head over race. Hardin pointed to the "assumption that there is no Negro problem and that agricultural policy has no effect on it" as the precipitating valuative issue. The excuse or precipitating cause was a community study, in this case a study of migration that included Coahoma County Mississippi, the county including Clarksdale, which was one of the sources of the Great Migration of Blacks to the north (as well, of course, as the home of the blues). Frank D. Alexander, later a Professor of Rural Sociology and Extension at Cornell,[3] produced a "Cultural Reconnaissance of Coahoma County, Mississippi" in 1944. The report was not published, and indeed was not public. Thirty-five copies were dittoed, largely for the internal use of the USDA. When Congressman Jamie Whitten became aware of the report, he turned it into a cause célèbre; calling it an "indictment of fine folks" (quoted in Hardin 1946:653), and suggested ulterior motives. The motives went to the heart of the rural sociology project. In questioning an official he asked:

> Again, I have not put these matters in the record because I did not want to spread an indictment of fine folks, regardless of the types and character of folks that may have made it, or the motives they may have behind them in this report.
> (Whitten quoted in Hardin 1946: 653)

The offending paragraphs noted that:

> At present the militant Negro leadership in urban centers of the North is making its opinions felt on the rural Negroes of Coahoma County, for a number of them subscribe to northern newspapers which do not hesitate to emphasize injustices done to Negroes.
> (Whitten quoted in Hardin 1946:654)

They added that the school system of Clarksdale was segregated and provided amenities for Whites not available to Blacks.

> The city of Clarksdale has a highly rated white school system and a junior high school for Negroes. The municipal swimming pool for whites is located on the campus of the white high school. The school system maintains a free kindergarten for white children of preschool age. The superintendent of the white school is strongly opposed to employing Negro teachers who come from the North or who have been educated in northern schools.
> (Whitten quoted in Hardin 1946:655)

These facts themselves were not matters of reasonable dispute. But mentioning them went beyond the limits of what was politically acceptable. Rural sociologists studying community had always had to negotiate, and sometimes test, these limits. And they normally internalized a strong sense of what was acceptable and productive, but this constrained this kind of research.

Whitten got his way. USDA appropriations after 1946 came with a rider that banned land-use planning and social surveys. A way was found around this rider, but the damage was done. Rural sociology as a whole turned away from this kind of study and focused on areas that were safer: survey research with samples, individual questionnaires, and demography. The model of feeding back community information to the community was already compromised, by the 1930s when it became directed to policy rather than community edification. Studies instead focused on particular problems in a community, such as aging or access to healthcare. In this respect rural sociology followed the path of the Survey Movement itself. Yet the Survey Movement petered out by the late 1920s, and the rural sociology form of it hung on. Increasingly, however, it hung on in the form of work for clients or agencies concerned with development.

What happened to the leading idea of community, and to community research? A good indicator of the change from Galpin to the later period was a textbook produced by two rural sociology faculty members entitled *Human Community* (Hassinger and Pinkerton 1986). The book retained a much attenuated sense of speaking to the public, and even a sense of commitment. In the Introduction the authors write that "While we have attempted to be analytical and descriptive in this book, we are not neutral about outcomes" (1986:iv). But the link to the past is broken. The book makes no reference to Galpin, whose methods of illustrating social ties are vivid and are a form of network analysis, which was then coming into vogue, or to the long tradition in rural sociology of community studies. Instead, the historical references are to the classical sociologists, Émile Durkheim, Ferdinand Tönnies, to Robert Redfield. Their examples of past community studies are all studies of urban or middle-size towns, notably the Lynd's *Middletown*. All references to villages and trade centers are anonymized, which marks a complete transformation from Galpin's studies: there is no intent to feed back to the communities themselves; the intention is to make a general point about communities. What had been a distinctive mode of public engagement had become indistinguishable from textbook general sociology.

The Heart of Rural Sociology

During the postwar period at the University of Missouri, as I experienced it and heard about it, many of the patterns of the 1930s persisted, in part because the people were still there. The rural department had a graduate of Ohio State with a 1928 degree, an MA from the department from the 1930s, who taught methodology and statistics, two Ph.D.s from the department from the early 1950s, and another from a later period, as well as some younger faculty from other Rural Sociology programs. The faculty members followed the pattern of the founders, in some key respects. They were older when they received degrees, came from the country (or more often small towns), and had worked in rural institutions before coming to sociology—rural schools, rural churches, or the extension service, for example. Even the middle-aged faculty could tell stories about being taught in one-room schools. One had been a minister in a rural church. Rural life was not an abstraction to them.

For the generation that was then in their forties or early fifties when I was a student, my impressions are strong. They were people who were personally committed to, comfortable with, and completely without cynicism about country people and small town life, or about their own calling. As one of the faculty members, Rex Campbell, recalled:

> I started my career as an extension agent. My job was to help improve agriculture by convincing farm operators they should follow the recommendations of the University of Missouri College of Agriculture. I was very aware that my role was to be a change agent. It was a noble cause to me.
> (Campbell 2004:161)

They did not, as did many of the students in general sociology from country backgrounds, have an ambivalent relation to rural life, or try to distance themselves from it. Neither did they put on faux rustic airs, as some of the general sociologists did. They knew the history of rural sociology, and what its traditional commitments had been, and tried to follow them in an environment that had changed, and was changing very rapidly. They were unmoved by the pecking order of general sociology, or by the controversies within the discipline that were raging at the time. If they had anxieties, they were about their relation to the school of agriculture, and the question of whether the Dean understood and appreciated them. This was an important motivation for research into things that might matter to the Dean and fit with the larger agenda of the College of Agriculture.

Strangely, these social origins were not all that different from at least some of the general sociology faculty, and the same could be said of the students. Many of the older faculty in the general sociology department came from farms or small towns, had been ministers, or had worked in typically "rural" jobs; similarly for the students in general sociology. There was, however, a cultural difference between students in rural and general sociology based on professional choices. And it was not a matter of choosing advisors: many of the general sociology students worked with Rural Sociology faculty on non-rural projects. It was instead a decision to enter into the very specific and largely closed career world of the agricultural complex, with its distinctive publication practices of experiment station bulletins, locally oriented research projects, and contact with the machinery of extension education and agricultural research.

The structure of this world was quite different from the world of general sociology, and the difference pervaded interactions and orientations. For the general sociologists, the discipline itself was the battleground, the job market was the great goal, and defining oneself within the discipline was one's task as a graduate student. One learned with shock about the differences. I served as student representative on a search committee for a rural sociologist. There were very few candidates. One had produced dozens of Agricultural Experiment Station Bulletins. (Ironically, as memory serves, these were about debt, which was about to become, in the 1980s, an issue that transformed Missouri agriculture.) I was impressed. When I got to the committee meeting, one of the general sociologist members of the committee commented that he had no publications. No one disagreed with this: there was a tacit understanding both among the rural sociologists and the general sociologists that a rural sociologist in a Ph.D. department had to publish in journals to be accepted. But it was also the case that one could have a career, as this candidate did, in the agricultural research world, as a rural sociologist, without doing this, or much of this, and indeed by ignoring general sociology. And there were always jobs, if not careers—state projects that were funded for years, AID projects that could take one to the other side of the planet, and work in state agencies. Sometimes general sociology students would cross over into this world, but without becoming true rural sociologists.

This tacit agreement concealed a deep divide. The departmental history, describing the two decades in which the departments of Sociology and Rural Sociology were administratively combined puts it, is anodyne:

> total integration of the two departments was never achieved. The diversity of values, interests of the faculty and missions of the two departments was the cause of continuous friction. The Rural Sociology faculty is administratively oriented toward conducting empirical research that contributes to the College of Agriculture's mission of improving the quality of living in rural areas, while the General Sociology faculty are primarily concerned with the development of the discipline. Dissent over administrative matters increased to the point where the deans of the respective

colleges (Agriculture and Arts and Science) decreed total administrative separation in 1981. Since then, cooperation in the graduate and undergraduate teaching programs and in research endeavors of the two departments has increased.

(University of Missouri 1988:15)

The frictions were the result of many causes, one of which, unsurprisingly, was money. Rural Sociology faculty were on full-time contracts, not nine-month contracts, and consequently made more money. They taught less, having their time assigned to various other activities, with the experiment station or extension. They had better secretarial support. Yet from the point of view of at least some of the general sociology faculty, they not only did less, but in some cases appeared to do virtually nothing. Indeed, for some of these faculty members in rural sociology, there was little publication in professional journals, even in rural sociology journals. The university did nothing to equalize resources: the College of Arts and Sciences was itself impoverished.

The Rural Sociologists were doing something, and in some cases a great deal. From their own point of view, and from the point of view of the College of Agriculture, they were performing a vast array of services to the college, the extension service, and through research to the state and rural community. A report written by Herbert F. Lionberger explaining the history and current status of the department laid this out.

> The Department staff being concerned with research in problem areas almost by decree, has produced a continuing crop of knowledgeable faculty members in areas of current public concern. These knowledgeable faculty members have served as consultants throughout the departmental history. C. E. Lively, Department Chairman from 1937 to 1961, was on many advisory committees for local, state and national agencies, mainly in the field of public health but also in matters relating to the conservation of natural resources and population movement and distribution with its attendant implications. This type of consultation has continued, with Robert L. McNamara and

> Edward Hassinger playing key roles in both the general areas of rural and public health; Rex R. Campbell and McNamara in population characteristics, distribution and movement; Lionberger in "diffusion" research and its applications; Daryl Hobbs in social change and the sociology of development; John S. Holik in local social organization and leadership; and J. A. Hartman in research methods; all in their respective areas of research competence. Also, each has served as research and organizational consultants in more general matters of administration and organization of effort in various fields of endeavor.
>
> ([1968] 1974)[4]

This was work. And much of the other research productivity consisted in putting information, such as census information, into usable forms. This was time-consuming, required thinking about the needs of clients and audiences, and often required a great deal of interaction with the audiences. Little of this effort could or would be translated into professional publication, though this too happened.

But what they were doing was itself undergoing a significant long-term change. The older Galpin model, of feeding knowledge back to the community, was a distant memory. Lively's model, of providing facts for policy makers, was alive. But the policy issues had changed, and changed in ways that called into question the specifically "rural" mission. By the 1980s, there was talk about the urbanization of rural life. The idea of a career in farming and therefore the idea of rural sociology as supporting these careers and improving the lives of those that pursued them, effectively disappeared, along with the students in the College of Agriculture who intended to be farmers. Campbell describes his experiences with the introduction to rural sociology class, taught in the college of agriculture for their students, in this way:

> When I started teaching forty years ago, about 20–25 percent of the students in my introductory classes said they planned to enter farming. Now, perhaps one out of fifty will say that. Many students will say they want to live in the country or on a farm, but that farming will not be their career. The decline in farming as a career after the farm crisis [of the eighties] was very dramatic.
>
> (Campbell 2004:228)

This was a part, and an important part, of the gradual disengagement of rural sociology from the original project of improving rural life. To be sure, concerns with rural health services, the rural aged, and similar issues was a form of this original project. But the drivers for these concerns were health and aging policies, not the community-oriented vision of a better farm life with which the early rural sociologists had begun.

During the period before 1970, the funding system, of small grants combined with agricultural experiment support, tied the research to the mission of the school of agriculture, the funding system of later years changed, in ways that made funding itself the object. This had the effect of directing money toward development work in other countries. This had been a long tradition within the College of Agriculture, and rural sociology had participated, especially by training students from Asia.

This was all to change. In 1970, the first Earth Day took place. The environment, meaning the rural environment, the problem of food, and everything related to them became a focus of student concern. A few of the rural sociology students were activists. The older focus on the quality of rural life shifted to a systemic understanding of the place of agriculture in the world. At the same time, and especially as a result in the farm credit crisis of the eighties, the traditional family farm was vanishing as an economic unit. Recruitment base changed, grant getting took over, and development work, especially in the Third World, became more important and attracted different students.

The chapters in this volume deal with lives and research in this new world of rural sociology. Autobiography is often the best way to understand complex changes and the way in which people respond. Hans Bakker used the collection Alan Sica and I edited, *The Disobedient Generation* (Sica and Turner 2005), as a model for this volume. That book addressed the effects of 68ers on the generation of theorists in sociology who were coming of age at that time. The effects were complex, deep, but not simple or mechanical. The experience did not merely produce "tenured radicals," though it did produce a few. Instead, the personal experiences were diverse, and the responses unpredictable. But taken together, the autobiographies captured a world, the world in which commitments were forged and ideas were developed. The present volume does something similar: it shows the diversity of experiences of rural sociology during a period of institutional transformation.

It is perhaps ironic that rural sociology, which always stood apart and never attempted to separate itself from its original progressivist (and ultimately conflicting) goals of improving the quality of rural life and promoting scientific agriculture, is today closer to its origins than ever—as the autobiographies in this volume attest, the combination of engagement, problem-focused research, and teaching not only remains, but has revived. The Golden era of cozy placement within the agricultural research, education, and extension complex, which blunted and channeled the field, but also allowed it to flourish, has now passed, and the broader perspective of the founders has returned. It is especially ironic that an analogous return to "public sociology" and engagement is occurring in general sociology, under the quite different influence of feminism and its ideas about engagement, and the demographic feminization of the field.

Rural sociology is, pardon the phrase, rooted in a set of concerns that are shared with the people they study, and reflect the same attitude of respect and sympathy with which the field began. The people have changed. The agricultural economy has changed beyond recognition. But something remains of the original idea of the founders of the field. Indeed, one may think of the history of rural sociology as a great experiment in the bringing of expertise to the solution of problems in the real world, in the development and maintenance of institutional structures that allowed this to happen, and in the politics of engagement —in facing the issues and dilemmas that arise from being officially sanctioned and politically dependent yet also pursuing an agenda of betterment. This book is a welcome contribution to the record of this experiment.

Thanks to Rex Campbell, Mary Grigsby, Mike Nolan, J. Kenneth Benson, and John Galliher for their input. They are not responsible for any interpretations given here.

Notes

1. The European discussion had deep roots: Arnaldo Momogliano provides an interesting intellectual history of the background to these discussions that shows the centrality of

agrarian issues, notably the emancipation of the serfs, to the European understanding of modernity itself (1994:225–236).
2. College of Agriculture University of Missouri-Columbia. 1988 June. "A History of Rural Sociology Special Report 361, p. 3. University Archives at the University of Missouri-Columbia." http://digital.library.umsystem.edu/cgi/t/text/text-idx?c=agext;cc=agext;sid=bb5ae999dc349705e42fdead040220a1;rgn=main;view=text;idno=agesr000361. Accessed 15 September 2014.
3. Alexander was much later to write a critical discussion of evaluation research on extension services, identifying the same conflict between the expectation that the researcher be an advocate and that they report the truth. 1965 *Journal of Cooperative Extension*.
4. Herbert F. Lionberger. [1968] 1974. "A History of the 'People Speciality' in the Missouri College of Agriculture: From Modest beginnings to Distinction." Department of Rural Sociology. University Archives, University of Missouri-Columbia, C: 3/31/7, Box1 RC # 73901.

Bibliography

Alexander, Frank D. 1965. "A Critique of Evaluation," *Journal of Cooperative Extension III* (Winter): 205–212.

Brunner, Edmund de Schweinitz. 1935. *The Study of Rural Society*. New York: Houghton Mifflin.

Brunner, Edmund de Schweinitz. 1955. *American Society: Urban and Rural Patterns*. New York: Harper.

Buttel, Frederick H., and Howard Newby. 1980. *The Rural Sociology of the Advanced Societies: Critical Perspectives*. Montclair, NJ and London: Allanheld, Osmun & Croom Helm.

Campbell, Rex. 2004. *A Revolution in the Heartland: Changes in Rural Culture, Family and Communities 1900–2000*. http://web.missouri.edu/~campbellr/Book/title.html (accessed 15 July 2014). Cornell University Library ecommons.library.cornell.edu/ (accessed 15 July 2014).

Curti, Merle Eugene. 1938. Review of *Morally We Roll Along* by Gay MacLaren; *Henry Ford and Greenfield Village* by William Adams Simonds. *American Sociological Review* 3(5): 760–761.

Galpin, Charles J. [1912] 1920a. "Social Privileges of Village or Small City," pp. 464–466 in *Readings in Rural Sociology*, edited by J. Phelan. New York: Macmillan.

Galpin, Charles J. [1912] 1920b. "A Method of Making a Social Survey of a Rural Community," pp. 484–489 in *Readings in Rural Sociology*, edited by J. Phelan. New York: Macmillan.

Galpin, Charles J. [1912] 1920c. "The Social Anatomy of an Agricultural Community," pp. 497–499 in *Readings in Rural Sociology*, edited by J. Phelan. New York: Macmillan.

Galpin, Charles J. 1918. *Rural Life*. New York: The Century Company. https://archive.org/details/rurallife00galpuoft (accessed 21 July 2014).

Galpin, Charles J. 1938. *My Drift into Rural Sociology: Memoirs of Charles Josiah Gilpin*. Baton Rouge, LA: Louisiana State University Press.

Hardin, Charles. 1946. The Bureau of Agricultural Economics under Fire: A Study in Valuation Conflicts. *Journal of Farm Economics* 28(3): 635–668.

Hassinger, Edward W., and James R. Pinkerton. 1986. *Human Community*. New York: Macmillan.

Hassinger, Edward W., John S. Hilik, and J. Kenneth Benson. 1988. *The Rural Church: Learning from Three Decades of Change*. Nashville, TN: Abington Press.

Hine, Lewis. [1913–1914] 1920. "Children or Cotton," *The Survey* 31 (February 7), pp. 589–592. Reprinted in *Readings in Rural Sociology*, edited by J. Phelan. New York: Macmillan, pp. 158–159.

Kellogg, Paul U. [1912] 1920. "Five Principles of Surveys," pp. 481–483 in *Readings in Rural Sociology*, edited by J. Phelan. New York: Macmillan.

Kellogg, Paul U., S. M. Harrison, and G. T. Palmer. 1912. *The Social Survey*, 2nd ed. New York: The Russell Sage Foundation, pp. 1–17. Reprinted from *The Proceedings of the Academy of Political Science* II (4), July, 1912.

Larson, Olaf F., and Julie N. Zimmerman. 2003. *Sociology in Government: The Galpin-Taylor Years in the U.S. Department of Agriculture, 1919–1953*. University Park, PA: Penn State University Press.

Larson, Olaf F., Edward O. Moe, and Julie N. Zimmerman. 1992. *Sociology in Government: A Bibliography of the U.S. Department of Agriculture's Division of Farm Population and Rural Life, 1919–1953*. Boulder, CO: Westview Press.

Lynd, Robert, and Helen Merrill Lynd. 1929. *Middletown: A Study of American Culture*. New York: Harcourt Brace and World.

Momigliano, A. D. 1994. *Studies on Modern Scholarship*, edited by G. W. Bowersock and T. J. Cornell. Translated by T. J. Cornell. Berkeley, CA: University of California Press.

Morgan, E. L., and O. Howells. 1925. *The Rural Population Groups of Boone County*. Columbia, MO: University Archives of the University of Missouri-Columbia.

Nelson, Lowery. [1948] 1969. *Rural Sociology: Its Origins and Growth in the United States*. New York: American Book Company. https://archive.org/details/ruralsociologyru00nels (accessed 7 July 2014).

Phelan, John. 1920. *Readings in Rural Sociology*. New York: Macmillan. https://archive.org/details/readingsinrurals00pheliala (accessed 22 July 2014).

Ross, E. A. 1916. "Folk Depletion as a Cause of Rural Decline." *Papers and Proceedings by American Sociological Society* 11: 21–30.

Sealander, Judith. 1997. *Private Wealth & Public Life: Foundation Philanthropy and the Reshaping of American Public Policy from the Progressive Era to the New Deal*. Baltimore, MD: Johns Hopkins University Press.

Sica, Alan, and Stephen Turner. 2005. *The Disobedient Generation: 68ers and the Transformation of Social Theory*. Chicago: The University of Chicago Press.

University of Missouri College of Agriculture. 1988. *A History of Rural Sociology*, Special Report 361, June. Columbia, MO: University Archives of the University of Missouri-Columbia. http://cdm.sos.mo.gov/cdm/ref/collection/agexptstn/id/39146 (accessed 21 July 2014).

Weber, Max. [1909] 1976. *The Agrarian Sociology of Ancient Civilizations*. Translated by R. I. Frank. Atlantic Highlands, NJ: Humanities Press.

Zimmerman, Julie N., and Olaf F. Larson. 2010. *Opening Windows onto Hidden Lives: Women, Country Life, and Early Rural Sociological Research*. Rural Sociological Society. Rural Studies Series. University Park, PA: Penn State University Press.

3
"I COULD TELL STORIES 'TIL THE COWS COME HOME"

PERSONAL BIOGRAPHY MEETS COLLECTIVE BIOGRAPHY

JULIE N. ZIMMERMAN, *UNIVERSITY OF KENTUCKY*

Storytelling as a way of communicating information and sharing experiences is as old as humanity. For individuals, their stories can be seen as a form of biography; communicating aspects of who they are and where they came from. When it comes to thinking about disciplines and scholarship, individuals' biographies can shed light on someone's professional journey as well as their intellectual approaches. Storytelling is also a way to convey the journey of a group and their collective experiences. This chapter extends the idea of individual biography to the idea of a collective biography. If individual biography or people's personal stories inform the construction of their intellectual enterprise, are there similar collective stories that inform the development of a field?[1]

You Never Know Where a Phone Call Might Lead

That's what I always tell graduate students. "You never know where a phone call might lead." I tell them this because, for me, a chance phone call is how I first got involved in rural sociology and where my own individual biography first intersected with a collective biography of rural sociology.

At the time, I was a graduate student in between graduate programs on the hunt for summer funding. While I was to begin the Ph.D. program in the fall at Cornell, I was not officially a student there yet. Still, the need for summer funding being what it still is even today, I was not willing to let any stone go unturned. So, I made a call from Providence, Rhode Island, to the main office of the Rural Sociology Department at Cornell, just in case.[2] Could there be any chance at all that someone might be needing to hire a graduate student?

As it turns out, there was. A retired faculty member was looking to hire a student to work on some research. The retired professor was Olaf F. Larson and he was documenting and assessing the work of the USDA's Division of Farm Population and Rural Life.[3] Even though I had no idea what "the Division" was, I eagerly accepted.

As I soon came to learn, "the Division" was the first time a unit of the federal government was devoted to sociological research (rural or otherwise).[4] Thirteen past presidents of the Rural Sociological Society (RSS) and three past presidents of the American Sociological Association (ASA) had worked in the Division at some time in their careers. Included among these was the first woman to be president of RSS and the first president of the ASA[5] to serve while being in a non-academic position (Margaret Hagood and Carl Taylor respectively). At the time, the Division's work was "by far the most dominant element in the field of rural sociological research" (Smith 1957:13).

For Olaf, working to rescue the Division's work was not just another research project. He was one of the past presidents of RSS who had worked in the Division and he spent about a decade in the unit working in several regional offices as well as in Washington, DC. The project also brought together others who had worked in the Division including Edward O. Moe and an advisory group (all former Division members).

It could have all ended there. Students come and go on research projects and working on the project began as some summer funding to help pay the bills. But even as I began the Ph.D. program at Cornell, I continued to work with Olaf as his RA. And, as I look back now, I realize how that chance phone call really was only just the beginning.

History Comes Alive (AKA: I Think I See Dead People)[6]

In writing about the role of biography in history, Barbara Laslett noted the importance of remembering that larger social changes do not simply occur or just emerge. Instead, "they were ... the result of concrete actions by real live actors within historically specific situations" (Laslett 1991:516). If there was one lesson from working with Olaf that has informed my work over the years, it is how history is populated by real people making real decisions in real time and in real contexts.

As for rural sociology as a field, my introduction came through the 53 years of the Division's research. Being Olaf's graduate research assistant meant that it was my job to read the Division's research publications and help in applying a system of keywords to the body of work. All together, Olaf had found over 1,500 products produced by the Division including restricted manuscripts, congressional testimony, journal articles, experiment station bulletins, books, and presentations. Of these, there were 986 research publications.[7]

Reading the contents of all of those publications was a lesson in itself. But even more important was the process of learning about rural sociology and its history through Olaf. He made it all come alive. After all, while this was all history to me, the people I was learning about were not just theoretical actors in a bygone past. They were Olaf's friends and colleagues.[8]

Just as individuals came alive through working with Olaf, so too did a larger sense of history itself. Events that had once been sections in history books were now populated by real people who were living those real events. In fact, it was one of those behind-the-scenes stories I learned from Olaf that became an ever-present and vivid reminder that there was more going on in the post World War II years.[9] There was another climate that we tend to forget about or overlook.

It was Olaf's story about how Division head Carl Taylor tried to take a distinguished professor from Fisk University to lunch in the USDA's executive dining room that made it all become so real. Because the facilities were segregated, Taylor and his guest were refused service. Taylor was so angry that, as Olaf put it, he "took initiatives which resulted in a widespread understanding that when the [new] cafeteria opened it would be on a desegregated basis" (Zimmerman 2006b).[10]

Even today stories like that about Carl Taylor catch my eye and there were hints that Carl's story was not alone. While preparing for the 75th Anniversary of RSS, I learned of another story. While Holik and Hassinger mentioned it in their multi-part series on the history of the RSS (1978b), like Carl Taylor's story, it likely isn't remembered today.

It happened at the 1945 RSS conference. The meeting was being held at the Morrison Hotel, a common location for the RSS when meeting in Chicago. That year, the Morrison Hotel refused to honor the confirmed room reservation of an RSS member: Dr. Charles G. Gomillion who was a professor at Tuskegee University. In response to the hotel's actions, RSS President Lowry Nelson sent both a letter of apology to Gomillion and a letter of condemnation to the hotel (Holik and Hassinger 1978b:159).

Two years after Gomillion's confirmed hotel reservation was refused, the RSS subsequently voted not to hold its conferences at establishments which did not allow all of its members to attend (Holik and Hassinger 1978b:161). While Holik and Hassinger attribute the resolution as following up on the Gomillion incident, since it was passed during the conference held at Fontana Village in North Carolina, there is likely more to the story.

In 1947, the RSS held its first conference at a nonhotel location. Fontana Village in North Carolina was the recreational facility created once the TVA (Tennessee Valley Authority) had completed construction on Fontana Dam.[11] While RSS members later reported that they enjoyed being at a nonhotel location (Tate 1947:457) there was an important drawback that attendees did not know about until after they arrived—Fontana was segregated.[12] Enraged, an RSS member spearheaded an effort for the Society to resolve not to hold its conferences at establishments that did not accept all RSS members. At the end of a series of more pro-forma resolutions, the resolution that passed during the 1947 conference read:

> Whereas the membership of the Society includes persons of other than the White race, *Be It Resolved* that meetings of the Society be held at places which are accessible to or which provide appropriate accommodations to other than those of the White race, and that all members be fully advised of this fact in advance of the meeting in order that none shall stay away for fear of a lack of accommodations.
>
> (Tate 1947:458)

Today, Dr. Charles Gomillion has a renowned place in history for his role in the landmark Gomillion v. Lightfoot legal decision that paved the way for the 1965 Voting Rights Act. For the RSS, it began holding its meetings in Chicago at a different hotel: often the Palmer House. In 1965, the Morrison was razed to make room for what is now the Chase Tower.

While this incident might have been the first time that the RSS sought to have its organization's actions match larger goals, it would not be the last. For instance, the RSS is credited for increasing funding for research at 1890 Institutions (Holik and Hassinger 1989; Mayberry 1977). Following multiple resolutions regarding gender discrimination and a 1975 resolution to use gender-neutral language in the Society's constitution and bylaws, in 1980 the RSS voted not to hold its conferences in states that had not ratified the Equal Rights Amendment (Holik and Hassinger 1989:33–35).[13] More recent resolutions addressed issues related to recycling, local foods, accessibility, and labor.

Behind-the-scenes stories like these continue to draw my attention. But one story in particular that grabbed my interest early on was that of the Coahoma County research study and how it led to a ban from the U.S. Congress on conducting "cultural surveys." While the congressional ban focusing on a specific type of research was extraordinary, it was the relatively ordinary nature of the study itself that, for me, made the story particularly intriguing.[14]

The Ordinary Becomes Extraordinary

If you are of a certain generation, Coahoma is a familiar story and in some ways is part of the folklore of rural sociology. But for younger generations, it's new. And, like a reality TV show, it is filled with power and intrigue that still resonate today. Since others have written about the Coahoma study and the resultant fallout that happened (e.g. Kirkendall 1966; Larson and Zimmerman 2003), I will keep to the "Twitter version."[15]

The Coahoma county research study was conducted by the Division in the mid 1940s. It was one of the 71 Cultural Reconnaissance surveys intended to contribute to building a broad knowledge base on rural America. Frank Alexander was at the Division's regional office in Atlanta.[16] Alexander was charged with conducting the survey of Coahoma County, Mississippi, for the project. As it turns out, his draft report happened to be the first of several that would be completed.

There was nothing particularly unique about Coahoma County—at least for the time. Social relations within the county reflected those found in other places in the South and were similar to what was described in other cultural reconnaissance surveys conducted in the region (e.g. Montgomery 1945; Pryor 1945; Raper 1944). In Coahoma, Alexander described how the separation of Whites and Blacks was an important feature of life in the county. Consequently, Alexander's report included issues like how law enforcement was left to the White plantation owners, and how Blacks were not allowed to vote, hold office, or participate in county organizations (Alexander 1944; Larson and Zimmerman 2003:51–53; Zimmerman 2008).[17] Daniel (1990) puts the study in context, including Ed Moe's earlier report on race relations in the region (1990:892–894).

There was nothing particularly unique about Alexander's report. It followed the same outline as the other studies in the project. Alexander described the county, its history, and the social organization of agriculture and community life. For anyone reading Alexander's draft report today, it is a straightforward description of the rural South at the time (1944). But that wasn't the reaction that Alexander's report got, especially once it hit the floor of the U.S. Congress.

Alexander's draft report raised the ire of interests in Mississippi who were already critical of the Division's parent unit—the BAE (Kirkendall 1966:235). In response, the newly appointed Secretary of Agriculture, Clinton P. Anderson, made assurances that the USDA would not be publishing the report and Alexander was reprimanded. However, the controversy did not end there.

During the USDA's Congressional appropriation hearings, BAE Chief Howard Tolley was grilled about the Division's study. Mississippi Congressman Jamie Whitten called the report "vicious attacks on a county and its people" (U.S. Congress, House 1946:238), "slanderous" (U.S. Congress, House 1946:235), a "gross misrepresentation," and an "indictment" of the "fine folks" of Coahoma county (U.S. Congress, House 1946:241). Whitten also countered that the people of the county were "getting along in perfect harmony" (U.S. Congress, House 1946:241) and told Tolley that the study "strays far from the facts and from the intended work of your Department" (U.S. Congress, House 1946:235).

Whitten was not alone. The American Farm Bureau Federation at the time joined the attack. During their congressional testimony, the Farm Bureau argued that the BAE should "serve the business interests of the farmers" (Kirkendall 1966:241), that the USDA unit should be prohibited from conducting "social surveys," "confined to statistical and fact-finding research," and that its regional offices should be eliminated (U.S. Congress, House 1946:1644).

In the appropriations bill that followed, this is exactly what happened. Among its prohibitions, the bill closed the regional offices, banned the BAE from using any of the funds for "cultural surveys," and cut the unit's funding. Before the first phase of the larger study could even be completed, the project was brought to an abrupt halt. None of the 71-county cultural reconnaissance reports were ever published by the USDA and only 31 internal draft reports have been found (Larson, Zimmerman, and Moe 1992).[18]

While Alexander's study of Coahoma County, Mississippi, was singled out in the Congressional hearings, it was not the only Division study that was garnering ire at the time. Meanwhile, at another regional office—this time in California—Walter Goldschmidt's study was also under fire.

If you have heard of the Goldschmidt hypothesis, then you are familiar with the research to which I am referring. To put it all too briefly, Goldschmidt conducted a study that compared two towns in California: Arvin and Dinuba. In his study, Goldschmidt found more favorable circumstances for the community with small-scale agriculture and farms compared with the community with large-scale agricultural production. Needless to say, there were agricultural interests in California who were not happy. Goldschmidt himself, and others, tell the story in greater detail, including how Goldschmidt learned of his subsequent termination.[19]

The impact of Coahoma and Goldschmidt reverberated for years to come. Even Olaf felt the impact of the post-Coahoma climate.[20] In 1953, Ezra Benson became the first Republican in two decades to be Secretary of Agriculture. Within less than a year of taking the position and by his order, the BAE, and with it the Division, was abolished.[21]

In some ways, these were only just the beginning. In 1955, Jamie Whitten again played a role in another incident in Congress in which rural sociology was singled out as among USDA research that was "nonessential and nonproductive" and as one of the areas that should not be funded by USDA monies:

> In view of the urgencies for research on basic problems, the Conference Committee insists that research projects of limited value, such as orchids of Guatemala, flora of Dominica, differences of clothing of farm and urban people, population dynamics, *rural sociology*, methodology, child rearing practices, and projects undertaken primarily for the benefit of employees doing graduate work, be discontinued in favor of more important work [. . .] (emphasis added).[22]

The years that followed Coahoma and Goldschmidt also saw the rise of McCarthyism, the House Committee on Un-American Activities (e.g. Badash 2000; Hutcheson 1997), and J. Edgar Hoover's FBI going after sociologists and the ASA (Keen 2003). But that's another story for another day.

For many, Coahoma and Goldschmidt were contributing factors in the subsequent climate in rural sociology. And they influenced not only the field of rural sociology but also the next generation to come.[23]

However, it was a different younger generation that led to the RSS becoming a reality. O.D. Duncan recalled the events as "[I]t was a case of men who were then young, at least younger than they are now, loading a meeting while the elder brethren slept on their own rights" (1953:412). Duncan should know. Not only was he there, he spearheaded the minority report that created the RSS in the first place. But I'm getting ahead of myself.

What Happened Between Rural Sociology and Sociology?

As Historian for the RSS, the question I probably am asked most often by graduate students is: what happened between rural sociology and sociology? Sometimes the question is posed in relation to the two professional organizations, but other times it is posed more broadly. While the search for an answer came years after my time as a graduate student working for Olaf, his influence still informed my search for an answer (or at least an understanding).

Over time, I had learned multiple accounts of, and explanations for, the particular relationship between sociology and rural sociology. Some of the shorthand versions included themes such as: rural sociology as a field was too applied when compared with sociology; sociology held a bias against rurality—questioning its generalizability or relevance; that rural sociology "left" sociology when it formed the RSS; and so on. Historical accounts more typically focused on the growth of rural sociology and the inability of the ASA to meet their growing professional needs (e.g. Holik and Hassinger 1986b; 1987a; Nelson 1969).

In different ways, all of these are correct. In the years leading up to forming the RSS, rural sociology had been growing. In response, the Rural Sociology section of the ASA was established in 1921 (the first section formed in the ASA) and in 1936 the section began publishing its own journal—*Rural Sociology* (Holik and Hassinger 1986b; 1987a).[24] However, even though having a section provided a mechanism for rural sociologists to formally organize and the journal increased publication opportunities, it did not resolve other limitations associated with the ASA.[25]

Although the idea of forming an autonomous professional organization had been discussed before, at the annual conference in December 1936, a formal committee was finally created. Referred to as the "Sanderson Committee," the group was charged to officially consider the possibility. The majority of the committee was reluctant to make the move and separate from the ASA, including Dwight Sanderson and Carl Taylor. Later referred to as the "Big Boys" (Collard 1984:329), both Sanderson and Taylor had close connections with the ASA and both went on to become president of the ASA.

However, a new generation was growing within rural sociology—one that had a different vision and a different viewpoint about staying with the ASA.[26] O. D. Duncan was the youngest on the Sanderson Committee and he had long favored separation. Realizing that he was the only committee member holding that opinion, he solicited the assistance of T. Lynn Smith at Louisiana State University (LSU). Smith organized a memorandum of support from the faculty at LSU and sent it not only to members of the Sanderson Committee, but also to other leaders within the rural group. With this support, O. D. Duncan drafted a minority report.[27]

At the following year's conference in December 1937, both the majority and minority reports from the Sanderson Committee were presented. While the majority report wanted to pursue constitutional amendments with the ASA so that the group could remain a part of the larger organization, the minority report read in part:

> that this group here and now declare itself to be an independent society and that as an organization its allegiance to the American Sociological Society in all matters of jurisdiction shall be regarded by this action as having come to an end.
> (Rural Sociological Society of America 1938:124)

Decades later, Sewell (who was there) described "the shock of the old guys" and how "[M]uch to everybody's surprise . . . practically everybody there was in favor of Duncan's report" (Fuguitt 2009:35; 30).

In the end, and after much debate, it was the minority report that won out and the Rural Sociological Society of America was born.[28] Many years later, Duncan looked back on the events as outgoing president of the RSS. Reflecting his well-known flourish for language (Fuguitt 2009:34), Duncan wrote:

> It is always young men who win the crucial issues. Old men may declare the war and dictate the terms of peace, but young men fight, and young men die for the causes in which they believe. Sometimes they win. December 28, 1937, was a day of victory for young men.
>
> (1953:412)

Befuddled Looks and Different Languages

It's easy to look inwards; to tell the story as if forming the RSS happened in a vacuum. But, in fact, part of Sanderson and Taylor's reluctance to form a separate professional organization stemmed from their concerns over the financial future and viability of the ASA (Holik and Hassinger 1987a; Zimmerman 2012a). At the time, not only was the ASA in financial straits, but the growth in regional sociological associations appeared to be threatening the national Society's membership base (Hertzler 1938). There were also growing and vigorous debates about the nature of sociology itself and, regardless of the RSS, sociology itself was undergoing a transition.

Years after he had first told me the story, a clue about the transition within American sociology came from Olaf. Following a vigorous campaign to elect Carl Taylor president of the ASA, Olaf recounted how Taylor's presidential address elicited strong reactions from parts of the membership. Curious, I read it (Taylor 1947). And, just like when I read Alexander's report on Coahoma County, I didn't get it. Why would it have been so scandalous?

Titled "Sociology and Common Sense," in essence, Taylor argued for his version of a sociology of knowledge—one that reflected his approach in rural sociology. In his address, Taylor presented sociology as including common sense and, among other things, argued that knowledge held by the common man (*sic*) was useful for sociology.[29]

By today's standards, Taylor's approach does not sound out of the ordinary. But at the time, things were different.

In her decisive analysis of the 1935 ASR rebellion, Lengermann (1979) helps shed some light on what was going on. At the same time (literally) that the RSS was forming, a sea change was fomenting within the ASA. In addition to factors such as a changing labor market, personality conflicts, anger over the perceived influence of the University of Chicago, and a leadership overthrow within ASA,[30] another transition was underway.

While related to the growth of quantitative analyses, the transition was more fundamental and wide ranging than just a research method. I don't recall where I read the suggestion, but hidden in a footnote somewhere, an author suggested reading the presidential addresses of Luther Lee Bernard (1932) and William F. Ogburn (1930) back-to-back as a way of gaining an understanding of the epistemological differences represented in the transition. Whoever it was that made the recommendation truly got it right![31]

Abbott calls it a movement from a contextualist interactionist approach to a variables way of thinking (1997). Within this movement, the unit of analysis shifted from "actors in social relations" to notions of a decontextualized social facts "abstracted from" their context and where "causal meaning" was the same regardless of its context (Abbott 1997:1152). In addition to transforming the system or way of thinking about social relations and social phenomena, it also had implications for definitions of what constituted "good sociology" (Lengermann 1979:192).

In the two presidential addresses of Bernard and Ogburn, my favorite quotes are those that encapsulate some of the differences between their perspectives. While Bernard states "I am a strong believer that research should have a close and intimate relation to life" (1932:3), Ogburn on the other hand clearly differentiated the production of scientific knowledge as a distinct and separate enterprise. Although sociological research may be useful for nonscientists, Ogburn wrote that "[S]ociology as a science is not interested in making the world a better place in which to live [. . .]" (1930:2). Needless to say, for Ogburn, science should be done for other scientists and "no attempt will be made to make these articles readable for shop girls or the high-school youth" (1930:3).[32]

When Carl Taylor gave his presidential address to the ASA in 1946, even though it was more than a decade after Ogburn and Bernard, the fundamental issues were still alive. Taylor summed up his presidential address by saying "[G]ood sociology is a combination of science and common sense" (1947:9). Since we know which side won out in the battle (at least for a while), no wonder Taylor got the reaction Olaf described.[33]

For rural sociology and the RSS, larger changes in sociology such as the founding and growth of the regional societies, and debates over the proper content and role of sociology were also important because they provided a lens through which the action of creating the RSS (and the work of rural sociologists) would be interpreted (Zimmerman 2012b).

Over the years, while rural sociology was "initially and until World War II one of the field's [sociology's] largest branches" (Calhoun 2007:3), it was also seen as a "splinter group" and part of the fragmentation of sociology and the ASA (Collard 1984:333–334). In his history of American Sociology, Howard Odum characterized how rural sociology's 'departure' through forming the RSS was appropriate given its inclusion of nonacademics (1951:300). In more recent years and using a different approach, Turner and Turner reasoned that rural sociology's "separation . . . from the rest of the discipline" came as a result of its "distinct resource base" which had made its research methodologies either "peculiar" or "biased" (1990:52–53).

Twenty years after the RSS was formed, Deutscher (1958) argued how rural sociology was "one of the best examples" of the way in which concerns external to sociology were creating specializations and how these specializations were a threat to the continuity of knowledge accumulation within sociology (1958:35). As a result, even though rural sociology (and others) may have made contributions to real life issues, Deutscher specifically named rural sociology when he wrote: "their contributions to the general body of sociological knowledge have been small in comparison to their relative numbers and the relative quantity of research they have produced" (1958:35).[34]

Years after he was president of the ASA, Charlie Loomis reported having conducted a survey of members "at regional meetings of the ASA" (1981). The results, Loomis revealed, were that 35 percent "believed the field of sociology would be better off without the Rural Sociological Society and that it should be abolished" (1981:59). Other results included that "sizeable proportions of American non-rural sociologists would not accept a rural sociologist in such status-roles as 1) office mate, 2) co-author of a book or monograph and 3) "chairman or head of your department or unit" (Loomis 1981:59).

While Holik and Hassinger questioned why the rural sociologists of the mid 1930s "appeared to have a minority group complex" (1987a:15), years later Friedland still noted rural sociology's "second-class citizens" status (2010). In the long run, perhaps the feeling was not entirely unfounded. Or, more importantly, perhaps the two were increasingly speaking different languages.[35]

For me, coming to some way of understanding "what happened between rural sociology and sociology" meant understanding some of the uniqueness of rural sociology's history,[36] but it also meant understanding the larger context of sociology itself. And, while it was years later, Olaf's story about Carl Taylor's presidential address to the ASA is what first set me on that journey.

There are so many other stories to tell—like what led to the USDA burning the farm population estimates one year (Rosenbaum 1965); how Charlie Loomis was one of the founders of the Society for Applied Anthropology (van Willigen 2013); or how the SSSP sought to configure its organization modeled on the RSS (Skura 1976:23). And those don't even cover our more recent generations![37]

Conclusion

I could tell stories til the cows come home. Thanks to Olaf, I know why Carle Zimmerman's publications at one time can be the most excruciatingly detailed, dry things you ever read to being one of the most animated the next.[38] How E. L. Kirkpatrick loved working with graduate students and even married one. Or, how Edmund de S. Brunner helped play a role in the number of women who were members of the early RSS.

If biography informs one's personal journey, then in a way, the behind-the-scenes stories like these can also lift the curtain on the history of a disciplinary field. They reveal qualities of its culture and values. They uncover another aspect to the collective journey—beyond the theories, methodologies, and research products—they reveal a kind of collective biography.

History is not just about dead people. It's about personalities, struggles, and challenges. Some are unique to our (or their) times and some are more ubiquitous. In 2005, Jess Gilbert wrote in his review of *Sociology in Government*:

> About twenty-five years ago, a "new," critical rural sociology arose in the United States. Young radicals were reacting to what they saw as the relatively staid, uncontroversial research of their elders. Except for the case of Goldschmidt, who republished his work in 1978, young rural sociologists did not know of the "purges" and tribulations that had occurred within the discipline at the end of World War II. They thought that they were the first rural sociologists to challenge the agricultural status quo and advocate serious reform. They (rather, we) were wrong [. . .]
> (Gilbert 2005:243)[39]

Everyone has their stories. While some may get published, most won't. My own introduction to rural sociology came through the 53 years of the Division's research and my introduction to thinking about our history came through Olaf. Even though I have done work in other areas, including rural poverty and applied population work in Cooperative Extension, historical research was my dissertation focus, and I have continued in my historical pursuits. In December 2010, Olaf and I published another book and in 2013 it was nominated for the ASA History of Sociology Section's Distinguished Scholarly Publication Award. I even became the first woman and second youngest person to serve as Historian of the Rural Sociological Society. Who knew how fateful that one phone call would turn out to be? In the words of Dudley Duncan:

> I foresee a rural society which we cannot study without new concepts, new units of measurement, new ideas of basic rural

groups, and new senses and ideas of relationships between rural people and other human groups. We must see agricultural society in the light of a new function in the total society . . .

Never cease looking for the unexpected, despising not the old nor fearing the new . . .

The things which we know are never true for a much longer time than it took us to learn them. In the future, social change will be so rapid that what we learn will have become obsolete before we are sure of it. Such is the prospect which we must face with a realistic determination. Carry on!

O. D. Duncan (1953)

Notes

1. Space precludes being able to do more than pose the question in a rhetorical manner, but some good related reads on biography and personal narrative include Sica and Turner (2006), Laslett (1991; 1999) and Abbott (2005). To read in their own words about how some of the early rural sociologists got into the field, check out the last section of Nelson (1969:165–185). As a complement to his history of rural sociology, Nelson wrote and asked many of the pioneer rural sociologists "How did you happen to become a rural sociologist?" He includes the responses in his book section titled "Memoirs."
2. Today, the department at Cornell is called the Department of Development Sociology.
3. As I write this, Olaf just celebrated his 104th birthday. In 2010, he saw his fifth and sixth books come out in print (Larson 2010; Zimmerman and Larson 2010). Olaf is not only the last person remaining who worked in the Division, he is the last person who was present at the founding of the Rural Sociological Society (Fuguitt 2009). Today, "it's not just Olaf's students, but the students of his students who are now being counted among the senior rural sociologists" (Zimmerman 2013:5). To learn more about Olaf Larson, see also Voth (1985) and Zimmerman (2005; 2006a; 2006b). Olaf's video welcome for the RSS 75th anniversary is available on the Historian's section of the RSS website: www.ruralsociology.org/
4. Today, what had been the Division is now the USDA's Economic Research Service which was established in 1961. For more on the transition from what had been the BAE and the DFPRL, see Bogue (1990) and Bowers (1990).
5. The ASA was originally named the American Sociological Society. Concerns over the acronym led to a petition in 1959 and the name was changed to the American Sociological Association (Martindale 1976:125; Rhoades 1981:76). While not historically accurate, for ease of reading and reference, I will use ASA throughout—even if the official name was the American Sociological Society at the time.
6. The phrase "I see dead people" comes from the 1999 movie *The Sixth Sense*.
7. The full bibliography of the Division's work is in Larson, Moe, and Zimmerman (1992). While materials were found in libraries, others came from personal files, book-shelves, and even attics of surviving relatives. With new electronic search tools (and some dumb luck), I have occasionally discovered even more articles and publications by Division staff. Some of these are included in Zimmerman and Larson (2010).

8. In fact, Olaf either met or knew many of the big names of the era. Though I really had no clue as to their importance, I even got the chance to meet some of the well-known names in the Division's and rural sociology's history. As Olaf's graduate student, he included me in a meeting of the project's advisory panel. As a result, I met some of the people whose names would later become so familiar. At the time I had no idea who these people were, but as the saying goes—if only I knew then what I know now!
9. While the impact of World War II was an important research area (e.g. Alexander 1945; Ensminger 1943; Frame 1945), we often forget that the war also had practical implications for the way research was done (Schuler 1944).
10. There was only one African American to work in the Division: Edward B. Williams. Yvonne Oliver interviewed Williams for Larson and Zimmerman (2003). In his interview, Williams noted that while "the BAE was probably the least racist part of the USDA, and among the least racist in the federal government," it was still "a product of its time" (2003:184).
11. Fontana Village is still a recreational destination today. To read more, go to: www.fontanavillage.com/history/ and to http://digitalheritage.org/2010/08/fontana-dam/
12. To see a sampling of Jim Crow Laws, visit the University of North Carolina at Chapel Hill School of Education's website LEARN NC at www.learnnc.org/lp/editions/nchist-newcentury/5103
13. There is more on the role of women in the RSS and the work of the Women's Caucus. In addition to Holik and Hassinger (1989), see Willits, Ghelfi and Lipner (1988) and Flora (1972; 1974).
14. From nearly its beginnings, Division research encountered challenges (Larson and Zimmerman 2003:49–56; Zimmerman 2008). One of the earliest incidents was Galpin's research on the use of time on farms. Intended to be helpful for planning activities directed at farm families, the chair of the House Committee on Printing spoke from the floor "booming, 'this is the stuff the Department of Agriculture wants to print. It tells the farmer that the sun rises in the morning and sets in the evening'" (Galpin 1938:41–43). USDA historians Wayne Rasmussen and Gladys Baker later wrote: "of all the Department's research bureaus, the Economic Research Service and its predecessor, the Bureau of Agricultural Economics, have engendered the most controversy" (1972:77).
15. Twitter is a social networking service where users can send text messages in a global online environment. Begun in 2006, public texts are limited to 140 characters and are called "tweets."
16. Even though Frank Alexander went on to a distinguished career, it was his involvement in the Coahoma study for which he is best remembered (Broadwell, Lawrence, and Larson 2010).
17. If you are thinking that the Coahoma study might stand out for being the first research conducted by the Division to describe race-based inequalities, it is not. During the early years of the Division, race was included in analyses of the social organization and relations among Blacks and Black communities (e.g. Doggett 1923). Under the headship of Carl Taylor, however, Division research placed a greater focus on the effects of structural inequality and the relations between Blacks and Whites. This approach was likely a reflection of Taylor's own views, for which he found himself in trouble before coming to the Division (Larson, Williams, and Wimberley 1999). For more on the reconnaissance studies, see Larson and Zimmerman (2003:104–108).

18. There was one exception: Oscar Lewis's book *On the Edge of the Black Waxy* (1948). While his book was based on his cultural reconnaissance survey of Bell County, Texas, it was published outside the Division. Still, results from the unpublished reconnaissance surveys did not go unused. They provided a basis for other research within the Division (e.g. Raper 1946), and may have been reconfigured to be used as part of the "impact of the Second World War" studies (e.g. Alexander 1945; Frame 1945).
19. The controversy surrounding the Arvin and Dinuba study has been reported in detail from the perspectives of the BAE economist who coordinated the set of Central Valley studies (Clawson 1946:330–332; 1987:150–160), an historian (Kirkendall 1964) and Walter Goldschmidt who conducted the research (1978a:467–473; 1978b). Decades after his original research, re-examinations of the Goldschmidt hypothesis can still be found (e.g. Green 1985; Lobao, Schulman, and Swanson 1993; Peters 2002).
20. Not long after the congressional hearings, the phrase "cultural surveys" came to symbolize trouble. Even the mere mention of the word "culture" caused alarm. Olaf had completed a comprehensive study of the RR-FSA (Rural Rehabilitation—Farm Security Administration) program. Before submitting Olaf's manuscript to be published, BAE Chief O.V. Wells stepped in. Wanting "insurance that it contained no terms such as "culture" or other language which could result in a political backlash costly to the BAE," Wells "insisted on personally reading and editing the 400-plus page manuscript (Larson and Zimmerman 2003:54). In the end, only a few mimeograph copies were produced and "made available to interested research workers, administrators, and to libraries" (Larson 1947: Foreword). It was not until nearly five years later that the Indian Society of Agricultural Economics reissued Olaf's report (Larson 1951).
21. Since Benson moved quickly, some called it a sneak attack (Hardin 1954:218) and the ending of the BAE came as a "shock" for both former BAE chiefs Henry Taylor and Howard Tolley (Wells et al. 1954:12, 14). Benson's reorganization cut up the BAE (Baker et al. 1963:463–466, 498–501) such that Henry Taylor asked: "What considerations led to the breakup of the already very small Division of Farm Population and Rural Life and assigning part of its activities to the Agricultural Research Service and part to the Agricultural Marketing Service?" (Wells et al. 1954:15). In his analysis, Hardin noted that "the general orientation of the Department's high command is toward business" (1954:210) and that the "dismembering of the BAE" was part of Republican moves to "break up apparently unfriendly concentrations and to create their own positions of strength" (1954:227). In 1961, with another reorganization, the current Economic Research Service was established (Bowers 1990; Koffsky 1966).
22. To read the Conference Report and reactions from those in the RSS, see the display book "Congress Strikes Again: The Era of the 'Big Chill'" created for the RSS 75th anniversary (Zimmerman 2012a).
23. In at least one graduate program in the 1960s, Coahoma was taught in the context of civil rights and Goldschmidt was taught in relation to agriculture. Including Coahoma and Goldschmidt, Friedland (2010) recounts two other stories of "persons violating the established norms" as well as the impacts on the climate in rural sociology.
24. Since the ASA Rural Sociology section saw their journal *Rural Sociology* as addressing all the issues in sociology, just in a rural context, in its first year the section requested to have their journal listed among those that ASA members could choose from. However, the request was rebuffed. Relationships between the journal and the ASA arose again nearly three decades later. After the initial sponsorship by LSU, university sponsors/publishers changed about every five years or so. In 1962, the upcoming transition brought

a desire for greater stability and prompted the question of asking if the ASA would publish the journal. The idea never went very far and the response revealed larger antagonisms. Indeed, Talcott Parson's letter suggests that the decision from ASA would have been to the negative. The summary of events by Allan Beegle, as well as Parsons's letter, indicate that larger issues of relations between the ASA and RSS were also at hand as the ASA would have required that the RSS resume its section status. Copies of the original documents are available in *Creating the Journal: Rural Sociology* (Zimmerman 2012a).

25. The ASA restricted section members to only one conference presentation. This meant that if a person presented a paper in the section on Rural Sociology (or any other section), they were not allowed to present a paper in any of the general sessions or in another sections' sessions. Another issue was that the ASA required all members of sections to first be members of the larger society. As a result, nonsociologists or those with few interests in the larger academic discipline of sociology had no mechanism through which to join the rural group (e.g. Collard 1984:327).

26. "Youngest" is a relative term. As Sewell described in his interview, professional culture at the time was marked by more deference and young referred more to time in a post-Ph.D. professional position than to chronological age (Fuguitt 2009:33).

27. A copy of the original letters and correspondence are available in "Establishing the Rural Sociological Society" (Zimmerman 2012a).

28. In order to allow time for Sanderson to determine if the RSS could remain within the ASA while also being an independent organization, the RSS began its first year as the Rural Sociological Society of America with a provisional constitution and bylaws (Rural Sociological Society of America 1938). Sanderson presented his proposed amendment to the ASA Executive Committee (and it was twice published to the ASA membership). In the end, the question was shunted to the ASA Committee on Regional Societies. Eventually, in 1942, the ASA constitution was changed and the RSS was given representation on the ASA Executive Committee (Holik and Hassinger 1987a:13–16). To see copies of some of the original documents, see "Establishing the Rural Sociological Society" (Zimmerman 2012a).

29. Since it was not typical of other ASA presidential addresses, as if to "stir the pot," Taylor invited Robert Redfield and Samuel Stoffer to respond to his address (Redfield 1947; Stouffer 1947).

30. While not acknowledged as such, there were rural sociologists who Lengermann identifies as being a part of the ASR rebellion within the ASA (1979:189). In addition, Dwight Sanderson and John H. Kolb were both elected vice-presidents as part of the subsequent leadership change (1979:188). For more on the relationship between rural sociology and the ASR rebellion, see Zimmerman (2012b).

31. If you can't put your hands on the ASA publications, both Bernard's and Ogburn's presidential addresses can be found online on a website called "The Mead Project." Luther Lee Bernard's "Sociological Research and the Exceptional Man" is at www.brocku.ca/MeadProject/Bernard/Bernard_1933.html and William F. Ogburn's "The Folkways of a Scientific Sociology" is at www.brocku.ca/MeadProject/sup/Ogburn_1929.html. For more on Ogburn, a good read is Laslett (1991). For Bernard, he was a leader in the ASR rebellion (Lengermann 1979) and went on to create the original *The American Sociologist* as an alternative publication and outlet for opposing and critical assessments of the ASA (Galliher and Hagan 1989).

32. Highlighting how the shifting logics within sociology was not limited to methodological techniques, Ogburn goes on to say that scientific sociology is about one's approach, how

"[I]t will be necessary to crush out emotion" (1930:10), and that while he expected statistics to grow, that for at least a time, "a goodly portion of research in sociology will make no use of statistics" (1930:5). Luther Bernard, on the other hand, emphasized that even statistics required "well-filled minds to direct and interpret" the research (1932:9). As a result, as Bernard continues, "[T]hat is why some men's random observations are better than the most pretentious quantitative researches of other men" (1932:9).

33. For much more on sociology and the rise of positivism, Steinmetz is always a good read (e.g. 2005, 2007). Of course, rural sociology was not insulated from these movements or debates. For instance, Falk and Gilbert point out that Sanderson's approach to sociology was more "conservative" and "consensual" than that of Taylor's more action oriented, "engaged rural sociology" (1985:564). In what is my favorite RSS presidential address, Tom Ford reflects back on the epistemological shift represented by Bernard and Ogburn as it affected rural sociology. Tracing through the presidents' addresses that came before him, Ford eloquently lays out the various criticisms and issues that had faced rural sociology over the years. Included and key among them was the shift rural sociologists made to "utilizing more sophisticated procedures and designing their research to test sociological theory" (1985:529). In the end, Ford comes full circle and ends with echoes of an earlier era when he wrote: "It will be sadly ironic if, after discarding the dream [to create a better world] in order to better our research products, we learn that what society values most highly is not the scientific quality of our knowledge but our willingness to pursue the dream itself" (1985:536).

34. A similar critique made its way into rural sociology itself; variously portrayed as "relatively crude descriptions" (Stokes and Miller 1985:557) or researchers themselves colorfully referred to as "fact-finders" and "privy counters" (Sewell 1965:441). Additionally, while early research was not limited to community studies, a general critique of early rural sociology research cannot be disconnected from the specific critique of community studies as "flimsy," "impressionistic" (Newby 1980:77–80), and whose "contribution to the discipline is nil" (Sanders and Lewis 1976:47).

35. Turner's chapter in this volume includes some of the differences between sociology and rural sociology in universities. In addition, Camic's (2007) analysis of sociology's reactions in the interwar years includes comparisons with rural sociology and provides a good glimpse into some of the concrete implications that the different approaches in sociology and rural sociology.

36. There is not enough space to do it justice, but mention has to be made of the impact on rural sociology of its institutional location within Land Grant Universities. To learn more, be sure to read Buttel (1987), Busch and Lacy (1983), and Falk (1996). Later, Friedland speculated that "by moving toward quantification, rural sociology could relate itself simultaneously to the broader mainstream of the discipline while talking a language understandable to those elements dominating the institutional network of which it is a part" (2010:84).

37. In addition to the chapters in this book, there have been other venues such as special issues of journals like those dedicated to Bill Freudenberg (*Journal of Environmental Studies and Sciences*) or Bill Heffernan and the University of Missouri (*Southern Rural Sociology*). Over the years, a common place where commentaries and the history of rural sociology have been published was in *The Rural Sociologist* (*TRS*). In 2012, RSS ended the publication in favor of electronic means for communicating the Society's news and announcements but it remains a unique resource. In the near future, searchable pdf files of issues of *TRS* and its predecessor *Newsline* will be available on the RSS website. For

more on the history and contents of *TRS*, see Zimmerman (2011). Since history and its proscriptions for the future are interpreted and reinterpreted through the eyes and lives of each successive generation, some good reads also include Theodori (2009), Hooks (1983), Hooks and Flinn (1981), and Falk and Gilbert (1985).

38. From nearly my first days working for Olaf, I used to get asked if I was any relation to Carle Zimmerman. As far as I know, I don't think so. But the question became so ubiquitous that, for a while, Olaf would introduce me as "Julie Zimmerman—no relation." Eventually, the disclaimer was no longer needed. Not because I had established my own reputation, but because the number of people who remembered Carle were fewer and fewer. For more on Carle Zimmerman, see Smith (1978) and Fuguitt (2009:34–35).

39. Some of the critique and context to which Gilbert is referring include Newby (1980), Picou, Wells and Nyberg (1978), Bealer (1975), and his own (Gilbert 1982). While not published until much later, Friedland's "Who Killed Rural Sociology" was also written during this time (2010). Bonanno's chapter in this volume provides a good look into the shifting theoretical issues during this time.

Bibliography

Abbott, Andrew. 1997. "Of Time and Space: The Contemporary Relevance of the Chicago School." *Social Forces* 75:1149–1182.

Abbott, Andrew. 2005. "The Historicity of Individuals." *Social Science History* 29:1–13.

Alexander, Frank D. 1944. "Cultural Reconnaissance Survey of Coahoma County, Mississippi. For administrative use." Dittoed. Atlanta, GA: U.S. Department of Agriculture, Bureau of Agricultural Economics (Division of Farm Population and Rural Welfare).

Alexander, Frank D. 1945. "A Rural Community in Time of War: The Valley Community in Rabun County, Georgia." Mimeo. Atlanta, GA: U.S. Department of Agriculture, Bureau of Agricultural Economics (Division of Farm Population and Rural Welfare).

Badash, Lawrence. 2000. "Science and McCarthyism." *Minerva* 38:53–80.

Baker, Gladys L., Wayne D. Rasmussen, Vivian Wiser, and Jane M. Porter. 1963. *Century of Service: The First 100 Years of the United States Department of Agriculture*. Washington, DC: USDA, Centennial Committee.

Bealer, Robert C. 1975. "Theory and Rural Sociology." *Rural Sociology* 40:455–477.

Bernard, Luther Lee. 1932. "Sociological Research and the Exceptional Man." *Publications of the American Sociological Society* 27:3–19.

Bogue, Allan G. 1990. "Comment: Policy Making in the USDA." *Agricultural History* 64:244–251.

Bonanno, Alessandro. 2015 [forthcoming]. "Globalization and "Research Nationalism" in Rural Sociology." In Bakker, J. I. (Hans) (Ed.) *The Methodology of Political Economy: Studying the Global Rural-Urban Matrix*. Lanham, MD: Lexington Books (Taylor and Francis).

Bowers, Douglas E. 1990. "The Economic Research Service, 1961–1977." *Agricultural History* 64:231–243.

Broadwell, George J., James E. Lawrence, and Olaf F. Larson. 2010. "Frank DeWitt Alexander. November 16, 1903—November 20, 1983" in *Memorial Statements of the*

Cornell University Faculty 1868–2009. The Internet-First University Press: Cornell University. Retrieved March 6, 2014 (http://ecommons.cornell.edu/bitstream/1813/18859/2/Alexander_Frank_DeWitt_1983.pdf).

Busch, Lawrence, and William B. Lacy. 1983. *Science, Agriculture, and the Politics of Research*. Boulder, CO: Westview Press.

Buttel, Frederick H. 1987. "The Rural Social Sciences: An Overview of Research Institutions, Tools, and Knowledge for Addressing Problems and Issues." *Agriculture and Human Values* 4(1):42–65.

Calhoun, Craig. 2007. "Sociology in America: An Introduction," pp. 1–38 in *Sociology in America: A History*, edited by C. Calhoun. Chicago, IL: University of Chicago Press.

Camic, Charles. 2007. "On Edge: Sociology during the Great Depression and the New Deal," pp. 225–280 in *Sociology in America: A History*, edited by C. Calhoun. Chicago, IL: University of Chicago Press.

Clawson, Marion. 1946. "Discussion." *American Sociological Review* 11:330–332.

Clawson, Marion. 1987. *From Sagebrush to Sage: The Making of a Natural Resource Economist*. Washington, DC: ANA Publications.

Collard, Clyde V. 1984. "The Founding of Rural Sociology and the Rural Sociological Society." *The Rural Sociologist* 4(5):324–335.

Daniel, Pete. 1990. "Going Among Strangers: Southern Reactions to World War II." *The Journal of American History* 77:886–911.

Deutscher, Irwin. 1958. "Specialization in Sociology: A Logical Inquiry." *The Midwest Sociologist* 21:34–38.

Doggett, Allen B., Jr. 1923. "Three Negro Communities in Tidewater Virginia." Hampton, VA: Hampton Normal and Agricultural Institute. *Bulletin*, Vol. 19, No. 4. Contributed by School of Agriculture. U.S. Department of Agriculture, Bureau of Agricultural Economics, Division of Farm Population and Rural Life cooperating.

Duncan, Otis Durant. 1953. "A Communication from the Retiring President." *Rural Sociology* 18:412.

Ensminger, Douglas 1943. "The Impacts of the War on the Rural Community." *Social Forces* 22:76–79.

Falk, William H. 1996. "The Assertion of Identity in Rural Sociology." *Rural Sociology* 61:159–174.

Falk, William W., and Jess Gilbert. 1985. "Bringing Rural Sociology Back In." *Rural Sociology* 50:561–577.

Flora, Cornelia B. 1972. "Women in Rural Sociology." *Rural Sociology* 37:454–462.

Flora, Cornelia B. 1974. "A Letter to the Editor." *Newsline* 2(1):22.

Ford, Thomas R. 1985. "Rural Sociology and the Passing of Social Scientific Chivalry." *Rural Sociology* 50:523–538.

Frame, Nat T. 1945. "Rushmore: Village Centered Community in the Cornbelt in Wartime." Mimeo. Milwaukee, WI: U.S. Department of Agriculture, Bureau of Agricultural Economics (Division of Farm Population and Rural Welfare).

Friedland, William H. 2010. "Who Killed Rural Sociology? A Case Study in the Political Economy of Knowledge Production." *International Journal of Agriculture and Food* 17:72–88.

Fuguitt, Glenn. 2009. "William Sewell on the Founding of the Rural Sociological Society." *The Rural Sociologist* 29(2):30–36.

Galliher, John F., and Robert A. Hagan. 1989. "L. L. Bernard and the Original *American Sociologist*." *The American Sociologist* 20:134–143.
Galpin, Charles J. 1938. *My Drift Into Rural Sociology*. Baton Rouge, LA: Louisiana State University Press.
Gilbert, Jess. 1982. "Rural Theory: The Grounding of Rural Sociology." *Rural Sociology* 47:589–608.
Gilbert, Jess. 2005. "Review of Sociology in Government: The Galpin-Taylor Years in the U. S. Department of Agriculture, 1919–1953 by Olaf F. Larson and Julie N. Zimmerman, assisted by Edward O. Moe." *Agricultural History* 79:241–243.
Goldschmidt, Walter R. 1978a. *As You Sow: Three Studies in the Social Consequences of Agribusiness*. Montclair, NJ: Allanheld, Osmun & Co.
Goldschmidt, Walter R. 1978b. "Reflections on Arvin and Dinuba." *Newsline* 6(5):10–19.
Green, Gary P. 1985. "Large-Scale Farming and the Quality of Life in Rural Communities: Further Specification of the Goldschmidt Hypothesis." *Rural Sociology* 50:262–274.
Hardin, Charles M. 1946. "The Bureau of Agricultural Economics under Fire: A Study in Valuation Conflicts." *Journal of Farm Economics* 28:635–668.
Hardin, Charles M. 1954. "The Republican Department of Agriculture. A Political Interpretation." *Journal of Farm Economics* 36(2):210-227.
Hertzler, J. O. 1938. "American Regionalism and the Regional Sociological Society." *American Sociological Review* 3:738–748.
Holik, John S., and Edward W. Hassinger. 1986a. "The Rural Sociological Society: Its Beginning." *The Rural Sociologist* 6(5):331–348.
Holik, John S., and Edward W. Hassinger. 1986b. "The RSS: Coming to Formalization." *The Rural Sociologist* 6(6):407–420.
Holik, John S., and Edward W. Hassinger. 1987a. "The RSS: The Ties that Bind." *The Rural Sociologist* 7(1):3–18.
Holik, John S., and Edward W. Hassinger. 1987b. "RSS During the Depression and World War II Years." *The Rural Sociologist* 7(3):154–165.
Holik, John S., and Edward W. Hassinger. 1989. "The RSS: Toward Greater Participation." *The Rural Sociologist* 9(1):32–40.
Hooks, Gregory. M. 1983. "A New Deal for Farmers and Social Scientists: The Politics of Rural Sociology in the Depression Era." *Rural Sociology* 48:386–408.
Hooks, Gregory M., and William L. Flinn. 1981. "Toward a Sociology of Rural Sociology." *The Rural Sociologist* 1(3):130–138.
Hutcheson, Pilo A. 1997. "McCarthyism and the Professoriate: A Historiographic Nightmare?" pp. 610–627 in *The History of Higher Education*, 2nd edition, edited by L. F. Goodchild and H. Wechsler. Reno, NV: University of Nevada Press.
Keen, Mike Forest. 2003. *Stalking Sociologists: J. Edgar Hoover's FBI Surveillance of American Sociology*. Edison, NJ: Transaction Publishers.
Kirkendall, Richard S. 1964. "Social Sciences in the Central Valley of California: An Episode." *California Historical Society Quarterly* 43:195–218.
Kirkendall, Richard S. 1966. *Social Scientists and Farm Politics in the Age of Roosevelt*. Columbia, MO: University of Missouri Press.
Koffsky, Nathan N. 1966. "Agricultural Economics in the USDA: An Inside View." *Journal of Farm Economics* 48:413–421.

Larson, Olaf F. 1947. "Ten Years of Rural Rehabilitation in the United States." Mimeo. Washington, DC: U.S. Department of Agriculture, Bureau of Agricultural Economics (Division of Farm Population and Rural Welfare).

Larson, Olaf F. 1951. "Ten Years of Rural Rehabilitation in the United States: Summary of a Report." An abridgement by Sri B. S. Mavinkurve from the full report by the same title. Bombay, India: Indian Society of Agricultural Economics.

Larson, Olaf F. 2010. *When Horses Pulled the Plow: Life of a Wisconsin Farm Boy, 1910–1929.* Madison, WI: University of Wisconsin Press.

Larson, Olaf F., and Julie N. Zimmerman (with the assistance of Edward O. Moe). 2003. *Sociology in Government: The Galpin-Taylor Years in the U.S. Department of Agriculture, 1919–1953.* University Park, PA: Penn State University Press.

Larson, Olaf F., Edward O. Moe, and Julie N. Zimmerman. 1992. *Sociology in Government: A Bibliography of the U.S. Department of Agriculture's Division of Farm Population and Rural Life, 1919–1953.* Boulder, CO: Westview Press.

Larson, Olaf F., Robin M. Williams, Jr., and Ronald C. Wimberley. 1999. "Dismissal of a Sociologist: The AAUP report on Carl C. Taylor." *Rural Sociology* 64:533–553.

Laslett, Barbara. 1991. "Biography as Historical Sociology: The Case of William Fielding Ogburn." *Theory and Society* 20:511–538.

Laslett, Barbara. 1999. "Personal Narratives as Sociology." *Contemporary Sociology* 28:391–401.

Lengermann, Patricia Madoo. 1979. "The Founding of the American Sociological Review: The Anatomy of a Rebellion." *American Sociological Review* 44:185–198.

Lewis, Oscar. 1948. *On the Edge of the Black Waxy: A Cultural Survey of Bell County, Texas. Social and Philosophical Sciences*, No. 7. St. Louis, MO: Washington University Studies, New Series.

Lobao, Linda M., Michael D. Schulman, and Louis E. Swanson. 1993. "Still Going: Recent Debates on the Goldschmidt Hypothesis." *Rural Sociology* 58:277–288.

Loomis, Charles P. 1981. "Parochialism in the ASA." *The American Sociologist* 16(1):59–62.

Martindale, Don. 1976. "American Sociology Before World War II." *Annual Review of Sociology* 2:121–143.

Mayberry, B. D. (Ed.) 1977. *Development of Research at Historically Black Land-grant Institutions.* Jefferson City, MO: Association of Research Coordinators Land Grant 1890 Colleges and Universities.

Montgomery, James E. 1945. "Reconnaissance Survey of Union County, South Carolina (Summary)." For administrative use. Mimeo. Atlanta, GA: U.S. Department of Agriculture, Bureau of Agricultural Economics (Division of Farm Population and Rural Welfare).

Nelson, Lowry. 1969. *Rural Sociology: Its Origins and Growth in the United States.* Minneapolis, MN: University of Minnesota Press.

Odum, Howard W. 1951. *American Sociology: The Story of Sociology in the United States through 1950.* New York: Longmans, Green & Co.

Ogburn, William F. 1930. "The Folkways of a Scientific Sociology." *Publications of the American Sociological Society* 24:1–11.

Oliver, Yvonne. 2003. "The Division and Black Populations," pp. 171–187 in *Sociology in Government: The Galpin-Taylor Years in the U.S. Department of Agriculture, 1919–1953,* by Olaf F. Larson and Julie N. Zimmerman (with the assistance of Edward O. Moe). University Park, PA: Pennsylvania State University Press.

Peters, David J. 2002. *Revisiting the Goldschmidt Hypothesis: the Effect of Economic Structure on Socioeconomic Conditions in the Rural Midwest.* P-0702–1, Missouri Economic Research and Information Center. Jefferson City, MO: Missouri Department of Economic Development.

Picou, J. Stevens, Richard H. Wells, and Kenneth L. Nyberg. 1978. "Paradigms, Theories, and Methods in Contemporary Rural Sociology." *Rural Sociology* 43:559–583.

Pryor, Herbert. 1945. "Cultural Reconnaissance: Avoyelles Parish, Louisiana." For administrative use only. Dittoed. Little Rock, AR: U.S. Department of Agriculture, Bureau of Agricultural Economics (Division of Farm Population and Rural Welfare).

Raper, Arthur F. 1944. "Cultural Reconnaissance: Greene County, Georgia." For administrative use. Dittoed. Washington, DC: U.S. Department of Agriculture, Bureau of Agricultural Economics, Division of Farm Population and Rural Welfare.

Raper, Arthur F. 1946. "Uses being made by Rural Families of Increased Wartime Incomes: Based on Current Field Reports made by Professional Observers in a National Sample of 71 Counties." Mimeo. Washington, DC: U.S. Department of Agriculture, Bureau of Agricultural Economics (Division of Farm Population and Rural Welfare).

Rasmussen, Wayne D., and Gladys L. Baker. 1972. *The Department of Agriculture.* New York: Praeger Publishers.

Redfield, Robert. 1947. "Sociology and Common Sense: Discussion." *American Sociological Review* 12:9–11.

Rhoades, Lawrence J. 1981. *A History of the American Sociological Association 1905–1980.* Washington, DC: American Sociological Association.

Rosenbaum, Walter A. 1965. *The Burning of the Farm Population Estimates.* Inter-university Case Program Series No. 83. Indianapolis, IN: The Bobbs-Merrill Company.

Rural Sociological Society of America. 1938. "News Notes and Announcements." *Rural Sociology* 3:123–128

Sanders, Irwin T., and Gordon F. Lewis. 1976. "Rural Community Studies in the United States: A Decade in Review." *Annual Review of Sociology* 2:35–53.

Schuler, Edgar A. 1944. "Suggestions for Rural Sociological Research under Wartime Restrictions on Travel." *Rural Sociology* 9:59–62.

Sewell, William H. 1965. "Rural Sociological Research, 1936–1965." *Rural Sociology* 30:428–451.

Sica, Alan, and Stephen Turner (Eds.). 2006. *The Disobedient Generation: Social Theorists in the Sixties.* University of Chicago Press: Chicago.

Skura, Barry. 1976. "Constraints on a Reform Movement: Relationships between SSSP and ASA, 1951–1970." *Social Problems* 24:15–36.

Smith, T. Lynn. 1957. "Rural Sociology in the United States and Canada: A Trend Report." *Current Sociology* 6:5–75.

Smith, T. Lynn. 1978. "The Life and Work of Carle C. Zimmerman," pp. 1–7 in *Sociocultural Change since 1950. In Honor of Carle C. Zimmerman, Professor Emeritus, Harvard University*, edited by T. Lynn Smith and Man Singh Das. Vikas Publishing House: New Dehli, India.

Steinmetz, George. 2005. "The Genealogy of a Positivist Haunting: Comparing Prewar and Postwar U.S. Sociology." *Boundary 2* 32(2)109–135.

Steinmetz, George. 2007. "American Sociology before and after World War II: The (Temporary) Settling of a Disciplinary Field," pp. 324–366 in *Sociology in America: A History*, edited by C. Calhoun. Chicago: University of Chicago Press.

Stokes, C. Shannon, and Michael K. Miller. 1985. "A Methodological Review of Fifty Years of Research in *Rural Sociology*." *Rural Sociology* 50:539–560.

Stouffer, Samuel A. 1947. "Sociology and Common Sense: Discussion." *American Sociological Review* 12:11–12.

Tate, Leland. 1947. "News Notes and Announcements." *Rural Sociology* 12:456–166.

Taylor, Carl C. 1947. "Sociology and Common Sense." *American Sociological Review* 12:1–9.

Theodori, Gene L. 2009. "Modification and Adaptation in Rural Sociology: Part 1." *Southern Rural Sociology* 24:1–13.

Turner, Stephen Park, and Jonathan H. Turner. 1990. *The Impossible Science: An Institutional Analysis of American Sociology*. Newbury Park: Sage Publications.

U.S. Congress, House. 1946. Hearings before the Subcommittee of the Committee on Appropriations. Agriculture Department Appropriation Bill for 1947. 79th Congress, Second Session. Washington, DC: Government Printing Office.

van Willigen, John. 2013. "SfAA Oral History Project: Conversation with one of SfAA's Founders: An interview of Charles P. Loomis" *SFAA News: A Publication of the Society for Applied Anthropology* 24(1):25–30.

Voth, Donald E. 1985. "Comments on Olaf F. Larson: Distinguished Rural Sociologist." *The Rural Sociologist* 5(5):363–364.

Wells, O.V., John D. Black, Paul H. Appleby, H.C. Taylor, Howard R. Tolley, Raymond J. Penn and Theodore Schultz. 1954. "The Fragmentation of the BAE." *Journal of Farm Economics* 36:1–21.

Willits, Fern K., Linda M. Gelfi, and Michele E. Lipner. 1988. "Women in the Rural Sociological Society: A History." *The Rural Sociologist*. 8(2):126–141.

Zimmerman, Julie N. 2005. "A Conversation with Olaf Larson: Part 1." *The Rural Sociologist*. 25(4):30–32.

Zimmerman, Julie N. 2006a. "A Conversation with Olaf Larson: Part 2." *The Rural Sociologist*. 26(1):32–34.

Zimmerman, Julie N. 2006b. "A Conversation with Olaf Larson: Part 3." *The Rural Sociologist* 26(2):13–15.

Zimmerman, Julie N. 2008. "Voices from the Past, Lessons for the Future: Learning from the History of Sociology in Government." *Equal Opportunities International (Now: Equality Diversity and Inclusion—An International Journal)* 27:132–146.

Zimmerman, Julie N. 2011. "A Long and Winding Road: Assessing The Rural Sociologist's Past in Order to Inform its Future." Rural Sociological Society (RSS). November.

Zimmerman, Julie N. 2012a. "The American Sociological Society's Section on Rural Sociology," "Creating the Journal: *Rural Sociology*," "Establishing the Rural Sociological Society," "Congress Strikes Again: The Era of the 'Big Chill,'" "Organizing the 1st World Congress of Rural Sociology: The Beginnings of the International Rural Sociological Association." Rural Sociological Society (RSS). July.

Zimmerman, Julie N. 2012b. "What's Rural Got To Do With It? Rural Sociologists and the ASR Rebellion in the American Sociological Association." Paper presented at the Rural Sociological Society Annual Meeting. Chicago, IL. July, 2012.

Zimmerman, Julie N. 2013. "A Rural Sociologist for Almost Eight Decades: Olaf F. Larson." *ASA (American Sociological Association) Footnotes* 41(7):5.

Zimmerman, Julie N., and Olaf F. Larson. 2010. *Opening Windows onto Hidden Lives: Women, Country Life, and Early Rural Sociological Research*. University Park, PA: Penn State University Press.

Part II
CANDID ACCOUNTS

4
AN ACCIDENTAL RURAL SOCIOLOGIST

MICHAEL D. SCHULMAN,
NORTH CAROLINA STATE UNIVERSITY

Prologue

I never intended to become a rural sociologist. I grew up in a Jewish neighborhood in the middle of Chicago. My standard one-liner about my background is that my dad had 1/4000th of an acre, all in pasture. I think the closest I was to a farm while growing up was visiting a zoo in Chicago where they had a cow and a few barnyard animals. So my academic profession really has nothing to do with my parents, my hometown, or any formative experiences as a youth. I became a rural sociologist by osmosis, serendipity, adaptation to my environment, networks, and labeling. I am an accidental rural sociologist.

Osmosis and Serendipity

I finished my undergraduate degree at a small liberal arts college on the West Coast. There were three sociologists and two or three anthropologists in the social sciences. One of the professors was a Harvard Ph.D. who had taken theory classes with Talcott Parsons. I remember taking a class in Community from one of the anthropologists. That is about as close to rural sociology as I ever got during my undergraduate career. Classes were relatively small with a strong emphasis on sociologist theory. It was also the late 1960s, so critical theory was the rage. Everyone had a copy of Marcuse's ([1955] 1964) *One Dimensional Man* and Domhoff's (1967) *Who Rules America* in their backpacks along with granola and other organic substances.

I arrived at the University of Wisconsin-Madison in the fall of 1970 having very little idea about the nature and organization of professional sociology. I took a general methods class and an intro statistics class in my undergraduate program, but never thought of them as core until I landed in Wisconsin. It was quite a shock to realize that quantitative methods and statistics, not classical or contemporary theory, were the core of graduate training.

I also learned that Madison was quite unique in having two sociology departments, but one graduate training program. The main department, in a contemporary building, was located high on Bascom Hill overlooking woods and the lake. The rural sociology department was down the hill, towards the center of campus, in a classic land grant building dating from 1902. My first graduate advisor was from the rural sociology faculty, but I was really interested in political sociology and social organization. I really paid very little attention to the rural sociology faculty until I needed a summer job. Rural sociology had some part-time hourly jobs, and I was able to obtain one.

The job was with the Wisconsin Population Laboratory. I was calculating county level statistics on population change. It was in the attic of Ag Hall, which was a windowless space that baked in the Wisconsin summers. For each county in Wisconsin, I took data from the Census volumes and calculated percentage changes from 1960 to 1970 using an old Monroe calculator. I had weekly meetings with my supervisor, but otherwise had considerable flexibility in terms of my hours. I soon discovered that there was one major advantage to being in rural sociology—you were much closer to the ice cream in Babcock Hall on the agriculture part of the UW-Madison campus than working in the social sciences building. A 2 pm break for ice cream became our "happy hour" for those of us working in the rural sociology department.

People must have been pleased with the population work I did because I was also asked to be an interviewer on a county fair survey that the extension sociology faculty was conducting. Each county in Wisconsin had its own fair, some small, others large with midways and concerts. To many of my graduate student colleagues, this was a non-prestigious job. I thought it was great. I traveled throughout the state and had my travel expenses covered by the project. The State of Wisconsin put government funds into these local fairs, and the project was designed to gather feedback and public opinion about their local fairs. We worked late afternoons and evenings at a tent near the entry/exit of the fair. With a clipboard and a printed survey, I interviewed fair attendees. In exchange for their time, those who completed the interview received a wooden yardstick.

Again, people must have been pleased with my work because I received a research assistantship appointment in rural sociology. I remember working on issues of rural poverty and underdevelopment with Professor Gene Havens, especially with regard to the Northern part of the state, known as the "cut-over." It was here that I first met Fred Buttel, another graduate student, who was working on surveys of environmental attitudes with Professor Bill Flynn. They graciously allowed me to use some of the data on political attitudes and beliefs from their statewide surveys for my dissertation. I was working in political sociology but living in rural sociology.

My teaching experiences also developed in the rural sociology program. Another graduate student, Pat Smith, was working with Extension sociology. Somehow, he managed to get permission to teach some introductory sociology classes in the Wisconsin prisons (Schulman and Canak 1976). I taught an introductory sociology in the minimum-security prison and then in the maximum-security prison. When Professor Flynn went on leave, I was hired to teach his introduction to rural life/community class as a part-time instructor. I taught it as a social problems class in the countryside. I remember using Hightower's (1973) *Hard Times, Hard Tomatoes* as one of the books. One of the students in the class must have talked to her father, because my

Department Chair called me in one day to talk about the class. Apparently, the student's father had mentioned my class to someone from the College when a Presidential candidate was visiting his farm. The Department Chair was very supportive of my efforts and wrote an excellent letter on my behalf and that was the last that I heard about the issue.

By the time I went on the job market, I thought of myself as political sociologist and social theorist. However, I had no success in finding any jobs in these areas. I did not realize that all my experiences and almost all my references were in rural sociology and therefore, I was labeled as a rural sociologist. So I became a rural sociologist in graduate school through a process of osmosis and serendipity.

Adaptation to the Environment

When I got off the plane in Raleigh North Carolina for my job interview at North Carolina State University, I thought I was interviewing for a position in comparative sociology and social change. The department was advertising several positions. While originally all the positions were in the College of Agriculture and Life Sciences, the growth of the university and the creation of the College of Humanities and Social Sciences resulted in new sociology positions. There was only one department, but some positions were in Ag and Life Sciences and others were in Humanities and Social Sciences. There was a long tradition of rural sociology at NCSU, dating back to the 1920s with the arrival of Carle Zimmerman, and Carl Taylor was on the faculty at NCSU in the 1930s.

The Associate Head soon informed me that I was interviewing for the rural sociology position in Ag and Life Sciences. Since it was a nine-month teaching position, just like the positions in Humanities and Social Sciences, I probably gave it very little attention. The Associate Head guided me through the interview and I managed not to say anything that tripped me up. I received an offer and, having no other alternatives, accepted it.

When I started as an Assistant Professor at NCSU, the Department was somewhat lopsided in terms of career stages. There were a group of senior faculty, mainly demographers and community development specialists, and a few people in the middle ranks. The department was hiring three or four assistant professors per year, some experienced and others new doctorates. The new assistant professors formed a reading group as a way of banding together and giving each other social support. I was teaching three classes per semester: mainly sections of introductory sociology but also another version of my rural social problems class.

It was through the rural social problems class that I first became acquainted with rural North Carolina. I would have students do a county level and community profile as one of their assignments. They could use demographic information but could also interview people about their community and how it has changed over time. A number of the students were from farm backgrounds or were actually working or operating a farm, so I would receive papers on tobacco production and on tobacco-dependent communities. Since I was in the College of Agriculture and was under pressure to start a research program on rural North Carolina, and since the sociology of agriculture was beginning its ascendance in the Rural Sociological Society, I started reading about tobacco and tobacco farming. The decline of African American farmers was also a major issue at the time, as evidence by a land loss prevention project at the North Carolina Central University Law School (the historically Black law school in the state). Through a long and somewhat convoluted process, I was able to collect survey data from small-scale, limited resources, and minority farmers in selected North Carolina counties (Schulman and Garrett 1990). The project provided data for publications on land loss and minority farmers and it established my rural sociology credentials at North Carolina State University (Schulman, Garrett and Luginbuhl 1985; Schulman, et al. 1985; Schulman and Newman 1991; Schulman, Zimmer, and Danaher 1994).

I was teaching classes in development sociology and reading the peasant economy literature, especially the debates about the definition of peasants and the differentiation of the peasantry. At the same time, I was involved in a study of small-scale limited resource farmers in North Carolina. The US Agricultural Census statistics were showing drastic declines in the number of African American farmers, and community organizations were highlighting the role of discrimination and racism in this decline. The article from the *Journal of Peasant Studies* (Schulman, Garrett, and Newman 1989) represents an attempt to combine these intellectual and political issues. I was able to collect multiple waves of survey data on low-income predominantly African American farmers in a tobacco-growing region in North Carolina. While Black farmers are not "peasants," the problem of socioeconomic and demographic differentiation throughout the life cycle is addressed in this article.

At the same time, one of the other new faculty members who joined the NCSU Department was interested in work and work organizations. In addition to tobacco, textile mills dominated the rural areas of North Carolina. One community, Roanoke Rapids where the J.P. Stevens Company had its plants, was receiving national attention because of a unionization effort and a national boycott pressuring the firm over its stance towards unions (Zingraff and Schulman 1984). Four of us, including faculty from other departments and institutions, formed a research group to do a community case study of Roanoke Rapids and the unionization struggle. We were able to secure a small grant to fund a research project and, using graduate student labor, collected survey data on textile workers in Roanoke Rapids. I went back and used many of the political attitudes and belief scales that I learned about while at Wisconsin. A set of articles and a co-edited book came of these efforts (Leiter, Schulman, and Zingraff 1991). My rural credentials were enhanced: not only was I studying tobacco, but I was also studying textile communities and rural workers. I received funding for another textile community study in the early 1990s: a study of Fieldcrest Mills and Kannapolis North Carolina. This was another traditional mill town experiencing rapid social change due to globalization, technological change, and in the middle of a unionization struggle.

The article published in *Rural Sociology* (Schulman and Anderson 1999) on social capital came from my second community study of a textile town. Our study community, Kannapolis North Carolina, was the home of Cannon Mills and was at one time the largest unincorporated community in the United States. The Cannon family sold the mills to R. Murdock, who operated them for a short period of time before selling the mills, but keeping a large amount of community real estate, to Fieldcrest. Fieldcrest was engaged in a unionization struggle in the community in the 1990s (Anderson, Schulman, and Wood 2001). The workforce was down to approximately 5,000 workers, partially due to technological change, when we conducted our study. We collected informant interviews from workers and townspeople, compiled historical data on the town, and sought to chart its historical transformation, with a concentration on issues of race, gender, and unionization.

There is a large literature on paternalism and another one, mainly coming from studies in Britain, on deference and the worker. Studies concerned rural mill and industrial towns, similar to the one that we were studying, so it seemed a natural fit to the case study of Fieldcrest Mills and Kannapolis. At the same time, the literature on social capital was taking off: many of the studies assuming an overwhelming positive approach to social capital as the glue that made social life and social organization possible. There were one or two commentaries on the negative or downside of social capital. I decided to apply the social capital perspective to our textile community case study, emphasizing the downside or the dark side (clearly a *Star Wars* knockoff) of social capital in the form of the paternalistic and deferential social relations characteristic of mill towns. It is an article that really has no traditional data: no charts or statistics. I still chuckle sometimes over a few of the sentences that contain *Star Wars* allusions.

The tobacco and textiles work carried me through the mid-1980s. I was also involved in NCSU international programs efforts on technological change and development. When the farm crisis of the 1980s enveloped the South, we asked for funds to emulate the farm household surveys that our rural sociology colleagues in the Midwest were conducting. We were able to do several years of statewide surveys, collecting data on health, well-being, employment, and the quality of jobs. Working with graduate students, we developed a set of publications on stress, well-being, and farm survival (Schulman and Armstrong 1989, 1990; Armstrong and Schulman 1990). In this work, we addressed questions from the social psychology of stress literatures, and also questions from the peasant differentiation debates. My adaptation to the North Carolina environment was now complete—I had become a rural sociologist, a sociologist of agriculture, and a scholar of textiles and tobacco (Falk, Schulman, and Tickamyer 2003).

Networks

In working on our North Carolina Farm and Rural Life Surveys, I was reading articles on rural health. An epidemiologist at the UNC School of Public Health who I consulted recommended including some questions on injury and occupational safety and health, given the high rates of injury among farmers and members of farm households. From these questions, I developed a paper that I submitted to the Surgeon General's Conference on Farm Safety and Health. At this conference in Iowa, I made contact with Dr. Carol Runyan, the Director of the UNC Injury Prevention Center. Even though we worked at institutions that are approximately 25 miles apart, we had no contact till the Iowa conference. We talked about our interest in work and young workers, and decided to see how we could work together in terms of future projects. This was entry into occupational injury and public health. Having always been interested in work and workers, this did not seem a big leap to me. Injury was simply a new dependent variable: a consequence of the social relations of production.

The collaboration with Dr. Runyan and the UNC Injury Prevention Center began in 1990 and started with a set of small-scale projects. We decided to direct our efforts at young workers, aged 14–18. We did the traditional academic process of reviewing existing data and studies. Sociologists had much to say about young workers in the status attainment and juvenile delinquency literatures, but few seemed to be studying occupational hazards and injuries. We started developing questionnaires and consent scripts for young workers and their parents. I remember getting permission to interview the teens attending the North Carolina 4-H Congress and administering a questionnaire about their farm and non-farm work experiences. A set of focus groups with young workers in the immediate geographical area yielded rich qualitative data about the hazard exposures and power relations in the workplace.

From these small-scale studies we were able to secure funding for a North Carolina statewide survey of young workers. A special set of questions for farm work was included in this survey and I was able to develop both basic and applied journal publications from the survey data (Schulman et al. 1997). We did one article where we looked at workplace hazards and jobs by gender (Evensen et al. 2000). Of course, for sociology, this is no big deal, but it was one of the first articles in public health to look at the gender division of labor and hazards among young workers. We were also able to secure funding for a study of teen workers in construction and for a study of Latino construction workers (Runyan et al. 2006). As part of the construction worker research, I conducted a survey of North Carolina construction firms that employed teen workers. The success of our small and medium-scale projects lead to a successful proposal for a national study of working teens and parents. I was now firmly in public health and injury prevention that resulted in my also having a foothold in rural health. Over time, my public health work grew and I was using the majority of my research time on injury control and prevention (Loomis et al. 2009; Runyan, Schulman, and Scholl 2011). Since one aspect of this work concerned young workers and farms, my deans and directors were quite pleased, although many of my sociology colleagues probably thought I was crazy since they did not see me publishing in the major mainstream sociology journals (Runyan, Schulman, and Hoffman 2003).

The studies in the *American Journal of Public Health* (Rauscher, Runyan, and Schulman 2008) and in *Pediatrics* (Runyan et al. 2007) are from our youth work and injury surveys. These were mainstream survey research and quantitative analysis public health research projects directed at identifying hazard exposures among youth working in both farm and non-farm settings. It was an emerging issue in injury control and prevention, but one where relatively little data existed at the time. Many of the big national data collection projects did not collect data from workers under 16 years of age. The growth in the youth labor force and youth employment, and news reports about youth injuries, especially in the agricultural sector, added to the currency of the project. Sociologists of work were addressing issues of race and gender through analyses of segregation and dual labor markets. I decided to add these perspectives to our empirical studies and investigate gender and race issues in teen work and hazard exposure. These articles represent attempts to bridge mainstream sociological concerns with race and gender with public health surveillance investigations of workplace hazards and injuries among youth workers. One of the articles from the North Carolina survey data on youth workers was originally submitted to a mainstream sociology journal. The editor of the journal called me about the paper a few days after submission. While the editor had a very positive review of the paper, he/she asked me to withdraw it because of concerns about negative evaluation from outside reviewers. After working with the public health and epidemiology folk, I had adopted their publication style that did not rely upon tracing the issue under investigation back to the original writings of one of the classic works in sociology. I understood what the editor was saying and followed her/his advice to withdraw the paper and find it a new publication home in another type of journal. So, apparently, I had transformed myself once again, away from sociology and into the field of public health (Costello, Schulman, and Luginbuhl 2003; Schulman and Slesinger 2004).

Keeping up Surprises

Throughout this intellectual and professional odyssey, I maintained an active role in the Rural Sociological Society. I was on council for two years and edited the monograph series, The Rural Studies Series, when it was first with Penn State University Press. I went to meetings, gave papers, and interacted with colleagues. I remember applying to be Editor of Rural Sociology, but was not selected. So it was a surprise when I was contacted and asked to think about applying to be Editor of *Rural Sociology*. The call came at an appropriate time in my professional career. We had finished a set of primary data-collection efforts on young workers and were analyzing the data and writing publications. I applied, not thinking that I would be selected. However, I was selected, and the journal came to North Carolina State University.

I was very fortunate to have a group of exceptional graduate students working with me as managing editors of Rural Sociology. One of my goals was to move to an on-line submission and review system. So, during my first year, we moved to the Allen Track system with Allen Press. Coincident with this transition, RSS Council was looking into finding a commercial publisher for *Rural Sociology*. A special committee was put together and proposals from commercial presses were reviewed. A recommendation to move the journal to Wiley-Blackwell was approved by RSS. So, in my second year as Editor, we started working with a new on-line submission and review system (Scholar-One) that was part of the Wiley-Blackwell contract. In fact, for several months we had manuscripts in the old systems as we finished our contract with Allen Press and manuscripts in the Scholar-One as we started to publish with Wiley-Blackwell.

Three years as Editor was fine. The first year is hectic as one is still learning about the process and the production system. The second year is fun. By the third year, the bureaucratic process is starting to get on your nerves. Seeing manuscripts develop and improve was rewarding and getting called all sorts of nasty names from folks who had papers rejected was part of the job. We started receiving large numbers of papers from international authors that were really not ready for submission to a referred journal. I was told that they were under pressure from their administrators to publish in indexed journals. We tried to give these authors some feedback so that they could improve their work even though the manuscripts were clearly not really ready for peer review. We transitioned the journal to the next editor and editorial office, and I thought my role in RSS was winding down. I was surprised when I received a call about running for President of RSS. Again, the timing seemed about right. I never really expected to be elected.

While I had known many RSS Presidents, I had little actual knowledge of what the job of RSS President actually involved and what the President actually did aside from the address at the annual meetings. With an excellent Executive Director and Business Office handling many of the details, selecting the main theme for the annual meeting and selecting members of committees seemed to be the major effort. Again, I underestimated the number and complexity of issues that come before a professional society, even one the size of RSS. First, there was trying to understand policies and procedures, which were more in the form of a track changes document. An effort to review and clarify all the changes had begun and it was important to continue this effort, realizing that it was going to take more than one year to get everything straight. Second, there were some regular activities that needed to be considered, such as starting the search for the next editor of Rural Sociology and reviewing our publication contracts. Third, the boycott of Hyatt Hotel properties by the hotel worker's union became a major issue because of contracts RSS had signed for future meetings with Hyatt properties. The Executive Committee and Council dealt with these issues in a deliberant manner, but not in a manner that pleased some of the parties involved in the dispute. We talked to both the union and the company to find out more information and details: apparently talking to the company was a mortal sin according to some parties and we were condemned to one of Dante's levels of Hell for our efforts. Lesson learned: nothing is simple or straightforward. At the same time, I was dealing with a serious illness in my family. Thankfully, my university department was very supportive of my efforts and I could put a number of other projects on hold while I prioritized the personal and professional issues.

Epilogue

In the Business sections of the newspaper, I read columns about work and careers. They all seem to propose a very rational choice model of professional development and career choice. Reflecting on my own career in rural sociology, luck and taking advantage of opportunities that present themselves seem to be as important, if not more important, than any rational choice model of status attainment. Being open to new ideas and being in the right place at the right time certainly helped my professional development.

   My career in rural sociology moved from basic to applied analyses of social problems. It also changed from the traditional hierarchical model of the professor to a team-based collaborative model of research. Rural sociology has always been interdisciplinary, so the move into public health was perhaps less drastic than for someone else. I would like to think that it models C. Wright Mill's statements on intellectual craftwork, but that again is at best a lucky outcome, rather than a controlled choice.

I remember reading many excellent articles and debates about what is rural and what is rural sociology. While I enjoy these articles and find them intellectually stimulating, over time they became less important to my identity as a rural sociologist. I have come down to a crass empiricist definition: rural sociology is what rural sociologists do. It is not that these debates about rural space and rural sociology are unimportant, but I found it difficult to live and function according to an abstract set of theoretical concepts and theories.

Acknowledgments

This chapter is based on a talk given at the NCSU Department of Youth, Family, and Community Sciences Departmental Graduation, May 2014. The author is solely responsible for the content, which may be a product of selective memory and the loss of grey matter. A large number of people have contributed to my success in rural sociology, too many to list, but I wish to thank them all.

Bibliography

Anderson, Cynthia D., Michael D. Schulman, and Phillip J. Wood. 2001. "Globalization and Uncertainty: The Restructuring of Southern Textiles." *Social Problems* 48:478–498.

Armstrong, Paula S., and Michael D. Schulman. 1990. "Financial Strain and Depression among Farm Operators: The Role of Perceived Economic Hardship and Personal Control." *Rural Sociology* 55:475–493.

Costello, Theresa, Michael D. Schulman, and Regina Luginbuhl. 2003. "Understanding the Public Health Impacts of Farm Vehicle Public Road Crashes in North Carolina." *Journal of Agricultural Safety and Health* 9:19–32.

Domhoff, G. William. 1967. *Who Rules America?* Englewood Cliffs, NJ: Prentice Hall.

Evensen, Christian, Michael D. Schulman, Carol Runyan, Ronda Zakocs, and Kathleen Dunn. 2000. "The Downside of Adolescent Employment: Hazards and Injuries among Working Teens in North Carolina." *Journal of Adolescence* 29:545–560.

Falk, William, Michael D. Schulman, and Ann Tickamyer (Eds.). 2003. *Communities of Work: Rural Restructuring in Local and Global Contexts*. Athens: Ohio University Press.

Hightower, Jim. 1973. *Hard Times, Hard Tomatoes*. Cambridge, MA: Schenkman.

Leiter, Jeffery C., Michael D. Schulman, and Rhonda Zingraff (Eds.). 1991. *Hanging by a Thread: Social Change in Southern Textiles*. Ithaca, NY: Institute of Labor Relations Press, Cornell University.

Loomis, Dana, Michael D. Schulman, John A. Bailer, Kevin Statnback, Matthew Wheeler, David Richardson, and Steven Marshall. 2009. "Political Economy of US States and Rates of Fatal Occupational Injury." *American Journal of Public Health* 99:1400–1408.

Marcuse, Herbert. [1955] 1964. "One Dimensional Man." Studies in the Ideology of Advanced Industrial Society.

Rauscher, Kimberly, Carol Runyan, and Michael D. Schulman. 2008. "U.S. Child Labor Violations: Findings of a National Survey of Adolescents Working in the Retail and Service Sectors." *American Journal of Public Health* 98:1693–1699.

Runyan, Carol W., Michael D. Schulman, and Christopher Hoffman. 2003. "Understanding and Preventing Violence against Adolescent Workers: What Is Known and What is Missing?" *Clinics in Occupational and Environment Medicine* 3:711–720.

Runyan, Carol, Michael D. Schulman, and Lawrence Scholl. 2011. "Adolescent Employment and Injury in the United States," pp. 189–214 in *Injury Prevention for Children and Adolescents: Integration of Research, Practice, and Advocacy*, 2nd ed., edited by K. Liller. Washington, DC: American Public Health Association.

Runyan, Carol W., Janet Dal Santo, Michael Schulman, Hester Lipscomb, and Thomas Harris. 2006. "Work Hazards and Workplace Safety Violations Experienced by Adolescent Construction Workers." *Archives of Pediatric and Adolescent Medicine* 160 (July): 721–727.

Runyan, Carol, Michael D. Schulman, Janet Dal Santo, J. Michael Bowling, Robert Agans, and Myduc Ta. 2007. "Work-Related Hazards and Workplace Safety of U.S. Adolescents Employed in the Retail and Service Sectors." *Pediatrics* (119):526–534.

Schulman, Michael D., and Cynthia Anderson, 1999. "The Dark Side of the Force: A Case Study of Restructuring and Social Capital." *Rural Sociology* 64 (3):351–372.

Schulman, Michael D., and Paula S. Armstrong. 1989. "The Farm Crisis: An Analysis of Social Psychological Distress among North Carolina Farm Operators." *American Journal of Community Psychology* 17:423–442.

Schulman, Michael D., and Paula S. Armstrong. 1990. "Targeting Farmers for Stress Reduction." *Journal of Extension* 28 (Summer):10–13.

Schulman, Michael D., and William L. Canak. 1976. "Pedagogy in Prisons: The Structure and Practice of Teaching Sociology in a 'Total Institution'." *The Wisconsin Sociologist* 13 (Winter):30–38.

Schulman, Michael D., and Patricia Garrett. 1990. "Socioeconomic and Demographic Differentiation Among Smallholders: Implications for Technology Development and Transfer," pp. 135–151 in *The World Food Crisis: Food Security in Comparative Perspective*, edited by Hans Bakker. Toronto: Canadian Scholars Press.

Schulman, Michael D., and Barbara A. Newman. 1991. "The Survival of the Black Tobacco Farmer: Empirical Results and Policy Dilemmas." *Agriculture and Human Values* 8 (3):46–52.

Schulman, Michael D., and Doris Slesinger, 2004. "Health Hazards of Rural Extractive Industries and Occupations." *Critical Issues in Rural Health*, 49–60.

Schulman, Michael D., Patricia Garrett, and Regina Luginbuhl. 1985. "Dimensions of the Internal Stratification of Smallholders: Insights from North Carolina Piedmont Counties." *Rural Sociology* 50:249–259.

Schulman, Michael D., Patricia Garrett, and Barbara Newman. 1989. "Differentiation and Survival Among North Carolina Smallholders: An Empirical Perspective on the Lenin/Chayanov Debate." *Journal of Peasant Studies* 16 (July):523–541.

Schulman, Michael D., Catherine Zimmer, and William Danaher. 1994. "Survival in Agriculture: Linking Macro-Level and Micro-Level Analyses." *Sociologia Rurales* 34 (2/3):229–251.

Schulman, Michael D., Patricia Garrett, Regina Luginbuhl, and Jody Greene. 1985. "Problems of Landownership and Inheritance Among Black Smallholders." *Agriculture and Human Values* 2 (Summer):40–44.

Schulman, Michael D., Christian Evensen, Carol Runyan, Lisa Cohen, and Kathleen Dunn, 1997. "Farm Work is Dangerous for Teens: Agricultural Hazards and Injuries Among North Carolina Teens." *Journal of Rural Health* 13:295–305.

Zingraff, Rhonda, and Michael D. Schulman. 1984. "Social Bases of Class Consciousness: A Study of Southern Textile Workers with a Comparison by Race." *Social Forces* 63:98–116.

5
FROM ESTATE AGRICULTURE TO THE INDUSTRIAL DIET

THE TRAJECTORY OF A CANADIAN RURAL SOCIOLOGIST

ANTHONY WINSON, *UNIVERSITY OF GUELPH*

The trajectory of a person's life is to some degree unfathomable, but notable experiences during the early years surely play some role in this trajectory. In my own case, being uprooted every three to four years and living in remote regions in diverse environments across the globe at a time when such transcontinental nomadism was a rarity no doubt had its effect. My father was a mining engineer who was open to new experiences and travel. His vocation offered opportunities for both. Before I was born, he and my mother had lived in small mining camps in British Guiana and Northeastern Ontario before moving to Southern Quebec where I was born. When I was three years old my father took up an offer by the American mining company he worked for to move to a small remote mining camp in Southern Rhodesia (now Zimbabwe). And so began my own life of serial transplantation.

Rural southern Africa was still a relatively wild place in those days, but other than serious warnings about staying away from water I do not recall much in the way of restrictions. I never wore shoes for years, was able to run on gravel with bare feet thanks to thick calluses, spent lots of time wandering in the bush with friends, went hunting with my father in the back of a pickup truck out on the "veld," and later sat around late into the night listening to stories while the men downed rum toddies, shandies, and the like. And there were rides in the small aircraft of my dad's friend, Stan Birch. But that ended (but not my dreams to be a pilot) when he crashed his plane and was killed. This was all before I was seven years old.

In those years I was a privileged white child in a deeply segregated country whose family had African servants, in a mining camp where Africans constituted the main workforce. Being the son of the mine manager I had the "opportunity" of seeing first hand the mining operations and conditions of work, including deep underground, a truly frightening experience for a five-year-old. I visited from time to time, with my father, the "compound" that the company had built for its African workforce, complete with school and hospital clinic. Even then mining companies wanted a workforce that was somewhat literate and healthy. I also attended their festivities, pretended to talk with the men in their local language (which they found amusing, or so I remember) and played every day with the older African boy who was the caretaker for my baby brother and me. In less than four years this near idyllic life (for me) ended. After several months in Australia living with my aunt's family where I attended school and became integrated into Australian ways, we returned to Canada by ship to live in the small Quebec mining community where I was born, and where no one could imagine and few cared about my African or Australian experiences.

While I should not over-emphasize the impact of these early life events in shaping my scholarly interests in rural societies later, they should not also be entirely ignored. I was exposed to coexisting cultures outside the temperate climate zones of the planet, and in particular a rural community highly segregated by race and class, two very different cultural worlds living side by side. We brought the music and artifacts of southern Africa back to Canada, and the memories too, regularly reinforced in my mind by annual photo nights as we revisited my father's extensive Kodachrome archives. In rural Quebec a segregation of sorts was my reality as well, that one encapsulated by Hugh MacLennan's ([1945] 1967) classic Canadian novel *Two Solitudes*, the anglophone, and the francophone, side by side in a not always easy coexistence. The inequity of this reality was also palpable. In those days the entire management structure of the American-owned mine was exclusively anglophone beyond the level of the shop-floor foremen. Some years later we had moved to Northern Ontario to small remote communities where a somewhat more complex ethnic stratification prevailed.

As an undergraduate I was adrift, pushed by parents to consider a career in law like my maternal grandfather, while I nurtured a lifelong dream for a career in aviation. I had secured my private pilot's license as a teenager, flying off frozen lakes in Northern Ontario under the guidance of my hard-bitten flying instructor, Alex Marshall. He was a Spitfire pilot, I was told, who had survived the war and was determined to make sure his students survived their flying career.

While I managed to master a variety of different small aircraft and even later tried my hand at aerobatic flying at an abandoned World War II airstrip near London Ontario, a career in aviation was not to be my future. Deteriorating vision in one eye put an end to that, dashed my dreams, and made me despondent about the future. About the same time I had the first glimmer of intellectual inspiration taking a sociology class with Peter Archibald.

Peter was to have a considerable influence on me later on. Peter was one of the few Canadians teaching sociology at the University of Western Ontario in a department that was in the 1970s heavily dominated by American sociologists. Peter had earned his doctorate at the University of Michigan and had a thoroughly positivistic training, but one that took an unconventional trajectory. He had become fascinated with the Frankfurt School, and later with much of Marx's *oeuvre*. He had read the latter's *Grundrisse* and other significant works and we discussed these at length. I was interested in gaining a more profound understanding of technology and the context of its development and in reading courses he had me exploring this subject from the conservative take of Jacques Ellul to the then much talked about (if little read) radical analysis of Herbert Marcuse. Peter was most interested in bringing the insights of Marxism to social psychology, however, and I was to develop a well-rounded critical appraisal of the literature on worker job satisfaction studies and worker alienation as a research assistant to Peter and another very bright University of Wisconsin trained Canadian sociologist, John Gartrell. Alongside these figures, I was impressed with the scholarship and teaching of James (Jim) Rinehart, an American sociologist of radical leanings who had strong ties to the local labour movement. Jim's scholarship blended well-argued theoretical analysis and careful empirical investigation. His work was a potent antidote to the theoretically vacuous positivism that characterized much of the department's published output. Rinehart's *Tyranny of Work* (1987) became an early and accessible classic in the literature on the sociology of labor alongside the contributions of Harvey Braverman, Michael Burawoy, and numerous others.

Along the way I was influenced by a few other American sociologists at Western, including Carl Grindstaff and Joan Stelling. Both were demanding of high standards of work, taught us to consider sociology as a craft, and both were excellent and inspiring teachers. It was in Carl's social demography class that I had a chance to explore social developments then convulsing Latin America. It was this subject that was to engage me in my graduate school years, as it turned out. But before I graduated, my academic pursuits were to be temporarily sidetracked by more starkly political undertakings.

In my third undergraduate year fellow sociology students and I initiated "course unions" in the various social science departments in an effort to organize students and get them engaged with public intellectuals touring campuses in those years. Among those we sponsored on campus were Scottish psychiatrist R. D. Laing, with his radical views on psychiatry, as well as speakers who could critique the questionable views of Arthur Jensen and his race-based theories of intelligence. These were the heady years after the turmoil of May '68 in France, the protests on American campuses, the riots of Watts and Detroit, and the winding down of the debacle that was the Vietnam War. Canadian students were somewhat on the sidelines of these struggles, but many had absorbed the atmosphere around them. I certainly had.

Toward the end of this year I became heavily involved in a student confrontation with the Administration over the latter's plans to deny tenure to a popular female sociology professor. When student efforts to negotiate a different outcome failed, we opted to occupy the Sociology Department to press our demands. This action convulsed the university for some time and made the nightly news before we reluctantly abandoned the occupation. I mention this incident because it was significant in my intellectual formation. As one of the leaders of this occupation, I learned much about how university power structures worked in a very short period of time, knowledge that was to be of some use later in my academic career.

Toward the end of my undergraduate years I had more or less resolved to pursue graduate studies with a focus on Latin America. Like many others, I suppose, my growing interest in the region was further kindled with the short-lived social experiment in Chile with the election of Salvador Allende. The 1973 military coup d'état in which Kissinger, the U.S. Nixon Administration and ultra-conservative Chilean generals played their various roles was profoundly disturbing to me as it was to many others.

In the end, despite the disappointment for hopeful change in Chile, I resolved to pursue my Latin American interests. While I received more attractive offers of financial support elsewhere, I accepted the University of Toronto's offer of admission, with no promise of support, because of the prospect of working with noted Latin American scholars there. I moved to Toronto with the partner I had been living with for two years in late summer of 1975. For a boy used to small towns in remote regions, Toronto was a difficult adjustment.

As it turned out, beginning my graduate career in sociology at Toronto was well timed, for not only was it possible to begin coursework with a few extraordinary resident scholars, but my arrival coincided with the hiring of a couple of noted Argentine intellectuals who were to become very influential in shaping my studies and orientation. The most important for me was Miguel Murmis, who introduced me to the serious study of political economy and the analysis of agrarian social structure. He was eventually to attract a large graduate student following impressed by his sharp mind and his personal integrity. The latter was not especially widely distributed in academic circles I was to discover.

The other Argentine scholar I learned much from was José Nun. He introduced me to a more profound understanding of politics in Latin America, and especially the significance of Antonio Gramsci's contribution to a materialist analysis of politics in more advanced capitalist societies where liberal democratic politics held sway. Working under the tutelage of Murmis and Nun was not always comfortable. The polite niceties of Canadian culture were foreign to them, and shoddy work below the standard they felt I was capable of was likely to attract a disdainful comment, or worse. Painful though it might have been at the time, looking back I can now see that their attitude and the standard they demanded were what I needed to become a serious scholar.

In addition to this Argentine influence, other scholars that influenced me at Toronto included the Mexicanist Richard Roman and African scholar Jack Wayne, as well as Irving Zeitlin, an inspiring teacher and social theorist whose courses were often tumultuous, argumentative, and rarely dull. Outside the department, I had the privilege of being exposed to the insights of the development economist Gerald Helleiner and Cranford Pratt in political science, both of whom had achieved international acclaim in the emerging field of development.

Sociology at the University of Toronto was rather unique in those days, and this uniqueness left a profound stamp on us. It was an activist hotbed, and I had the opportunity to become completely immersed in that political ferment. The department's staid and conservative ways had been seriously disrupted by the hiring of several progressive American academics who, bolstered by a strong contingent of left-wing graduate students, were to implant what was, by most university standards, a radical democratic administrative process in the department. Virtually all department committees were to have an equal number of students and faculty, including the hiring committee, while major departmental decisions went to a general assembly where students again had a major presence and vote.

Hiring decisions being among the most significant decisions any department makes, I was keen to be involved in the process and was for two long years. Hiring was definitely where the "rubber hits the road" as far as political struggle in the academic world is concerned. As it turned out, the conversion of the position of my advisor, Miguel Murmis, from a visiting to a tenured faculty position was to be the most contentious hiring issue of those years. I found my own future to be very much tied up in the outcome. The Murmis hiring decision was to convulse the department for some time. While a clear majority of the hiring committee had voted to grant him a tenured position, the reactionary old lumber lurking in the department would have none of it. Never willing to abide by the norm of democratic decision-making that then prevailed, a few of these influential faculty made clear their opposing view to the Dean and to those higher up in the Administration. The decision, and my budding academic career, ground to a halt.

As it turned out, my organizational experience as an undergraduate proved to be very useful in the subsequent student struggle to have the department hiring decision respected. The process took many months to be resolved and, when it was, Murmis was nearly prevented from taking up his position because of the political machinations of the Argentine military dictatorship that ruled that country in those years. In the end, my own efforts to secure his position had taken up most of a year of my graduate studies. Nevertheless, in time I was able to proceed under the tutelage of the figure who had a major influence on my graduate and post-graduate career.

Working with Miguel Murmis and his colleagues on agrarian social structure and having several enthusiastic fellow students with this substantive focus helped to cement my resolve to forge ahead with doctoral work in the area. While research on peasant movements and agrarian reform was especially popular at the time, I was influenced by Murmis's interest in large landholders and their enduring impact on economic policy and politics in many of the Latin American countries. He had me read the work of Guillermo Flischmann on Argentina's landholding structure, that of Cristobal Kay on Chile, George Beckford on the Caribbean plantation system, and Edelberto Torres Rivas on Central America, among numerous other scholars.

The work of Torres Rivas (1971) was an inspiration to consider Central America as a locus for my own research. I had available to me also the agrarian census from each of the countries of the region compiled in a volume published by the Economic Commission on Latin America (ECLA). That data, together with a scouring of every bit of scholarly research I could get my hands on covering agrarian change in the region resulted in my first published piece, which found a home in *Latin American Perspectives* (1978). The article documented a disruptive process of capitalist development in the countryside in contexts where large landholdings were very dominant. In particular, what Lenin had called attention to in the Russian context years before the revolution there—the mass peregrination of rural labor—was very much part of agrarian change in Central America, with the tremendous social disruption and extreme poverty it produced. My article predicted major social unrest in the countryside. It was published in 1978, a year before the Sandinista uprising in Nicaragua and the escalation of revolutionary conflict in El Salvador.

For a while I was fascinated with research that compared Central America with developments within Latin America and even farther afield. Indeed, Toronto was probably unique as a department where historical and comparative research was considered not only legitimate, but given considerable status, within the context of sociology.

In time, this broader comparative and historical interest ran up against the necessity of finding a doable doctoral research project. This was going to require a more realistic and defined focus. At the time (late 1970s) Central America had become a tinderbox, with violence and repression by its various military dictatorships escalating every year. It was becoming clear that few countries offered an environment that was safe for the kind of research I had in mind. Costa Rica stood out as the exception.

The influence of large landholders in Costa Rica was considerable, as elsewhere, a fact that the comprehensive study by Samuel Stone (1976) made abundantly clear. Yet this country was famous throughout Latin America for its relatively successful liberal democratic process. The role of large landowners elsewhere in Central and South America in undermining the democratization process was fairly well documented in the literature and among specialists in political affairs of the region, so why had this class not had the same impact in Costa Rica?

This question seemed like as good a one as any to hang my thesis research on.

It is easy to forget today how difficult it was to secure up-to-date information, and particularly scholarly research, from regions of the global South before the Internet age. Fortunately, I did have access to the best research library in the country and my advisor brought back books and reports whenever he travelled to Latin America. All this helped, but with nothing yet available digitally, one had to arrange to spend considerable time in the place one wished to research to explore local archives and libraries, and talk to a variety of key informants. There was no other way. There was also no money, or at least very little.

I do recall a modest $800 travel grant from the university's small development studies program. With that, and the stipend from my Canada Council doctoral fellowship, I bought a (very) used Dodge van and converted it into a kind of camper van that would allow for inexpensive travel to Costa Rica to conduct my doctoral research and provide an inexpensive means to get around the country once there.

The five-week road trip I made with my partner of those days to San José, Costa Rica was an extraordinary adventure, an engrossing educational immersion in various Latin American cultures and, at times, a frightening encounter with the brutal economic and political realities of the region. I was ever-attentive to see how the conditions of people in the rural areas of the different countries we passed through met up with my earlier impressions gained from the extensive reading I had done. The realities of landless workers and their families in El Salvador were especially stark, as I remember, and validated what I had read and deduced from agrarian data in the many months of study before this extended road trip.

We traversed Nicaragua north to south in one grueling and stress-filled day in late May, 1979 and were stopped, interrogated and searched at gun-point six separate times by the dictator's troops, some only teenage boys. At one point we got lost in the maze of streets in a small town and almost collided head-on with a Sherman tank. As it happened, a week after our passage the Sandinista Front for National Liberation (FSLN) launched full-scale attacks on several fronts to bring down the Somoza dictatorship. At the same time a popular uprising in the cities saw the massive spread of armed combat between thousands of poorly armed citizens and the National Guard troops, well supplied as it was by Uncle Sam.

Regular detailed newscasts of this six-week armed conflict to topple Nicaragua's dictatorship and the momentous changes that were to accompany the Sandinista revolution afterwards were the distracting backdrop to my own private efforts to get my doctoral research in Costa Rica underway, and indeed get as much accomplished before our limited funds ran out. Serendipitously, I had met the Costa Rican sociologist Daniel Camacho just before the road trip south, and upon recontacting him in San José, he offered the services of his able administrative assistant to set up interviews with some of the prominent members of the country's coffee growing elite and the director of the Coffee Office, the government institution that coordinated all manner of affairs around the nation's leading export activity. The Director of the Coffee Office was to later place a car and driver at my service for several days so I could see first-hand how coffee was grown and processed in different parts of the country, and talk with personnel in the field and in the coffee-processing plants. I was nothing more than a Canadian doctoral student, yet I felt like I was being treated as a visiting dignitary, at least for a short time.

Many hours were spent in newspaper archives in the National Library, and many more reading theses and other works in the university library and in the library of financial institutions, and so on. Anything of interest had to be photocopied in order to be taken back to Canada, and securing photocopies was itself an arduous task. Nevertheless, as the weeks rolled on I began to see some glimmers of light in my quest to understand what some have called Costa Rica's political exceptionalism. As our stay in Costa Rica was coming to an end, I could see the outline of my dissertation argument taking shape.

Many of the better-off Nicaragua families had fled to Costa Rica once the war erupted, and we befriended some of them. I got to know fairly well a prominent Nicaraguan doctor and his family, and this family became even more prominent when the husband of one of his daughters became a member of the revolutionary directorate of the new government, representing the pro-Sandinista business interests.

We participated in the regular mass rallies and cultural events held by pro-Sandinista forces in San José and followed with great interest the expanding war in that nation just a few hours' drive to the north. I had no idea that I was to get the chance to participate more directly in the events that were to transform Nicaragua in the very near future.

In a one-month period at the end of 1981 I moved, got married, defended my doctoral dissertation, and left Canada for Nicaragua to take up a postdoctoral fellowship. The year prior I had applied for postdoc funding from the SSHRC to work with the agrarian reform center of the new revolutionary government in Nicaragua. I felt very fortunate to get the fellowship as the job prospects for faculty positions in Canada at that time were almost non-existent. I recall three tenure track positions advertised in 1981–1982 in sociology, and none of them remotely matching my own limited expertise.

On the other hand, the opportunity to become involved with research around the rapidly evolving agrarian reform process in a new revolutionary society was probably the most exciting prospect I could have imagined. My short stint at the Centre for Investigations and Studies of the Agrarian Reform (CIERA) in Managua was eventful. Miguel Murmis had put me in touch with a young and very bright Argentine economist, Eduardo Baumeister, with whom I was to work. The working conditions were primitive, I recall, but the experiences were rich and varied, both with the research and living in a society that was experiencing many positive transformations.

My background in the analysis of agrarian social structures was useful and valued, although the fact that I had a newly minted doctorate mattered not at all. The latter took some getting adjusted to. A Nicaraguan sociologist whom I had read, Jaime Wheelock (1975), was now a leading political figure and Minister of the Agrarian Reform. Another sociologist, Orlando Nuñez, was head of our research institute, itself linked to the Ministry of Agrarian Reform. I was working with a number of social scientists from different parts of the world, including the U.S., France, and various Latin American countries. We were all aware that we had a privileged opportunity to participate in the changes that were receiving the attention of the world at that time.

Not long after I arrived, I attended a ceremony in the countryside that distributed the first land titles to poor farmers. The land was part of the vast tracts of land confiscated from the ruling Somoza family that had amassed property over its thirty-plus years of iron-fisted rule. The staff of the Centre travelled by bus to a distant farm where the ceremony took place. It was the first of many land-redistribution ceremonies in revolutionary Nicaragua.

In my off hours I socialized with new friends from around the world. Managua seethed with journalists in those days as it was viewed as a leading hotspot, especially once the so-called Contra war started soon after Ronald Reagan became President. I gained considerable knowledge of what was happening beyond the capital from a good Canadian friend who had become a sought-after "fixer" for visiting correspondents. I shared meals under the stars in rustic café's with Salvadoran refugees who recounted the endless atrocities of the El Salvadoran military they had witnessed or heard about.

My own research in Nicaragua centered on the cotton-growing and processing sector which had become an important source of export earnings by that time. I mapped out the structure of landholdings in this sector, tediously compiled statistics, analyzed data on credits to producers and the frequency of repayments of credits by size of grower, and many other facets of the agrarian economy as it related to cotton production, processing, and commercialization. Over time we built up a picture of the behavior of different classes and class fractions of the agrarian society vis-à-vis the policies the new revolutionary government was pushing forward. This research became more significant as the most reactionary elements of the large landowners and agribusiness capitalists began to actively decapitalize their enterprises as the extraordinary privileges they had traditionally enjoyed were being challenged. On the other hand, we found evidence that smaller and medium-size landowners had a more positive response to the policies of the new government. There were some unexpected twists and turns in my life upon returning home, and the need for some serious additional archival research, but I eventually managed to publish a long journal piece on themes related to my work and experience in Nicaragua (1985).

The honeymoon of the new revolutionary society was brief as the new Reagan Administration began to prosecute its illegal covert war against the Sandinista Government. Nicaragua began to move onto a war footing. As my time there came to an end, the Contra mercenaries[1] were attacking installations within thirty miles of the capital. Nevertheless, I left with hopes of returning soon.

On my return to Canada I put a priority on publishing the theoretical chapter of my dissertation on Costa Rica that sought to bring a better understanding of the role of landowning capitalists and the large estate economy that supported them, so significant in many regions of the Third World, in undermining not only the development process, but also efforts to establish more democratic forms of governance. My efforts to theorize much more completely Lenin's brief outline of the so-called "Prussian path" of agrarian development and establish the contemporary relevance of this model for understanding the underdevelopment and authoritarian nature of a number of Latin America societies did finally bear fruit. My work in this area had been inspired by the recent publication of a previously "lost" chapter of Marx's *Capital* on the subsumption of the labor process by capital in the transition to capitalism,[2] and also by Keith Tribe's (1979) translation into English of important work by Max Weber on East Elbian labor relations. A revised version of my dissertation chapter was accepted without revisions in the English journal *Economy and Society* in early 1982.

As it turned out, my return to Nicaragua was to be delayed some years. For a number of reasons, among them family obligations and the dire hiring prospects for a teaching position in Canada at the time, upon my return to Canada I opted to take up a position as the new research director of a small research institute for Atlantic Canada studies in Halifax. Henry Veltmeyer, then Chair of the Sociology Department at Saint Mary's University, had championed my candidacy for the job after hearing a presentation of my work on the Prussian model of agrarian development. Fortunately for me, I had during my brief academic career path up to that time completed some minor work on issues of agrarian development in the Canadian context. In any case, there was some appetite at Saint Mary's for a sociologist with a political economy of development focus to take on the position of research director of what became the Gorsebrook Research Centre for Atlantic Canada Studies. I took up the position in September of 1982 and began a very different chapter of my academic life.

My three years in Halifax entailed some fairly heavy administrative duties, but alongside these I nurtured my scholarship as well, for I came to appreciate that the position I had was unlikely to be long term. I also became increasingly aware that while I could master the administrative duties required of this position, they brought me little joy and seemingly endless frustration. In the meantime, I was among the most avid of sailors in the inner and outer reaches of Halifax harbor for several years, and sailing helped me deal with the surprising number of stressful situations that I encountered in my job as research director.

My brief years in Halifax were filled with rich experiences. I found especially rewarding the various public forums I organized on the institute's behalf to further public discussion around key issues facing the community and broader Atlantic region, from the emerging crisis of the cod fishery to the very problematic manner by which the Conservative government of Nova Scotia was choosing to develop its offshore hydrocarbon resources. I became involved with research on the Atlantic fishery as well, and helped get underway some substantial research projects in the area. For myself, I began a serious investigation of agricultural development in the Atlantic region. Before I left Halifax I submitted to the SSHRC (the Canadian federal granting agency) a proposal to study the agro-food complex in the region, and was successful. Funding for this research project proved to be a seminal development in steering my career for many years to come. The funding approval was most timely, as by 1985 there was a parting of ways between myself and certain members of my board of directors around policy direction for the institute I was managing. As it turned out this was a sort of blessing in disguise.

While research funding for the next year had been secured, the bleak prospect of unemployment loomed up just as my son was about to be born. I traveled back to Central America to conduct more research in the quest to turn my dissertation into a book manuscript. On this occasion I first returned to Nicaragua. By 1985 Nicaragua was on a complete war footing as Mr. Reagan's Contra War ground on, with mounting costs to social infrastructure and people's lives. In my short visit there I was saddened by the contrast with the ebullient days of my postdoctoral work in Nicaragua just three years before. Later in Costa Rica I received word of an offer for a contractual position at the University of Western Ontario, which, although a stop-gap, offered generous teaching conditions and helped to refloat my hopes for a full-time academic post with tenure prospects down the road.

For some years I seriously tried to keep up my scholarship on both the Latin American and Canadian contexts. For a few years it worked, but ultimately I had to make the hard choice to leave most of my Latin American interests behind. In large part thanks to the efforts of my future Guelph colleague, Nora Cebotarev, I was able to keep up some links to the region via research projects with cooperatives in Nicaragua during the late 1980s and some work with *ejido* communities near Texcoco, Mexico, ten years or so later. There was also an innovative and useful IDRC-funded project I was invited to participate in by a soil scientist—Paul Voroney—which sought to support small organic bean farmers and coffee growers in different regions of Costa Rica. More recently, my interest in the enormous impact of tourism in poor countries has led to a small project examining the prospect for better outcomes from this major economic activity with the advent of ecological tourism. I chose Cuba as a case study for this project after a number of visits to the island including a study tour with a group of undergraduate students. Cuba proved to be a fertile site for such a study for a number of reasons, including the high priority given to the environment by the government, the sugar industry's legacy of environmental destruction over several centuries, the fact that it was one of the only socialist societies still existing, and the high priority Cuba began to give to international tourism (and the foreign exchange it could provide) as its sugar industry stagnated with the demise of its chief market, the Soviet Union. Interviews and on-site visits from one end of this large island nation to another yielded a complex picture of the realities of ecological tourism on the island (see Winson 2008).

Before I shifted most of my research efforts to the Canadian context in the late 1980s, I was able to finish the lengthy process of updating and rewriting my dissertation as a book. The journey getting it published was painful, but ultimately successful. Some years earlier the chief editor of Princeton University Press had shown real enthusiasm for my manuscript and had immediately sent if off for review. The Press had a policy of soliciting a single reviewer at that time. The possibility of publication by an Ivy League press buoyed my hopes immensely, especially given my precarious employment situation, and the reviewer's assessment was greatly anticipated. When it came it was with a sharp jolt of disappointment. I will never forget the opening line of the reviewer's assessment, which read "this manuscript should be published, but not by Princeton!" While in time I accepted that some of the criticisms were valid, it was apparent then and upon reflection later that the assessment was in large part an ideologically driven hatchet job. I was to learn from others in the years afterwards that my experience with this publisher was hardly unique.

In the end, what became *Coffee and Democracy in Modern Costa Rica* found a home with the Macmillan/St. Martin's presses, who were encouraged to take it on after a positive recommendation from Robert Brym, the outstanding University of Toronto political sociologist who I had met years earlier. While this book took some years to get published, it did finally receive positive reviews in various journals, among those a review in the prestigious *Latin American Research Review*, and one by a Latin American social scientist I had never met but whose work I respected highly—Carlos Vilas. This helped make the difficult journey of this book seem worthwhile.

By 1985 I had reluctantly moved back to Ontario from Nova Scotia. Nevertheless, SSHRC funding allowed me to return to Nova Scotia to carry out research on the food processing-farming complex there, which was very much under-researched. Not long afterwards I received further funding to extend my project to the Ontario context, and on a larger scale.

These years were marked by the continual hunt for a teaching position with some security. It was a time when sociology departments were attempting to rectify the deficit of female faculty on staff and consequently a tough time to be a male candidate. Many a promising job interview came to naught. At long last, and before I had completed my three-year contract at Western, a position came up at the University of Guelph with an emphasis on rural sociology, a rare occurrence in the Canadian context. The Department at Guelph voted to hire me, but there was a seemingly endless delay in receiving an offer, which caused considerable stress on my part. I was to later learn there was lobbying for another candidate by the faculty outside the department, and this was blocking the approval of my appointment. Finally, Wayne Thompson, the department Chair, took a stand with the Administration to uphold the decision of the department, and it worked.

Upon taking up my position at Guelph, I was to launch into my research on the food-processing–farming complex in Ontario with several months of extensive fieldwork. My work on the rural sociology of Canada had begun in earnest. Looking back, I realize that some good decisions were made with respect to research assistants that paid off handsomely with a wealth of valuable data from farm operators in the province. Both my assistants had farm backgrounds, which proved very valuable in gaining access to farm operators and establishing the rapport needed to gain the rich data we sought.

This research project proved pivotal for future research and recognition, but it almost floundered on the shoals of bureaucratic small mindedness. To secure a representative sample of farm operators—an important component of this project—I was going to need a list of farmers supplying fruit and vegetable processors across the province to draw from. For this I sought out the assistance of a high-level bureaucrat in the Ministry of Agriculture and Food (OMAF) who was in charge of agriculture reps in the various counties. These ag reps were my key to securing the list of relevant farm operators to draw my sample, or so I believed. I was variously shocked, dismayed, and angered when he told me in no uncertain terms in our first and only meeting and without any apparent reason that not only would he not give me the list, but he would be sending a letter to all his agriculture reps that they were not to assist me with my project. I was later to find out that this particular individual had nothing but contempt for social scientists and their research. His ability to pour cold water on my research project was a wake-up call to the charged political nature of the agriculture and food system, and the role bureaucratic gate-keepers had in preventing anyone from investigating the underbelly of what has become a corporate controlled agro-food complex. In the end, and after considerable agonizing, I decided that following bureaucratic protocol was playing into the power games of such bureaucratic gatekeepers. I opted for a more "grassroots" approach, and contacted each county's horticulture representative directly. They not only had lists of the kinds of farm operators I wanted, but were more than happy to be helpful. This put a triumphant end to my crisis.

By the end of the 1980s I had completed most of my research on the farming-processing complex and was looking to expand my research interests. A trip to Scandinavia got me intrigued with pursuing some comparative work there after discussions with a former Norwegian minister of agriculture in Tromsö, Norway, visits with staff of the Swedish ministry of agriculture in Jönköping, talks given to faculty and students at the Norwegian Agricultural University at Ås, and talks with Norwegian farmers in northern Norway where my partner's family originated. As it happened, tentative plans to return and possibly collaborate with my old friend and fisheries specialist Svein Jentoft on a comparative research topic were not to pan out. The death of my partner in a traffic accident the following year put my life into turmoil for some time, and ultimately resulted in changes to the course of my research.

Instead of building a Scandinavian connection, I slowly embarked on a new book project to deepen and extend the work I had begun related to Canadian rural sociology, and notably on the food-processing–farming complex. I was inspired, in part, after a visit to Paris where I had fruitful discussions with different researchers working with the Institute National de Recherche Agronomique (INRA). At the time they were conducting innovative research in the different branches (filières) of the French food system. They offered to host me should I plan to return to France and work on a collaborative project together. They also introduced me to the work of Louis Malassis and his approach to the "système agro-alimentaire." Despite the obvious attraction of a sabbatical in Paris, family obligations were once again to keep me closer to home. But the work of the French had inspired me to write on what I conceptualized, following Malassis, as the Canadian agro-food complex. This was to result in *The Intimate Commodity*, about which a few comments are in order.

My book *The Intimate Commodity: Food and the Development of the Agro-Industrial Complex in Canada* (1993) was an attempt to put my research on the food-processing–farming complex into a larger historical context. My intentions initially were largely to use secondary sources to write up the historical background to the contemporary relationships that had developed between farm operators and food-processing corporations. This was not to work out exactly as planned. Substantial topics I wished to summarize from published studies, such as the role of important early agrarian movements and leaders in shaping rural institutions, and the details of the emergence of marketing boards and supply management in Canada, were not well researched, it turned out. I spent a good deal more time in the archives studying primary sources than I had planned, which delayed the writing up of the book considerably, of course. This book was very nearly scuttled early on by the scathing criticism of my manuscript by the first editor I worked with. After considerable angst and reflection, I decided that this editor and his press were toxic for me and the success of my book, and I sought out an alternative. Fortune smiled upon me as Peter Saunders, with his fledgling Garamond Press, saw value in my project and was very supportive throughout.

This book project taught me the importance of editorial support if the long and tedious journey of a book manuscript was ever to see the light of day, and also the value of undertaking one's own promotional efforts to get the word out. Publishers in the academic world have limited attention spans when it comes to promoting your book, and unless you are willing to put some effort into this end of things, chances are that your book will be quickly forgotten. As it turned out, *The Intimate Commodity* was to garner sustained interest among the relatively small audience that cares about the political economy of agriculture and food in the Canadian context, and is still in print more than twenty years after its first publication.

Research for *The Intimate Commodity* opened up for me a window onto the turmoil that was besetting small rural communities that had been sustained for decades by small manufacturing firms. The deep and destructive recession of the early 1990s, accompanied as it was by a neoliberal political economic agenda that promoted contingent labor, lax regulations, and capital flight to offshore low-wage jurisdictions was having a serious effect on Ontario's manufacturing base. A significant portion of this base was located in smaller communities across the southern part of the province. Very little research had been done in these communities and virtually none focused on the role of manufacturing there.

I received funding at this time to investigate economic restructuring in several communities under the auspices of a large research grant focused on agro-ecosystem health directed by Barry Smit, a geographer, and David Waltner-Toews, an unorthodox veterinary scientist. This was the beginning of a ten-year project examining the restructuring of manufacturing in small rural communities that were being convulsed by shutdowns and down-sizing of the industrial firms that had sustained them for decades. The research was along the lines of that conducted by Janet Fitchen (1991), and Margaret Nelson and Joan Smith (1999) in the rural United States, and also drew on the work of Barry Bluestone and Bennett Harrison (1982) on American deindustrialization, among many others.

It was a stroke of luck, for me, that we had recently hired Belinda Leach, an English anthropologist who had been transplanted to Canada years before. Belinda had a keen interest in gender and work issues within the critical political economy framework that was well entrenched in Canadian social science. Her interests dovetailed with mine very nicely and we began a collaboration on the rural community research. A successful application for more SSHRCC funding allowed us to expand the research to cover a wider variety of manufacturing dependent communities, and include those involved in high-technology manufacturing and a single industry community in a more remote northern region I was familiar with.

This in-depth research in five different communities proved to be a daunting exercise, fraught with numerous frustrations and delays. As with my research with farm operators years earlier, finding a dedicated research assistant who could connect with respondents proved to be tremendously important in our ability to generate rich and insightful interviews with displaced plant workers in particular.[3]

Ultimately, we felt a book-length monograph that utilized detailed transcriptions illustrating the lives of displaced and down-sized employees caught up in the tsunami of industrial restructuring in the countryside was what we wanted to be the outcome of this project. The result was *Contingent Work, Disrupted Lives: Labour and Community in the New Rural Economy*.[4] While this was an especially long and drawn-out publication project, in the end the book garnered the John Porter book prize of the Canadian Sociology Association for 2003, a sweet reward for our efforts.

After almost ten years looking at rural communities I was ready for something completely different. I was looking for stimulation in new research areas where I might make some useful contribution. In the end this proved to be a return to the issues around food initially explored in *The Intimate Commodity*, albeit with a new focus on the political economic determinants of diet and nutrition. Intrigued with the emerging crisis posed by population-wide weight gain and obesity, I became convinced that the social sciences were ultimately where real policy solutions were to come from. First, however, it would be necessary to demonstrate how the tools of social science could be useful. Here my earlier work on the food retail sector of the Canadian food system proved to be relevant. I conceived of a project that would endeavor to measure the preponderance of nutritionally questionable edible products in the most important food environment in developed countries—the supermarket chain store. Preliminary results of this research were very well received when they were presented to the annual meetings of the Agriculture, Food, and Human Values society. Publishing the results of my study in the society's journal proved to be much more daunting, however, but I chose to pursue the matter to the end and finally did get the study published there. It has proven to be the second most highly cited publication of my career.

I followed up my pilot study of supermarket food with a small study of high-school food environments in a regional school district nearby. This was another largely unresearched topic in the Canadian context, and took place just as some provinces (provinces have jurisdiction over education) were about to make sweeping changes to the food guidelines in schools. Upon completing this pilot study I was intent on investigating further the forces shaping school food environments and followed up with an application for substantial funding to the SSHRC to do just this. When this application was not successful I was forced to rethink entirely where I wanted to go with my research on food environments. Future applications for funding in this area from the federal funding body, the SSHRC, were being put into jeopardy by the Council's decision to force all applicants who had a possible health dimension to their research to apply to another funding council dominated by medical researchers. This has had major implications for many social scientists, including myself.

The path I took out of this dilemma was to think in grander terms. Instead of pursuing a narrowly defined research project on school food environments, I decided instead that a book project with a much broader purview was worth pursuing. And pursue this I did for several years thereafter. Writing what became *The Industrial Diet: The Degradation of Food and the Struggle for Healthy Eating* (Winson 2013)[5] coincided with the rapid blossoming of the interdisciplinary study of food in Canada, and elsewhere. Canadian sociology has been slow to take up this development, but the formation of the Canadian Association for Food Studies[6] provided a home for an eclectic rural sociologist like myself who had a strong interdisciplinary bent in any case. I have been gratified to be part of the flourishing of the interdisciplinary study of food in Canada and to be a part of a successful attempt to put together the first edited collection of Canadian food studies scholarship (Koc, Sumner, and Winson 2012).

All in all, it has been a long and somewhat tortuous journey from a passion for understanding the structural dynamics and wider significance of estate agriculture in Central America to researching and writing about the degradation of whole foods in the industrial food system. Underlying my research journey has, nevertheless, been a keen interest in shedding light on how some aspect of the social world actually works, the power relationships at play, and the differential impacts of existing arrangements on people's lives. And in all my work I have generally found that situating my research subject within its historical context, and bringing into the research a comparative dimension, proved to be the most fruitful path to illumination.

Notes

1. The Contra army was also being reinforced with mercenary elements from the armed forces of the Argentine military junta who worked hand-in-hand with American covert operations.
2. Published as "Results of the Immediate Process of Production" and as an appendix in the Martin Nicholas translation of *Capital*, vol. 1, New York: Vintage Books, 1977.
3. Our assistant Sandra Watson had, among other qualities, the empathetic understanding of her interviewees' situation that allowed for the development of the trust needed to establish the frank and detailed dialogue we were ultimately able to secure from most of our respondents, many of whom were displaced semi-skilled female employees.
4. 2002, University of Toronto Press.
5. See also www.theindustrialdiet.com
6. More familiar to most as CAFS: http://cafs.landfood.ubc.ca/en/

References

Bluestone, Barry, and Bennett Harrison. 1982. *The Deindustrialization of America: Plant Closings, Community Abandonment and the Dismantling of Basic Industries*. New York: Basic Books.

Fitchen Janet. 1991. *Endangered Spaces, Enduring Places: Change, Identity, and Survival in Rural America*. Boulder, CO: Westview Press.

Koc, Mustafa, Jennifer Sumner, and Anthony Winson (Eds.). 2012. *Critical Perspectives in Food Studies*. Toronto: Oxford University Press.

MacLennan, Hugh. [1945] 1967. *Two Solitudes*. New York: Duell, Sloan, & Pearce.

Marx, Karl. 1977. "Results of the Immediate Process of Production." in *Capital*, Vol. 1, Appendix translated by Martin Nicholas. New York: Vintage Books.

Nelson, Margaret, and Joan Smith. 1999. *Working Hard and Making Do: Surviving in Small Town America*. Berkeley, CA: University of California Press.

Rinehart, James. 1987. *The Tyranny of Work: Alienation and the Labour Process*, 2nd ed. Toronto: Harcourt Brace Jovanovich.

Stone, Samuel. 1976. *La Dinastia de los Conquistadores*. San Jose: Editorial Universitaria Centroamericana.

Torres Rivas, Edelberto. 1971. *Interpretacón del Desarrollo Social Centroamericano*. San José (Costa Rica): EDUCA.

Weber, Max. 1979. "Developmental Tendencies in the Situation of East Elbian Rural Labourers." Translated by Keith Tribe. *Economy and Society* 8 (2):177–205.

Wheelock, Jaime. *Imperialismo y Dictadura: Crisis de una Formacion*. Mexico City: Siglo Ventiuno.

Winson, Anthony. 1978. "Class Structure and Agrarian Transition in Central America." *Latin American Perspectives*, Vol. V, No. 4, pp. 27–48.

Winson, Anthony. 1985. "Nicaragua's Private Sector and the Sandinista Revolution," *Studies in Political Economy*, no. 17, Summer.

Winson, Anthony. 1993. *The Intimate Commodity: Food and the Development of the Agro-Industrial Complex in Canada*. Toronto: Garamond Press.

Winson, Anthony. 2008. "Ecotourism and Sustainability in Cuba: Does Socialism Make a Difference?" *Journal of Sustainable Tourism* 14 (1):6–23.

Winson, Anthony. 2013. *The Industrial Diet: The Degradation of Food and the Struggle for Healthy Eating*. Vancouver: UBC Press and New York: New York University Press.

Winson, Anthony, and Belinda Leach. 2002. *Contingent Work, Disrupted Lives: Labour and Community in the New Rural Economy*. Toronto: University of Toronto Press.

6
THE INTERSECTION OF BIOGRAPHY AND WORK AS A RURAL SOCIOLOGIST

LINDA LOBAO, *THE OHIO STATE UNIVERSITY*

In his classic volume, *The Sociological Imagination*, C. Wright Mills (1959) stresses the unique perspective that newcomers to sociology gain when they become aware of the connection between their own personal experiences and the structural forces that surround them. My work as a rural sociologist has been defined by my working-class origins and subsequent experiences in living in different regions within the U.S. and abroad. At heart, I believe I have always aimed to understand the intersection between class and context, particularly geographic context. The general theoretical framework that speaks to this issue is critical political economy as it has evolved to understand inequalities generated by capitalism across time and space. While I have taken other approaches in my work, I invariably find political economy as shedding the most intriguing light on the research questions in which I am most interested.

My father was a clear contributor to the Fordist industrial and agricultural economy. He started out as a farmer, introducing Green Revolution petrochemical technologies to his parents' farm in Massachusetts. They had come to the U.S. from the Azores and followed the Portuguese practice of primogeniture—whereby only the eldest son inherited the farm. My dad was among the youngest of a dozen children. Although he both managed and labored endlessly on the farm, by the time he was in his late 20s, he was forced to leave it to make a living. He had met my mother who was a bookkeeper at International Harvester, which sold farm equipment. Without much education—he made it to sixth grade—he became a skilled machinist. My mother finished high school, the daughter of a factory worker. My father worked at the Watertown Arsenal where machinists initially had a great deal of control over the design of their products. Then numerically controlled designs came in which contributed to the deskilling and loss of power of machinists. My father was sent from Massachusetts to the Midwest to teach machinists at other plants how to work the new numerically controlled designs being introduced. Looking back on this, when I read Harry Braverman's classic *Labor and Monopoly Capitalism* as a graduate student, I remember that my father must have contributed to the deskilling of his fellow machinists.

I grew up in Massachusetts off Route 128 between the period of deindustrialization and the rise of high-technology economy. Growing up in that context, I was little aware of class differences—public schools were of high quality and there seemed to be little if any gap in the respect and care shown for members in the community whether rich or poor. The place-context was much like described in Cynthia Duncan's book (1990), *Worlds Apart*, where she contrasts a New England community one in Appalachia and another in the Mississippi Delta. Much more egalitarian relationships characterize the New England community and hence being disadvantaged in that context is far less devastating to daily life and to future mobility.

Class-consciousness was more awakened when I attended college at Boston University majoring in sociology. With scholarships and work-study, waitressing, and other jobs, I paid my way through college. I had roommates and friends from middle-class, urban backgrounds who had had far different lifestyles than me. They were accustomed to Florida and European vacations and had no need to work during college. My summers were spent waitressing in New Hampshire, working as a maid in a hotel in the Catskill Mountains, and working in a designer dress store in New York City. At Boston University (BU) I met Susan Eckstein, a well-known Latin American sociologist. She helped to inspire my interests in development and class-related politics. And she was instrumental in the next phase of my life.

At one of my summer jobs I had met a Brazilian man and when I graduated from BU, we decided to move to the city of Curitiba in the state of Parana. I taught English as a second language. We lived in a house on the outskirts of town with no electricity or running water. Curitiba is cold during the winter and sometimes it snows. In our suburb I had observed new families coming in from rural areas in Parana—farms were becoming industrialized and consolidated, and rural people were migrating into the city for better opportunities. These new in-migrants were relatively well-off in that they could afford to buy small houses; they were not the classic impoverished migrants who lived in the favelas, the Brazilian slums. The process of development started to pique my interests. My husband and I decided we would go back to the U.S. for a few years. I would start graduate school in the Sociology Department at the University of South Florida in Tampa, choosing that program because my parents had moved down to Florida after my father retired. We planned to return to Brazil where I would potentially take a job at a university. Susan Eckstein had always encouraged me about graduate school and she provided a letter of support. I was offered a research assistant position on a development project dealing with innovation-diffusion, then the hot topic being funded by a wide range of development agencies. Our study analyzed the adoption-diffusion of new farm technologies in Guatemala. Today, I teach a course in innovation-diffusion, a field which has a long history at Ohio State University—two major figures in this field, Everett Rogers and Lawrence A. Brown, were professors at Ohio State and carved out their research here.

During graduate school I saw marriages break up typically because spouses became aware of divergent ties and interests. I vowed my marriage would not—but it did. Having no place to live and being new to the city, my son and I were homeless for about four months and lived in a shelter. A faculty member, Roy Hansen at South Florida, helped me out and some wonderful graduate students did likewise. In the 1980s, real-estate in Florida was booming and Roy had invested. I was his apartment complex manager, a research assistant, took a full load of classes and was a single mom. But life was good. There was a nice closure to the help I had experienced when many years later my son wrote his MA thesis on homeless shelters and the importance of their location.

After I finished my Master's degree, I needed to make money. I became a sales representative for the Revlon Corporation in its health and beauty division. Being a new sales rep, my accounts were small, family-owned stores, and with experience I would be offered larger accounts. Working with small businesses, I quickly observed how Revlon offered them such poor deals relative to the deals that were cut with large volume stores. My sales territory was the west coast of Florida from Tarpon Springs in the north to Marco Island in the south—an extremely affluent city. My territory also spanned south-central Florida running through the Everglades and Immokalee (an industrialized farm town with many poor people and weak sales of Revlon products). I gained an insiders' view of the private sector, including its various excesses with expense accounts and various deals that sales representatives were able to cut on the side to pad their wallets. There were many perks with this job besides income. I used to slip a bathing suit underneath my dress suit and head for the beach after sales calls. But the job was boring—simple "uping your numbers" in sales was the goal— and I was getting brain-dead. I had not thought about going on for a Ph.D. until Gene Summers (a rural sociologist) showed up in the Department of Sociology at South Florida to give a lecture. It was late in the year and he indicated that North Carolina (NC) State University's Department of Sociology still had research assistantships available. I knew nothing about rankings and fit with a program—I applied there and also to Case Western (a faculty member had had a connection there as well). Both offered me RA positions. I chose NC State mainly because the current chair at the time, Ronald Wimberley, spent so much time trying to convince me to come. It was one of the best decisions I ever made in my life.

At North Carolina State, I was Ron's research assistant, funded on a project that was novel at the time: it addressed a new field in rural sociology, the sociology of agriculture. The project's objectives were to examine the restructuring of American agriculture and the growth of large-scale industrialized farms and relative decline in moderate-size family farming. My work on the project took it a bit further, when I decided to write my dissertation on the impacts of these changes in farm structure on socioeconomic disparities in communities across the United States. In conducting this research, I soon observed gaps in the literature pertaining to theory that could address the manner by which economic and political processes unfolded across space. This required going outside sociology and reading literature in geography and regional studies. When I did so, I discovered the wealth of critical, Marxist-oriented radical political economy that extended the study of capitalism and class spatially. I was hooked. David Harvey's critical Marxist geography and attention to social justice, Doreen Massey's work on the spatial divisions of labor, and Neil Smith's analysis of uneven development framed my ideas. In sociology at the time no one to my knowledge had strayed outside the discipline to read geography. It was a period when sociology occupied a more hegemonic position among the social sciences and interdisciplinary work was far less common. But to some degree this is still the case even when sociologists address spatial issues. And this stance has been taken vice versa, as rural geographers today similarly do not appear to engage that much with the rural sociological literature.

At North Carolina State, I also had the chance to work with Michael Schulman and Donald Tomaskovic-Devey, both inspirations for the political economy work I have undertaken. I also studied with Gerhard Lenski at the University of North Carolina who had produced major work on global stratification and was a pivotal figure in sociology for moving the discipline away from structural-functionalism to conflict theory.

My doctoral experience was liberating in providing the freedom and support I needed to conduct my own research. I used course term-paper requirements to write papers for publication. By the time I graduated, I had two single authored journal articles published plus others with faculty members. NC State graduate students were supportive and intellectually engaged. Faculty treated us like colleagues (this was in the day when that was often not the case). One of the early pieces of advice I received has steered the direction of my research continually. In trying to decide upon a dissertation topic, I had initially thought about analyzing some deeply specialized questions about micro-relationships on the farm. Ron Wimberley tried to help me out with my decision and gently raised the question: do you want to take on a big-picture question that would make a broader disciplinary contribution or are you aiming for a more narrow focus? I liked the big-picture idea and this has continued to that day.

Still working on my dissertation, I was offered a tenure-track position in rural sociology at Ohio State University. I began as instructor then finished my dissertation there within a few months and was appointed to an assistant professor position.

The previous experiences set the path of my future research—path dependency exists in our careers and interests. My first book, *Locality and Inequality: Farm and Industry Structure, and Socioeconomic Conditions*—brought it all home—my dad's farm background, the deindustrialization social change, and class inequality I had observed, and the importance of a political economic and geographic lens to interpret sociological relationships. In this volume, I examined one of the significant research questions in the sociology of agriculture at the time, the movement away from family farming to large-scale industrialized farming and thus differentiation among farm enterprise and the petite-bourgeois class location of American farmers. This question was expressed more popularly as the classic Goldschmidt hypothesis about the detrimental effects of industrialized farms on communities. But Goldschmidt had taken more what was then judged to be a populist (non-Marxist) stance which appeared to elevate farm industrialization and farm scale per se above class relationships as causal determinants. I worked to recast the Goldschmidt hypothesis more in political-economic terms to deal with class and the movement of capitalism in American agriculture and industry more broadly. I questioned how both farming and industry had changed over time and their impacts on populations' well-being across localities. I aimed to extend the sociology of agriculture literature by bringing in critical political economic perspectives from literatures in economic/industrial sociology and geography. I read in all three fields. I thought a great deal about their overlap, how I could better synthesize them, and the new directions in research such a synthesis would bring. Wimberley's advice to focus on the big-picture in terms of casting a research question paid off: it kept me excited in continuing and extending this research path.

At Ohio State, at the beginning of my career, I pushed deeper into the analysis of farm structure, and while I work less in this area at present, it will always be a source of interest and engagement. As one pushes deeper into a substantive area, an academic reputation for working in that area follows. Sometimes these areas catch fire in their timeliness—and then you are there, at the critical point where you can make a difference. As I was studying farm structure, a full-blown farm crisis was still in progress and there was a great deal of interest in survival strategies on the farm. With important work by Carolyn Sachs and Rachel Rosenfeld, there was also interest in gender roles on the farm that had previously not been explored from a feminist standpoint. Now the various facets of the neoliberal stage of development have piqued scholars' interests. In cases like these, when research hits at the ripe time, openings can be made in being able to push rural sociological research into major sociological journals and beyond, to have a broader public influence.

The timeliness of research particularly can open opportunities beyond the academy that allow engagement with policy-makers. I experienced one of those rare instance in which the research I was producing was important to court cases that had sprung up in the Midwest regarding industrialized farms. The South Dakota Attorney General's office asked me to serve as an expert witness in a federal court case where an amendment to the state's constitution was at stake. By a wide margin, the state's voters had authorized an amendment to restrict the operation of corporate farms held by entities outside the state. This was challenged by the South Dakota Farm Bureau which maintained the amendment was unconstitutional because it violated part of the Commerce Clause of the U.S. Constitution. The source of this challenge came from integrated livestock producer/processors seeking to expand operations and encountering barriers due to existing legislation.

When corporate farming laws are challenged, one of the legitimate public interests that can be used to support these laws is that industrialized farming can harm communities, requiring evidence as to the presence or absence of adverse community effects. So I was asked to use my research and to compile the many other studies by rural sociologists and other social scientists to demonstrate their conclusions as to the effects of industrialized farms. In this case, rural sociological research did its job—the court held that we had provided sufficient evidence of the adverse effects of industrialized farming. But the challenge was supported because the manner in which the amendment was written appeared to restrict some populations from farming. The outcome was appealed by the South Dakota Attorney General's office and the case wended its way up to U.S. Supreme Court, which in 2003 had declined to hear it. This was an era where the tides had shifted nationally—we had a Republican president still riding high in the aftermath of September 11 where large corporations had gained even greater clout. I was disappointed in the outcome until I heard from some activists from family farm and environmental organizations who had been involved in the case. They indicated in some ways it was a victory: the length of time the case took to wend its way through the court system discouraged the agribusiness corporations in question from entering the state and in fact they moved internationally, to Australia. This work on the South Dakota case is described in an article Curt Stofferhan and I published in *Agriculture and Human Values*.

Over time, I began to develop more of an interest in the general processes of stratification across geographic space (Lobao 1996). I have continued to carve out this interest in the geography of inequality with a focus on the state and market forces that produce it. I have come to see rural sociology as fundamentally concerned with space. Our focus is unique for sociology as a discipline because much research addresses development at the subnational scale, the area between the city and the nation-state at large. Ann Tickamyer, Gregory Hooks and I in our edited volume, *The Sociology of Spatial Inequality* (2007) have referred to the subnational scale as sociology's "missing middle" because theorizing about inequality has been less formally developed at this scale. Rural sociology's major subfields such as poverty and inequality, the sociology of agriculture, environmental/natural resources sociology, and demography can all be seen as concerned with the subnational scale and this unites rural sociology as a whole. The previous subfields all ask questions about the impact of change on the well-being of populations across places. In that sense, they all address the issue of spatial inequality at the subnational scale. For example, the Goldschmidt tradition in the sociology of agriculture channeled rural sociologists' interests toward the changing structure of agriculture and its impacts across communities. Environmental/natural resources sociology has a long tradition of studying the impacts of the extractive sector on communities' well-being. As I considered spatial inequality, I began to see how rural sociology brought a special lens to the study of stratification that was highly unique and important for sociology as a discipline. My presidential address to the Rural Sociology Society focused on this very issue (Lobao 2004).

More recently, as I have studied spatial inequality at the subnational scale, I have been particularly interested in how changes in the state can exacerbate or ameliorate disparities in well-being. At the subnational scale, the state has been given far less attention than shifts in the private sector. Such changes include the degree to which retrenchment in the social safety-net, cutbacks in public-sector employment, and general weakening of the state at all scales are occurring. These processes directly converge on questions about whether neoliberal governance across the U.S. is spreading and the degree to which there has been resistance. Neoliberal governance refers to free-market oriented government that is characterized by rollbacks in the social safety-net and interests in supporting private sector interests over those of the public good. In studying local governments, my colleagues and I have found evidence of their resistance to social service cutbacks and the general neoliberal agenda (Lobao, Adua, and Hooks 2014). This present work too takes me back to my biography. Without the social safety-net and social welfare programs I would never have been able to complete graduate school.

One of the great strengths of rural sociology is the field's respect for and interest in policy work as well as academic sociology. In addition to my work on the South Dakota federal court case, other foci of my work appear to have resonated with the interests of non-governmental and policy organizations. I have worked with The Kellogg Foundation, Anne E. Casey Foundation, National Association of Counties, Appalachian Regional Commissions, and other agencies outside the academy. Most, if not all of this work has led to publications in scholarly journals. It has also centered on how to improve the position of disadvantaged and disempowered populations. For that reason, I do not see there is any necessary gap between academic or professional sociology, policy work, and critical sociology that Michael Burawoy (2005) has argued generally exists. Moreover, I have always been puzzled by why one or the other of these goals in research needs to be valued over others. For example, one will often hear policy-oriented sociologists indicating that they have more impact on society through their policy work than they ever could with academic work. Possibly. But my experience particularly with the South Dakota case is that a strong portfolio of research in refereed journals is needed if the policy world is to take us seriously, such as in the case of being invited to serve as an expert witness. In this case, if you want to make a difference, you have to publish, preferably in major journals to convince the court that you know what you are talking about as an expert witness. Thus, I have always seen academic work as complementing policy work, each supporting the other.

An important part of rural sociologists' biography is institutional support and being able to collaborate and work among great colleagues, faculty, and graduate students. When I started at Ohio State, I was the only woman in a department of 40 men—most of them agricultural economists. Even though tension between economists and sociologists sometimes occurs at departmental levels, I have worked consistently with economists over the years and to use their language, their "value-added" to projects is great, and they cause little in the way of "externalities" that would deter working relationships. I have learned a great deal from them particularly in terms of addressing issues of causality (that is, endogneity or the ability to separate out cause from effect), methodology, and simply thinking through a research project. I also worked with Lawrence A. Brown, the geographer noted above for many years, until he passed away this spring. Interdisciplinary work is exciting when you have the right colleagues.

My approach to research can probably best be characterized tongue-in-cheek as "Marxist positivism." Much of my research is quantitative and focused on large populations, but it takes a critical political economic approach that, as I've noted above, stems from my class background and subsequent experiences. I am curious about things—I have hunches—I go with them. Sometimes I am wrong and that opens a host of nuanced possibilities in explanations.

I can't recall where I heard this saying: "if you want to destroy capitalism, you have to know how it works." Whether or not you are happy with capitalism, the message for sociologists is that you have to be dogged about confronting wrong turns and be dogged about uncovering where, why, and how a relationship works out. Critically analyze relationships rather than tell stories. So much can depend upon the research we do and one never knows when the openings will arise to do our part in social change.

References

Braverman, Harry. 1974. *Labor and Monopoly Capitalism*. New York: Monthly Review Press.
Burawoy, Michael. 2005 "For Public Sociology." *American Sociological Review* 70:4–28.
Duncan, Cynthia. 1999. *Worlds Apart: Why Poverty Persists in Rural America*. New Haven: Yale University Press.
Goldschmidt, Walter. 1978. *As You Sow: Three Studies in the Social Consequences of Agribusiness*. Montclair, NJ: Allanheld, Osmun.
Harvey, David. 1975. "The Geography of Capitalist Accumulation: A Reconstruction of the Marxian Theory." *Antipode* 7 (2):9–21.
Lobao, Linda. 1990. *Locality and Inequality: Farm and Industry Structure and Socioeconomic Conditions*. Albany, NY: The State University of New York Press.
Lobao, Linda. 1996. "A Sociology of the Periphery Versus a Peripheral Sociology: Rural Sociology and the Dimension of Space." *Rural Sociology* 61 (1):77–102.
Lobao, Linda. 2004. "Continuity and Change in Place Stratification." *Rural Sociology*. 69 (1):1–30.
Lobao, Linda, and Katherine Meyer. 2001. "The Great Agricultural Transition: Crisis, Change, and Social Consequences of Twentieth Century Farming." *The Annual Review of Sociology* 27:103–124.
Lobao, Linda, and Curtis W. Stofferhan. 2008. "The Community Effects of Industrialized Farming: Social Science Research and Challenges to Corporate Farming Laws." *Agriculture and Human Values* 25 (2):219–240.

Lobao, Linda, Lazarus Adua, and Gregory Hooks. 2014. "Privatization, Business Attraction, and Social Services across the United States: Local Governments' Use of Market-Oriented, Neoliberal Policies in the Post-2000 Period." *Social Problems* 61 (4):1–27.

Lobao, Linda, Gregory Hooks, and Ann R. Tickamyer (Eds.). 2007. *The Sociology of Spatial Inequality*. Albany, NY: The State University of New York Press.

Massey, Doreen. 1984. *Spatial Divisions of Labor: Social Structures and the Geography of Production*. London: Macmillan.

Mills, C. Wright. 1959. *The Sociological Imagination*. New York: Oxford University Press.

Smith, Neil. 1984. *Uneven Development: Nature, Capital, and the Production of Space*. Oxford: Basil Blackwell.

7
RURAL SOCIOLOGISTS AT WORK
DUAL CAREERS, SINGLE FOCUS

CORNELIA BUTLER FLORA AND JAN L. FLORA,
IOWA STATE UNIVERSITY

Beginnings

How do two people of very different backgrounds form a rural sociology team to attempt to make the world a better place, particularly for excluded people in the U.S. and around the world? How does the ethos of the generation of the 1960s carry over into academic careers that stress social justice, feminist activism, and working on the ground for change in a competitive academic environment? Part of the luck of generation is entering academia in the era of expansion. Another is a network of peers and colleagues around the world who set a high bar for integrity and social action. The Floras were blessed with both.

Jan's Path to Sociology

Jan was born and raised in western Kansas. After his parents married right out of high school, they went west to the Pacific Northwest and

California to make their fortune near the end of the Great Depression. Their first jobs were on a ranch in Idaho, where Leonard worked as a farm hand and Billie as the cook for the farm crew. They worked for a relative in San Francisco and eventually landed in southern California where Billie worked as a cook and Leonard as the gardener for a Hollywood director. But when Billie was pregnant with Jan, she and Leonard went home to Kansas, borrowed from her father to buy a section of land, and began dry land farming of wheat, sorghum, and cattle. Jan was the first grandchild on the maternal side, and all the aunts outdid each other to be sure he knew how to read and write, add and subtract, before he started first grade in a one-room school house. They moved to the land they had bought, which was closer to town, and, beginning in the second grade, he went to the consolidated school in town.

To earn money for college, Jan raised chickens and sold the eggs door to door in town. The summer after his graduation from Quinter Rural High School (1959) he worked as a bookkeeper's aide at the local farmers' cooperative, where his father served on the Board of Directors.

The Soviet Union launched *sputnik*, the first earth-orbiting satellite, in 1957, and Jan was swept up in the sputnik "hysteria." His choice of nuclear physics may have been related to his adherence to Barry Goldwater's apocalyptic views on nuclear war, expressed in his *Conscience of a Conservative*. The 4-H agent and Vocational Agriculture teacher convinced Jan that he should "go away" (a five-hour drive in those days) to Kansas State University (KSU), Kansas' Land Grant College. Jan leaned toward Fort Hays State University because it was nearer and cheaper, but he accepted the advice of his mentors.

Political Formation

After a heavy dose of calculus, engineering physics, and inorganic chemistry in Jan's first two years of university, Jan's desire to be a physicist faded. In the summer of 1961, he participated in a work group in a Mexican village in the State of Tlaxcala organized by the American Friends Service Committee—and it changed his life. He was exposed to vistas not usually open to a Kansas farm youngster. He was immersed in an agrarian society that little resembled the one he was accustomed to, with work group members from diverse parts of the U.S. with new ways of viewing the world socially, politically, and culturally. While he began the summer accepting the perspective of Barry Goldwater (hadn't he gotten an "A" on his review of Conscience of a Conservative in a political science class at K-State?), the young "Bohemian" couple from Minneapolis who led the summer work group in Tlaxcala introduced Jan to I. F. Stone's Weekly, which took an opposing view to Goldwater on almost every political issue.

Jan quickly shifted his occupational sights to community development in Latin America. He transferred to the University of Kansas in Lawrence which offered a major in Latin American Studies, where he started seriously studying Spanish and later Portuguese and steeped himself in the study of Latin American politics, history, and social structure. He perfected his Spanish first by a summer in Barcelona studying Spanish literature and grammar, and then a year at the University of Costa Rica. Jan decided that graduate school in sociology or rural sociology would prepare him to become a community developer. His advisor in Latin American studies suggested five schools. Cornell offered him an assistantship first, so he was New-York-State bound.

Cornelia's Path to Sociology

Growing up on a Navy research and development base in the middle of the Mojave Desert gave Cornelia a pretty straight view of male and female spheres during the 1950s. Men were scientists and engineers. Women were librarians, secretaries, and mommies. Cornelia's father was a physicist and her mother was a technical librarian. But because she was also a mommy, she took her reproductive responsibilities very seriously. She was the Girl Scout leader for her elder daughter's troops from fifth grade through high school. Cornelia's father included his two daughters in activities of the Rock Hounds and Toastmasters. They learned never to cross a picket line. Everyone in the family had productive, reproductive and community maintenance work, including the two Butler children. Cornelia and her sister Eugenia's productive work was to do well in school so they could go on to college and thus support themselves.

Had she been a boy, she would have become a physicist or an engineer, but because she was a girl, she became a sociologist. Like her husband-to-be, she figured that humans were even more interesting than molecules and protons, and that surely similar laws of nature influenced behavior. She was determined to discover those natural laws and to use them to make the world a better place.

During her time at Berkeley as an undergraduate, the teach-ins on campus made it obvious to Cornelia that the Vietnam War was a great mistake. She was outraged how the media trivialized an action for racial and worker justice in the Free Speech Movement, stressing the use of profane language more than goals. Her work as a cook for mule packers who took campers, fishers, and hunters into the wilderness area at Mammoth Lakes during summers while she was an undergraduate reinforced a gendered division of labor, although she added saddling horses to her cooking duties.

The Cornell Years

Jan came to Cornell to study Rural Sociology in the fall of 1964. His first year he had an assistantship with Frank Young, who offered a Durkheimean perspective on community development (Durkheim, [1895] 1992). Jan learned about centrality, differentiation and solidarity as collective, rather than individual attributes. His masters research was on intervillage systems in Puerto Rico during the summer of 1965. He was supported for the remainder of his graduate study by a National Defense Education Act fellowship (NDEA) in Portuguese. He was also affiliated with the International Population Program (IPP), which met regularly and had a focus on Latin America.

Cornelia received a National Defense Education Act fellowship in population studies, associated with the IPP, while in the Department of Rural Sociology, arriving in the fall of 1965. With Jan, she was involved in Latin American support work and anti-war activities. They married in August of 1967.

Jan became a leader in a national war resistance movement culminating in burning draft cards in Sheep's Meadow in Central Park in New York. He also got arrested at a demonstration at the Pentagon.

Cornelia changed the venue of her dissertation research from Chile, in the Southern Cone of Latin America, to Colombia so she would be nearer him when he went to jail.

However, Jan didn't go to jail. The grand jury did not indict him. The conjugal ABDs (All But Dissertation) each received Social Science Research Council dissertation grants and went to Colombia in Latin America to do their research. Jan was willing to do his research in the Cauca Valley because that was where Cornelia's research was already underway.

Cornelia was interested in social movements of excluded people. In 1966, she discovered that Pentecostals had more support in the poor neighborhoods of Bogotá than did the radical student groups with which she hung out, along with her fellow Cornellians there doing demographic research. So Pentecostalism—its sources, structure, and impact—became the topic of her dissertation. Women in the Colombian Pentecostal Church who served as evangelists accompanied her on some of her research trips, but the pastors and priests she interviewed were all males. She also interviewed community leaders in all the communities in the intervillage systems in the Cauca Valley, and then conducted a survey of members of the Pentecostal Church in a rural trade center and a comparison sample of non-Pentecostals. Jan continued his work on intervillage systems, visiting all the *cabeceras municipales* (county-seat towns) in the Cauca Valley to measure their differentiation, centrality, and solidarity.

By the time the Floras returned to Cornell from Colombia, the antiwar movement had broadened considerably. The Ohio National Guard's killing of four Kent State students on May 4, 1970, in a protest against the U.S. invasion of Cambodia, galvanized student protesters around the country, including Cornell. The Black Power movement and the Women's Movement had become intellectual centers on campus. Cornelia participated in one of the first women's studies courses in the country in 1969 while analyzing her data. As a result of these combined experiences, her life, and her work, were changed. She included women and their experiences as a key component of the Pentecostal movement in her dissertation. (See the book that resulted from her dissertation, C. Flora 1976, and her article on women in Pentecostalism, C. Flora 1975.) The part of her research on Pentecostalism that focused on changes in men's and women's roles continues to be used by scholars analyzing the gendered nature of this growing movement.

With the Floras' raised feminist consciousness, they determined to get a job where they both could be equals and to privilege Cornelia's job over Jan's. It seemed logical, as Jan's basic commitment to social justice made it easy to understand the power of patriarchy in the marketplace. They accepted appointments as Assistant Professors of Sociology at Kansas State University in 1971, doing teaching and research.

Jobs in hand and dissertations finished, the Floras decided it was time to start a family. The student health center at Cornell claimed that Cornelia was the first woman coming in to take a pregnancy test who *hoped* to be pregnant. They postponed starting their teaching until after the baby was born, using money Cornelia received as a whiplash injury settlement to do postdoctoral research in Colombia and to have the baby there. The Vietnam War was still in full force—the U.S. had just bombed Cambodia, so they wanted to give the child a choice of citizenship. Cornelia started work as Director of the Population Research Laboratory and Assistant Professor of Sociology at Kansas State University in July of 1970 so she would have health insurance to cover the baby after she was born.

While in Cali, Colombia, before and after Gabriela's birth, Cornelia took advantage of an offer by feminist sociologist Pauline Bart to contribute to a special issue on women for the *Journal of Marriage and the Family*. Pauline had to negotiate hard to get the topic into a journal on family at that time. Cornelia began research on the presentation of women in popular magazine fiction in the U.S. and Latin America. She figured she could do that research while recovering from childbirth —reading the stories while Gabriela nursed and coding while she slept. Unexpectedly, she acquired a research assistant when Jan took ill from Hepatitis A to which he was exposed through either food or water in Colombia. A colleague taught his course while he was sidelined for about three months (January to April 1971), during which time he coded *fotonovelas*—when he was not playing with Gabriela (C. and J. Flora, 1978).

Gabriela accompanied her parents in their anti-war and G.I. counseling activities, and to the meetings at Kansas State University where Cornelia helped set up the KSU Commission on the Status of Women and planned the establishment of the Women's Studies Program. From the time Gabriela's sister, Natasha Pilar, was born in September 1974 (delivered at home as a political act—a film of Jan delivering Natasha, *Born Among Friends*, resulted), she came to class. The Floras team-taught Introduction to Sociology to classes of 350 and took turns holding Natasha while the other lectured.

Natasha accompanied Cornelia to any number of feminist gatherings at professional meetings, in the community, and in Washington, DC with development agencies. She and Gabriela attended the Kansas meeting of International Women's Year, as well as the national meeting, carrying tote bags which proclaimed, "I'm a mini-feminist".

In Kansas, agrarianism was the emergent social movement, and the Floras began a series of research projects on the sociology of agriculture and rural communities. Cornelia's interest was focused on women in agriculture and rural communities, where, during the 1970s, women were increasingly moving to the foreground in the community work they had always done. With rural sociology colleagues, Jan published one of the earliest sociology of agriculture readers (Rodefeld et al., 1978). The farm crisis erupted in 1980 and Cornelia's presidential address to the Rural Sociological Society (C. Flora, 1990) documented the many parallels between the U.S. farm crisis of the 1980s and the international debt crisis.

Entering the Foundation World

As a result of Cornelia's research on rural women and her friendship with social anthropologist Susan Almy, a program officer for the Rockefeller Foundation, she was included in a Rockefeller-funded conference on the social aspects of agricultural development, which was also attended by representatives from the Ford Foundation. From those contacts, she received an invitation to apply to be Program Advisor for Agriculture and Rural Development for the Andean Region and Southern Cone of Latin America. Jan and Cornelia made a joint application, and were invited to an interview, which was an adventure. Cornelia convinced Jan not to wear his powder-blue polyester leisure suit and she purchased a new suit in New York, since she mistakenly left her suit in the western Kansas town of Pratt, where they presented the results of their study on in- and out-migrants to and from Pratt County on their way to New York.

The appropriate people in the Ford Foundation decided they could do the job. At the point of being hired, Cornelia's feminism and feminist scholarship was of relatively little interest. What mattered was the knowledge of Latin America, agriculture, and rural development. After unsuccessfully trying agronomists and agricultural economists in the post, the Ford Foundation determined that agriculture and rural development really dealt with social issues, which required the insights and expertise of sociologists. Next, they had to decide *how* to employ the Floras. The Floras told the Foundation that they wanted equal appointments so that either could talk to a grantee as the "real" program advisor. The Foundation hired each Flora full time with half-time leaves without pay. That worked particularly well the first year as both got sabbatical leaves (which were negotiated into an additional 1.5 years of leave without pay from Kansas State).

The family of four headed off to Bogotá. They arrived in Bogotá on September 18, 1978, Natasha's fourth birthday. Gabriela was seven. The dollar was at its historic low against other currencies in 1978, and a dramatic shift in the international terms of trade had taken place. The Floras' portfolios and geographic area of coverage increased, covering social science, education, human rights, and health and nutrition, as well as agriculture and rural development. The increase in breadth allowed an opportunity to integrate women into all program areas and to start women's programs in many countries. Cornelia took on the responsibility of setting up women's programs in the Caribbean and Central America, with some work in Brazil and Mexico. It was an incredible opportunity to help exceptional women get access to resources to both implement and legitimate their work to better the lives of women, particularly poor women, in the hemisphere.

The goal of a philanthropic foundation is to support the greater public good. Thus, a foundation can make decisions that are not based on profitability and net worth, which are the measures of success of a multinational corporation, or balance of trade, debt repayment and gross national product, which are measures of national and multilateral banks. Further, because they are non-governmental, grants do not need to be justified in terms of the national interest or specific foreign policy goals. Bettering the human condition is a requirement of the U.S. tax code, the articles of incorporation and, usually, their boards of directors.

Building a solid women's program was a challenge. Many of the most important feminist groups in Latin America were established and maintained by women active in parties on the left, very suspicious of all U.S. institutions. They assumed that the Ford Foundation was another arm of the U.S. State Department, CIA, or Department of Defense. It took time to build relationships to then build good programs.

Women researchers in male-led private research institutions in Ecuador, Peru, Chile, Uruguay, and Argentina were the first grantees. In the late 1970s and early 1980s, military governments dominated Latin America, and the only social science scholarship took place in private institutions, dependent on outside funding for support. For researchers in these institutions in 1978, studies of women provided the first chance they had to once again begin to do field research under highly repressive regimes. The subject of women seemed so trivial that the military governments did not feel it worth stopping the studies or repressing the women who participated, either as researchers or researched. However, the knowledge of potential repression—and friends who had "disappeared"—made taking on any field research somewhat dangerous.

It was harder to develop projects with key activists and scholars in Peru and the Dominican Republic. Their research on *fotonovelas* proved an entrée, as feminist groups sought new media to reach out to working-class women. In 1979 Cornelia was invited to attend a meeting in Chile organized by the feminist coordination group to work with them to develop fundable programs that addressed the related problems of international dependency and patriarchy.

Fascinated by the process of inserting women into the male world of international development, Cornelia conducted a study of Ford Foundation documents in 1981 to better understand and articulate the context in which she had worked and the women's movements emerging throughout Latin America (she describes these movements in C. Flora, 1982a, 1982b, 1984).

In the last year of the Floras' work with the Ford Foundation, Jan was invited to add Nicaragua to his portfolio. The Mexico office had made a commitment to fund progressive research and applied programs in health, agriculture, and education following the coming to power of the Sandinista government in 1979. He continued his work there over a three-year period as a consultant after the Floras returned to Kansas State University in January 1981. In collaboration with two North American activists who had advised and worked in the Nicaraguan Literacy Campaign, Jan wrote two articles on the impact of that campaign on the young *brigadistas* who went to the countryside, books and pencils in hand (J. Flora, McFadden and Warner, 1983; J. Flora and McFadden, 1984). As the Contra War, supported by the U.S. Government, heated up, Jan also became active in the U.S.-based movement against U.S. policy in Central America. He was a founder of the Manhattan (Kansas) Alliance on Central America (MACA), and co-organized and participated in a fact-finding trip to Honduras and Nicaragua with Congressman Jim Slattery and opinion leaders from Kansas's Second Congressional District. The trip convinced Congressman Slattery, largely through a discussion he had with the American ambassador in Managua, Nicaragua, that lasted late into the night. The ambassador, Harry Bergold Jr., had serious doubts about U.S. policy in Central America; the conversation and the trip itself helped ease Slattery into the role of a Congressional critic of that policy, and gave him experiences that lent legitimacy to his opposition to the Contra War.

Between visits to Nicaragua, Jan researched and later published a monograph on the roots of the Central American insurgency that addressed the question of why there were insurgencies in Nicaragua, Guatemala, and El Salvador, and not in Costa Rica and Honduras (J. Flora, 1987). He traced the difference in large part to the social inequalities resulting from very unequally distributed agricultural land in the first three countries, and the rise of an organized right-wing agrarian elite in those countries. Costa Rica experienced no insurgency, as land—coffee land in particular—was much more equally distributed.[1] He also edited a book with the dean of Guatemalan agrarian scholars, Edelberto Torres Rivas, which includes an introductory chapter by the two editors on this topic (J. Flora and Torres R., 1989). The book featured work by Central American scholars that had not previously been published in English.

Subsequent Application of the Lessons Learned at the Ford Foundation

The cumulative results of feminist and agrarian scholarship and action carried over in the Floras' subsequent research and development activities in both Latin America and in the U.S. As Latin Americanists, the Floras also sought where possible to conduct research and applied rural development work on and with Latinos in Kansas and later in Iowa. With Kansas State Agricultural Experiment Station funds, Jan brought a film team from Mexico to film a documentary called *The Invisible People* (Robinson, 1975) in Southwest Kansas, which had attracted Mexican immigrants, expelled by the violence of the Mexican Revolution, first to build the Santa Fe railroad, then to work in the sugar-beet fields, and by the 1970s to work in the feed lots and meatpacking plants. The Floras obtained a grant from the Kansas Council on the Humanities to share the film and discuss its implications with community groups in the communities where the film was made.

Work with communities was a critical part of the Floras' work in Kansas. Working with the concept of Entrepreneurial Social Infrastructure (ESI), they contested theories of rural development that stressed the importance of a "spark plug", showing that community structure, not individual charisma, contributed to community and economic development. To investigate this at a national level, they joined with RSS colleagues Gary Green and Fred Schmidt (who they met while graduate students at Cornell) to conduct field work and survey research to test the ESI theory (C. Flora et al., 1988; Green et al., 1990; J. Flora et al., 1992).

In 1989 the Floras took jobs at Virginia Tech, Cornelia as Head of the Sociology Department and Jan as Professor in the Agricultural Economics Department, where they continued their empirical work on Entrepreneurial Social Infrastructure, the basis of the Community Capitals Framework (CCF) (J. Flora et al., 1997). The Floras obtained a grant from the U.S. Information Agency to do a ten-day workshop on how to write and obtain grants for working-class women leaders from various parts of Peru in 1991. It included a weekend trip to nearby coal country, where they met with working-class women who played an important role in the 1989 Pittston Coal strike. The women had replaced their husbands and brothers' place on the picket line in order that the men should not be arrested for violating a restraining order that forbade workers from picketing. Both the Peruvians and the Virginians learned a lot from each other, with great appreciation of each other's lives.

While at Virginia Tech, Cornelia was asked to join a group of community development practitioners facilitated by the Aspen Institute that met regularly to discuss major issues of community development. Primarily from not-for-profit organizations (NGOs) and government agencies such as the Forest Service, participants shared approaches to community development practice and theories of change. This set the scene for moving ESI into the Community Capitals Framework (CCF).

In 1994, Cornelia was recruited as Director of the North Central Regional Center for Rural Development at Iowa State University. Both Floras became Professors in the ISU Sociology Department. Subsequently, Cornelia was appointed Charles Curtiss Distinguished Professor of Agriculture and Sociology and Jan added Extension community sociologist to a portfolio that already included teaching and research. The opportunity for working with Latinos was renewed. This culminated in research and Extension work on integrating Latinos into local food systems and Latino entrepreneurship in rural communities in Iowa (J. Flora et al., 2012). Jan and his graduate students studied the impact of a workplace raid on the Swift meatpacking plant in Marshalltown, Iowa, which occurred in 2006, measuring impact in relation to the seven community capitals (J. Flora, Prado-Meza, and Lewis, 2011; J. Flora, Prado-Meza, Lewis, Montalvo, and Dunn, 2011).

Self-Development, Social Capital, Advocacy Coalitions, and the Community Capitals Framework (CCF)

The Floras continued their research thrust on the social dynamics of rural community development at Kansas State University, Virginia Tech, and Iowa State University, successively conceptualizing key features of community development in terms of self-development, entrepreneurial social infrastructure, and bridging and bonding social capital, while at the same time collaborating with U.S. and Andean region colleagues on the SANREM CRSP in Ecuador, Peru, and Bolivia on research and application of entrepreneurial social infrastructure, social capital and advocacy coalitions mainly in indigenous communities in these Andean countries. Working with the USDA Forest Service as the agency sought to redefine their mission from board feet to successful forest communities, Cornelia worked with community development colleagues across the U.S. to develop a workbook for communities to use as part of their planning and accountability. While the most important accountability is to local residents, measures also had to be meaningful to other partners, including government agencies and private donors. The result was "Measuring Success and Sustainability" (C. Flora et al., 1999).

The Floras settled on the Community Capitals Framework (CCF) as the most useful framework for assessing and encouraging holistic local community development. The CCF owes a lot to community structural theory, designed to define and measure the underlying dimensions of collectivities, developed in the 1960s by Frank W. Young (1965, 1970, 1999), Ruth Young (1968), and Paul R. Eberts (1998) of the Cornell University Department of Development Sociology (Merschrod, 2008). The Community Capitals Framework emerged dialectically from practice, although it has diverse theoretical roots. Its theoretical base is rich and heterodox, bringing together symbolic structuralism, social constructivism, participatory action research, and appreciative inquiry. By focusing on collective efficacy, the CCF was developed as a tool for people in the field, including community members, to assess what key local resources to mobilize and invest in for a more sustainable collective future.

The Floras built on the concept of collective agency in community development, as emphasized by activist scholars in Latin America, reinforced by their own work in movements for social change. Their participation in the anti-war movement, work with colleagues in Latin America at a time when the Theology of Liberation stressed the preferential option for the poor and the women's movement raised a collective consciousness among women around the world all contributed to understanding that power and its various manifestations were a critical piece of understanding community. They studied and later taught the principles used by Saul Alinksy (1946, 1971), who organized for change in Chicago and Rochester, New York. They currently participate in an Industrial Areas Foundation affiliate in mid-Iowa, and seek to put into practices the principles of Alinsky's successors, Ed Chambers and Ernesto Cortés. They call this the power approach, which is contained within their definition of political capital. The term "conflict approach", which many scholars of community development use to contrast to such as approaches as "technical assistance" and "self-help" does not adequately describe the way that change occurs in rural communities, where open confrontation can—and has—divided communities for generations and made collective agency impossible.

As the Floras' concern with sustainability led them toward greater understanding of the importance of natural capital and its interactions with all the other capitals, they found materialist approaches inadequate to explain the stocks and flows of capitals within the community. In the course of empirical research that analyzed social structures to predict community outputs, they attempted to replicate the work of Goldschmidt (1947). In these analyses (J. Flora and C. Flora, 1988a, 1988b; C. Flora and J. Flora, 1988), they found the limitations of the materialist approach. At the same time, their work with rural communities in Kansas led them to believe that more than material structures allowed some communities to thrive while others fell behind, even as individuals within the latter communities may have acquired wealth. It became clear that summing individual wealth did not indicate the financial well-being of the community.

The CCF strategy is designed to meet the triple bottom-line goals of economic security, ecosystem health, and social inclusions. These goals, heavily influenced by European work on communities, avoid the assumption that growth should be an end in itself. Over the years as they have worked with colleagues in a variety of international, Federal and state agencies, as well as those in universities and the private sector, they have been reminded that growth generally increases inequality and environmental damage unless specific action is taken to protect ecosystem health and social inclusion. And, indeed, economic growth does not equal financial security for communities.

The CCF incorporates seven capitals defined as resources that are invested to create new resources. Investment is stressed over the tendencies of traditional societies to simply preserve and financialized societies to speculate (Tomaskovic-Devey and Lin, 2011). When one capital is privileged over another in community development strategies, all can be depleted and the triple bottom line is threatened. However, they have found that with balanced investment in all seven, communities can move forward to increasing all three aspects of the triple bottom line (J. Flora and C. Flora, 1991; Emery and C. Flora, 2006; C. Flora et al., 2007; C. Flora, 2008).

Natural capital includes the air, water, soil, biodiversity, and weather that surrounds us, and provides the possibilities and limits to community possibilities. Natural capital influences and is influenced by human activities. All community capitals must be mobilized to enhance natural capital (C. Flora, 2001b, 2011).

Cultural capital determines how we see the world, what we take for granted, what we value, and what things we think possible to change. Cultural hegemony allows one social group to impose its symbols and reward system on other groups, as Bourdieu (1986) makes clear. All groups as have cultural capital, although hegemony imposes one culture over another. Cultural capital can be a form of resistance as well as domination (C. Flora, 1986; C. Flora and J. Flora, 1988; O'Brien and C. Flora, 1992, C. Flora et al., 2009).

Human capital is the characteristics and potential of individuals determined by the intersection of nature (genetics) and nurture (social interactions and the environment). Human capital includes education, skills, health, and self-esteem (C. Flora and Gillespie, 2009).

Social capital involves mutual trust, reciprocity, groups, collective identity, working together and a sense of a shared future. Bonding social capital consists of interactions within a specific group or community, and bridging social capital consists of interactions among social groups (C. Flora, 2001, 2003; Mulale and C. Flora, 2006; C. Flora and J. Flora, 2012).

Political capital is the ability of a community or group to turn its norms and values into standards that are then translated into rules and regulations that determine the distribution of resources. Political capital is also mobilized to ensure that those rules, regulations, and resource distributions are enforced. This definition is based on the French Convention Theorists (Boltanki and Thévenot, 2006).

Financial capital includes saving, income generation, fees, loans and credit, gifts and philanthropy, taxes and tax exemptions. Financial capital is much more mobile than the other capitals and tends to be privileged because it is easy to measure. Community financial capital can be assessed by changes in poverty, in firm efficiency, diversity of firms, and increased assets of local people (C. Flora and Thiboumery, 2006).

Built capital is human constructed infrastructure. While new built capital is often equated with community development, it is only effective when it contributes to other community capitals. Built capital includes technologies, roads, bridges, factories, day-care centers, and wind farms. Built capital depends on the other capitals for maintenance and open access (C. Flora, 2004).

The theoretical focus of the CCF is on the interaction of structure and collective (rather than individual) agency: how communities work together for change. The notion of the collective conscience as a social phenomenon, rather than the sum of individual beliefs about right and wrong, is critical in the conceptualization of cultural capital and a justification for its separation from social capital.

CCF rejects the ecological and functional notions of moving from equilibrium to equilibrium and views systems in constant flux, consistent with current understanding of biophysical ecosystems.

Importance of an Asset-based Approach

The evolution of the CCF has also benefited from movement from a focus on deficits to a focus on assets (Kretzman and McKnight, 1993). However, the Floras reject the neoliberal thrust of the McKnight approach (MacLeod and Emejulu, 2014). Not only is it critical to retain the state as a major actor in providing for the general welfare and reducing poverty, organizing using the principles of Saul Alinsky (1971) is part of the CCF asset-based approach. Instead of individualizing problems, CCF provides a tool for collective analysis and solutions, providing non-market as well as market opportunities for holistic community development. Utilizing Polanyi's notion of the embeddedness of human action and institutions (1944), CCF does not separate land, labor, and capital, but sees them as highly interactive. Indeed, focusing on only one capital, such as financial capital, leads to the deterioration of all the other capitals through financialization.

We find that communities can strengthen each community capital by identifying appropriate bonding and bridging social capital linkages through market, state, and civil society actors[2] associated with that capital. The CCF goes beyond the usual asset-mapping exercise to identify not only the various capital assets within a community but also to collectively act to enhance tangible and intangible social capital assets associated with each other capital. This mapping process has already been institutionalized in several programs, providing greater breadth of resources for community and regional planning efforts. Although it starts with a holistic view of assets, communities then use it to address key issues, including poverty, social exclusion, and environmental deterioration. The Raccoon River Watershed Association uses the capitals as it confronts industrial agriculture in Iowa (C. Flora and Delaney, 2012).

CCF has also been very influenced by integrating key principles from Appreciative Inquiry (AI) into the understanding and application of the framework, particularly in moving from problem solving to solution seeking. Engaging people appreciatively in analyzing resources and assets across the capitals often brings new insights. In addition, the story-telling aspect of the Discover stage of AI creates narrative that can be deconstructed to identify resources related to each of the capitals that are invested to create additional assets resulting in a virtuous spiral.

The CCF is based in systems theory, stemming from the applied approach used in Farming Systems Research and Extension (C. Flora, 1992). The Floras empirical research base grew as the result of three major partnerships: one with the USDA Economic Research Service and colleagues Gary Green from the University of Wisconsin and Fred Schmidt from the University of Vermont, where they examined self-development in rural communities (Green et al., 1990; C. Flora et al., 1991; J. Flora et al., 1992; J. Flora et al., 1997), one with the USDA Forest Service, which partnered with the North Central Regional Center for Rural Development to determine the best ways to move communities beyond timber dependence (C. Flora et al. 1996) and one with USAID and the Sustainable Natural Resource Management Collaborative Research Support Program (SANREM CRSP) (Shields et al., 1996; C. Flora and Kroma, 1998; C. Flora, 2001b, 2001c). The CCF began to resonate internationally because of the underlying analysis of the conditions for sustainability (C. Flora 1998, 2000, 2001a, 2001b).

Market, state, and civil society are critical social actors for moving each of the capitals toward sustainability (C. Flora, 2003). Because of its grassroots-foundation and local-responsibility focus, the CCF can be charged with fostering a neoliberal approach that absolves the state from its responsibility in achieving the common good. On the contrary, the CCF does conceive of the state as a critical partner, but not the lead, in progressive movement toward a healthy ecosystem, economic security, and social inclusion. The Floras view the interaction of these three types of actors thusly: The market (consisting of the collectivity of for-profit firms and proprietors) can be an efficient and effective allocator of resources under certain conditions, particularly when no firm has undue political and economic power in the marketplace nor over the state or civil society. The State plays (or should play) a central role in regulating the market, making it profitable for the market to serve the common good, particularly by internalizing the costs of environmental degradation and social inequality. Without government involvement in promoting the common good, the unbridled market fosters environmental degradation and social and economic misery. The common good is articulated through the values that play out through civil society, often chaotically, but in a truly democratic society (what we might call *deep democracy*), each society's common good will be expressed through its laws, regulations, and the pattern of subsidies that it provides. Societies can serve their people and human kind and the earth itself without reaching that ideal, but it is a utopian vision that we must struggle toward if people are to live in dignity and civilization is not to perish.

Polanyi's work, *The Great Transformation* (1944), and the Latin American focus on *Vivir Bien* has informed the Floras' focus on the need not to separate the factors of production or to reify the notion of an unregulated market as the solution to all social and economic problems.

The Floras conclude: "We were privileged to be a part of several social movements, in both their national and international aspects—feminist, anti-war, ethnic, class, and sovereignty struggles. The movement for inclusion continues. The importance of informal connections, e.g. social capital in feminist communities of interest, continues to be critical for building toward a feminist and inclusive future. The impact on us as a family, as well as the continued activities of the connections formed in Latin America, Africa, and Asia, and between Latin American and North American scholars and activists, can hopefully continue to contribute to the process of changing the world—which is what we set out to do."

Notes

1. Honduras occupies a middle ground between Costa Rica and the other three countries, but is more like the latter three, both in terms of inequality of land ownership and coercive force used against exploited and human rights groups, both then and now, although no viable insurgency emerged there.
2. We find the three categories of market, state, and civil society (firm, agency, and organization) to be more useful than Kretzmann and Mcknight's individual, association, and institution triad.

Bibliography

Alinsky, Saul D. 1946. *Reveille for Radicals*. Chicago: University of Chicago Press.
Alinsky, Saul D. 1971. *Rules for Radicals: A Practical Primer for Realistic Radicals*. New York: Random House.
Boltanski, L., and Thévenot, L. 2006. *On Justification: The Economies of Worth*. BourPrinceton, NJ: Princeton University Press.
Bourdieu, Pierre. 1986. "The Forms of Capital." in *Handbook of Theory and Research for the Sociology of Education*, Ed. John C. Richardson, pp. 241–258. New York: Greenwood Press.
Durkheim, Emile. [1895] 1982. *The Rules of Sociological Method*, translated by W.D. Halls. New York: Free Press.
Eberts, Paul R. 1998. "POETS-PACS-LEDD: From Paradigm to Theory to Policy in Human Ecology Perspective," pp. 67–84 in *Continuities in Sociological Human Ecology*, edited by M. Micklin and D.L. Poston, Jr. New York: Plenum Press.
Emery, Mary, and Cornelia B. Flora. 2006. Spiraling-Up: Mapping Community Transformation with Community Capitals Framework. *Community Development: Journal of the Community Development Society* 37:19–35.
Flora, Cornelia B. 1971. "The Passive Female: Her Comparative Image by Class and Culture in Women's Magazine Fiction." *Journal of Marriage and the Family* 33:435–444.
Flora, Cornelia B. 1975. "Religion and Change: Pentecostal Women in Colombia?" *Journal of Inter-American Studies and World Affairs* 17:411–425.
Flora, Cornelia B. 1976. *Baptism by Fire and Spirit: Pentecostalism in Colombia*. Rutherford, NJ: Fairleigh Dickinson University Press.
Flora, Cornelia B. 1982a. "Incorporating Women into International Development Programs: The Political Phenomenology of a Private Foundation." *Women and Politics*. Winter, 2:89–106.
Flora, Cornelia B. 1982b. "Social Policy and Women in Latin America: The Need for a New Model." *Journal of Third World Societies*, May: 191–205.
Flora, Cornelia B. 1984. "Socialist Feminism in Latin America." *Women and Politics*, (Spring):69–93.
Flora, Cornelia B. 1986. "Values and the Agricultural Crisis: Differential Problems, Solutions, and Value Constraints." *Agriculture and Human Values* 3:16–23.
Flora, Cornelia B. 1990. "Rural Peoples in a Global Economy." *Rural Sociology* 55(2):157–177.
Flora, Cornelia B. 1992. "Building Sustainable Agriculture: A New Application of Farming Systems Research and Extension," pp. 37–50 in *Integrating Sustainable Agriculture, Ecology & Environmental Policy*, edited by R.K. Olson. Binghamton, NY: Haworth Press.
Flora, Cornelia B. 1998. "Sustainable Production and Consumption Patterns: Community Capitals," pp. 115–122 in *The Brundtland Commission's Report—Ten Years*. G. B. Softing, G. Benneh, K. Hindar, L. Walloe, and A. Wijkman (Eds.) Oslo: Scandinavian University Press.
Flora, Cornelia B. 2000. "Sustainability in Agriculture and Rural Communities," pp.191–207 in *Nachhaltigkeit in de Landwirschaft: Landwirtschaft im Spannungsfeld zwischen Ökologie, Ökonomie und Sozialwissenschaften*, edited by M. Härdtlein, M. Kaltschmitt, I. Lewandowski, and H.N. Wurl. Berlin, Germany: Erich Schmidt Verland.

Flora, Cornelia B., Ed. 2001a. *Interactions Between Agroecosystems and Rural Communities.* Boca Raton: CRC Press.

Flora, Cornelia B. 2001b. Access and control of resources: Lessons from the SANREM CRSP. Agriculture and Human Values 18(1):41–48.

Flora, Cornelia B. 2001c. "Access and Control of Resources: Lessons from the SANREM CRSP." *Agriculture and Human Values.* 18(1):41–48.

Flora, Cornelia B. 2003."Democracy: Balancing Market, State, and Civil Society," pp. 89–100 in *Walking toward Justice: Democratization in Rural Life*, edited by M.M. Bell and F. Hendricks. Bristol, England: JAI/Elsevier.

Flora, Cornelia B. 2004. "Social Aspects of Small Water Systems." *Journal of Contemporary Water Research and Education* 128:6–12.

Flora, Cornelia B. 2008. "Social Capital and Community Problem Solving: Combining Local and Scientific Knowledge to Fight Invasive Species," pp. 41–54 in *Learning Communities: International Journal of Learning in Social Contexts* (Australia), and *Kritis: Journal of Interdisciplinary Development Studies* (Indonesia). Biosecurity Bilingual Monograph.

Flora, Cornelia B., and Michael Delaney. 2012. "Mobilizing Civil Society for Environmental Protection in a Context Dominated by Industrial Agriculture: Avoiding Projects," pp. 201–213 in *Sustainability and Short-term Policies: Improving Governance in Spatial Policy Interventions*, edited by I. S. Sjöblom, K. Andersson, T. Marsden, and S. Skerratt Burlington, VT: Ashgate.

Flora, Cornelia B., and Jan L. Flora. 1978. "The Fotonovela as a Tool for Class and Cultural Domination," *Latin American Perspectives* 5:134–150.

Flora, Cornelia B., and Jan L. Flora.1988. "The Structure of Agriculture and Women's Culture in the Great Plains." *Great Plains Quarterly* 8: 95–205.

Flora, Cornelia B., and Jan L. Flora. 2013 (1992, 2004, 2008). *Rural Communities: Legacy and Change.* Boulder, CO: Westview Press.

Flora, Cornelia B., and Ardyth Harris Gillespie. 2009. "Making Healthy Choices to Reduce Childhood Obesity: Community Capitals and Food and Fitness." *Community Development* 40:114–122.

Flora, Cornelia B., and Margaret Kroma. 1998. "Gender and Sustainability in Agriculture and Rural Development," pp. 103–116 in *Sustainability in Agricultural and Rural Development*, edited by G. E. D'Souza and T. G. Gebermedhin. Brookfield, VT: Ashgate.

Flora, Cornelia B. and Arion Thiboumery. 2006. "Community Capitals: Poverty Reduction and Rural Development in Dry Areas." *Annals of Arid Zone*, 45 (3–4): 239–253.

Flora, Cornelia B., Corry Bregendahl, and Susan Fey. 2007. "Mobilizing Internal and External Resources for Rural Community Development," pp. 210–220 in *Perspectives on 21st Century Agriculture: A Tribute to Walter J. Armbruster*, edited by R.D. Knutson, S. D. Knutson, and D. P. Ernstes. Chicago: The Farm Foundation.

Flora, Cornelia B., Jan L. Flora, and K. Wade. 1996. "Measuring Success and Empowerment," pp. 57–74 in *Community Visioning Programs: Practices and Principles.* N. Walzer (Ed.) Westport, CT: Greenwood Press.

Flora, Cornelia B., Jan L. Flora, Gary P. Green, and Frederick E. Schmidt. 1991. "Rural Economic Development through Local Self-Development Strategies." *Agriculture and Human Values* 8:19–24.

Flora, Cornelia B., Matt Livingston, Iva Honyestewa, and Harrissa Koiyaquaptewa. 2009. "Understanding Access and Use of Traditional Food by Hopi Women." *Journal of Hunger and Environmental Nutrition* 4:158–171.

Flora, Cornelia B., M. Kinsley, V. Luther, M. Wall, S. Odell, S. Ratner, and J. Topolsky. 1999. "Measuring Community Success and Sustainability" (RRD 180). Ames, IA: North Central Regional Center for Rural Development.

Flora, Jan L. 1987. "Roots of Insurgency in Central America," *Latin American Issues: A Monograph Series on Contemporary Latin American and Caribbean Affairs*. Meadeville, PA: Allegheny College.

Flora, Jan L., and Cornelia B. Flora. 1988a. "Public Policy, Farm Size, and Community Well-Being in Farming-Dependent Counties of the Plains," pp. 76–129 in *Agricultural and Community Change in the U.S.: The Congressional Research Reports*, edited by L. E. Swanson. Boulder, CO: Westview Press.

Flora, Jan L., and Cornelia B. Flora. 1988b. "The Effects of Different Production Systems, Technology Mixes, and Farming Practices on Farm Size and Community: Implication for the Conservation Reserve Program," pp. 75–83 in *Impacts of the Conservation Reserve Program in the Great Plains*. USDA, Forest Service. General Technical Report RM-158, Ft. Collins.

Flora, Jan L., and Cornelia B. Flora. 1991. "Local Economic Development Projects: Key Factors," pp. 141–156 in *Rural Community Economic Development*, edited by N. Walzer. New York: Praeger Publishers.

Flora, Jan L., and Edelberto Torres Rivas, (Eds.) 1989. *Sociology of "Developing Societies": Central America*. London: Macmillan (published by Monthly Review Press in the U.S.).

Flora, Jan L., John McFadden and Ruth Warner. 1983. "The Growth of Class Struggle in the Nicaraguan Revolution: The Impact of the Nicaraguan Literacy Crusade on the Political Consciousness of Young Literacy Workers," *Latin American Perspectives* 10: 45–62.

Flora, Jan L., Claudia M. Prado-Meza, and Hannah Lewis. 2011. "After the raid is over: Marshalltown, Iowa and the Consequences of Worksite Enforcement Raids," Special Report. Immigration Policy Center, Washington, DC, January, pp. 1–21. Accessed on August 23, 2011 at www.immigrationpolicy.org/special-reports/after-raid-over-marshall town-iowa-and-consequences-worksite-enforcement-raids

Flora, Jan L., Mary Garcia Bravo, Cornelia B. Flora, and S. Andrango Bonilla, 2001. "Community sustainability in an Ecuadorian landscape: The role of economic, human, environmental and social capital," pp. 291–313 in *Bridging Human and Ecological Landscapes: Participatory Research and Eco-Development in an Andean Region*, edited by R. Rhoades. Dubuque, IA: Kendall/Hunt Publishing.

Flora, Jan L., Jeff S. Sharp, Cornelia B. Flora, and Bonnie Newlon. 1997. "Entrepreneurial Social Infrastructure and Locally-Initiated Economic Development." *Sociological Quarterly*. 38:623–645.

Flora, Jan L., Mary Emery, Diego Thompson, Claudia M. Prado-Meza, and Cornelia B. Flora. 2012. "New Immigrants in Local Food Systems: Two Iowa Cases," *International Journal of Sociology of Agriculture and Food*, Vol. 19, No. 1:119–134.

Flora, Jan L., Gary P. Green, Edward A. Gale, Frederick E. Schmidt, and Cornelia B. Flora. 1992. "Self-development: A viable rural development option?" *Policy Studies Journal* 20: 276–288.

Flora, Jan L., Claudia Prado-Meza, Hannah Lewis, Cesar Montalvo, and Frank Dunn. 2011. "Impact of Immigration and Customs Enforcement Raid on Marshalltown, Iowa," pp. 119–55 in *Latinos in the Midwest*, edited by R. O. Martinez. East Lansing, MI: Michigan State University Press.

Goldschmidt, W. R 1947. *As You Sow*. New York: Harcourt Brace.

Green, Gary, Jan L. Flora, Cornelia B. Flora, and Frederick E Schmidt. 1990. "Local Self-Development Strategies: National Survey Results." *Journal of the Community Development Society* 21:56–73.

Kretzman, John R. and John L. McKnight. 1993. *Building Communities from the Inside Out: A Path toward Finding and Mobilizing a Community's Assets*. Chicago: ACTA Publications.

MacLeod, Mary Anne, and Akwugo Emejulu. 2014. "Neoliberalism with a Community Face? A Critical Analysis of Asset-Based Community Development in Scotland." *Journal of Community Practice*. 22:4.

Merschrod, Kris. 2008. "A Sociology: The Dynamics of Collectivities and Their Application to Social Change and Development." Lulu.com

O'Brien, William E. and Cornelia Butler Flora 1992. "Selling Appropriate Development vs. Selling-Out Rural Communities: Empowerment and Control in Indigenous Knowledge Discourse." *Agriculture and Human Values*. 9:95–102.

Pescatello, Ann (Ed.) 1973. *Female and Male Latin America: Essays*. Pittsburgh, PA: University of Pittsburgh Press (published in Spanish in 1977, Mexico, D.F. Editorial Diana).

Polanyi, Karl. 1944 (1957, 2001). *The Great Transformation: The Political and Economic Origins of Our Time*. Boston, MA: Beacon Press.

Robinson, Scott, Director. 1975. "The Invisible People," 16 mm film, Grupo Cine Labor, Mexico City. (Funded by Kansas Agricultural Experiment Station, Jan L. Flora project director; available from KSU Minorities Center, Farrell Library.)

Rodefeld, Richard D., Jan L. Flora, Donald Voth, Isao Fujimoto, and James Converse, (Eds.) 1978. *Change in Rural America: Causes, Consequences; and Alternatives*. St. Louis: C.V. Mosby Co.

Shields, M. Dale, Cornelia B. Flora, Barbara Thomas-Slayter, and Gladys Buenavista. 1996. "Developing and Dismantling Social Capital: Gender and Resource Management in the Philippines."pp. 155–79 in *Feminist Political Ecology: Global Perspectives and Local Experience*, edited by D. Rocheleau, B. Thomas-Slayter, and E. Wangari. London: Routledge.

Tomaskovic-Devey, Donald, and Ken-Hou Lin. 2011. "Income Dynamics, Economic Rents, and the Financialization of the U.S. Economy." *American Sociological Review* 76:538–559.

Young, Frank W. 1965. *Initiation Ceremonies*. Indianapolis, IN: The Bobbs-Merrill Co.

Young, Frank W. 1970. "Reactive subsystems." *American Sociological Review* 35:297–307.

Young, Frank W. 1999. *Small Town in Multilevel Society*. New York: University Press of America.

Young, Ruth C. 1968. "A structural approach to development." *Journal of Developing Areas* 2:363–375.

Part III
Theory and Method

8
RURAL SOCIOLOGY
AN INTELLECTUAL CRESCENT WRENCH
RALPH B. BROWN, *BRIGHAM YOUNG UNIVERSITY*

Overview

My foray into rural sociology as a separate discipline somewhat distinct from general sociology was in search of an intellectual "crescent wrench" that would allow me to tackle any number of perplexing puzzles and issues on a practical basis. I was predisposed to think that the ability to apply sociology to problems of the real world was due to my upbringing in a blue-collar background and the hyper-Protestant work ethic environment of Mormonism. In this chapter, I provide an example of work I did for the Mississippi Wildlife, Fisheries, and Parks Department where the combination of conceptual frameworks and rigorous empirical methods employed by rural sociologists allowed me to provide a unique explanation for why different fishers in the Mississippi Delta had dramatically different experiences while utilizing well-stocked public reservoirs. I was able to solve the problem not by using just one specific research theory or one methodological technique, but by taking a more holistic historical approach that captured a seemingly isolated problem and recast it in the context of much larger social and economic shifts. My mouth waters when I see advertisements for a 24-drawer, 250-piece tool-box set from Craftsman. I have no idea what I would use half those tools for if I owned them, but I want them! Being more realistic, however, if I could only have one tool in my tool-box, I would want it to be the most adaptable, multifunctional tool possible. It would need to be a crescent wrench (or the "adjustable spanner" for our friends across the Pond). The fact that a crescent wrench is rather worthless for specialized applications is overshadowed by its broad utility for everyday issue and problem-solving. Hell, it can even be used as a hammer if needs be.

Background

My foray into Rural Sociology was in search of an intellectual "crescent wrench" that would allow me to tackle any number of perplexing puzzles and issues on a practical basis but with scientific precision. What Rural Sociology gave me was a keen sense of the futility of simplistic answers to complex issues or the absurd propensity of some academics to buy into dichotomies like "institution versus discipline," or "practice versus basic." Such dichotomies are meaningless when the purpose behind applying the scientific wrench is to solve some real-world problem.

Rural Sociology also gave me a greater appreciation for the value and uses of context. For purposes of this volume, I should give the reader context of a personal nature. I actually have a love–hate relationship with tools, having been introduced into the world of tools very early in my life. I get the metaphors; tools help you accomplish tasks that you otherwise could not with your "bare hands." I am a first-generation academic; the youngest of four boys reared in the 1960s and 1970s. My father managed a hardware and sporting goods store on the wrong end of a dying main street in Logan, Utah, a town of 40,000. Because of that store, I distinctly knew the difference between a customer versus a consumer long before writing about it in my dissertation and making a career about it in subsequent research on community satisfaction and attachment. I grew up working at the store assembling bicycles, wagons, motorcycles, mounting bindings on skis, etc. and pretty much hating every minute of it. To this day, while more than capable of assembling just about anything, I have a distinct distaste for doing so, but I can still look at a wrench and know immediately if it is a 14-millimeter or a 3/4-inch SAE. In my youth, work was something that became associated with tools.

Max Weber ([1905] 2002) introduced the concept of the Protestant ethic at the turn of the 20th century with no specific Protestant denomination in mind. Mormons (my faith background) took the concept and put it on steroids. A fundamental principle in the Brown household was that one had to be productive, and evidence of productivity was manifest in physical form; an assembled bike, a fixed tricycle, something that one could "kick," something that had been put together by the proper use of tools. For someone often lost in a world of ideas, figuring out how to create something at the end of the day that could be "kicked" as evidence of my productivity was a frustrating proposition. How do you kick an idea?

I was the first of my brothers to leave the store and work for someone else besides my father. This occurred in my senior year of high school when I became a shipping clerk for a local biological firm. Then, in 1979, I served a voluntary mission for the Church of Jesus Christ of Latter-Day Saints (the Mormon Church) for two years in Indonesia. I was exposed to a different set of tools associated with work—thinking, studying, reading, interacting, conversing, listening. I was also exposed to a world of social problems that needed fixing, not just *things* that needed it. Additionally, I saw a world that was not what people who had never been there told me (with great authority, no less) it was.

I was hooked. I knew I had to see more of that world and if I was to be a participant in "fixing" it, I had to understand it better and with different tools than I had grown up with. I had never planned to attend college, nor had I been encouraged to do so. In fact, the only guidance counseling I remember receiving to that point was sometime around 8th grade when I was asked what type of heavy machinery operator I wanted to be. I remember responding that "forklifts are cool." I returned to the States after two years in Indonesia knowing that if I was to get more insight into what I had seen and experienced there, I needed some different tools, I could only get them in college. Ironically, I funded five years of an undergraduate education at Utah State University by working swing shifts and graveyard shifts in a local cheese plant driving a forklift!

Academia

To say I was clueless about the world of academia is to give me more credit than I deserve. All I knew is that I wanted to get back to Indonesia and help solve problems. I was going to "fix" things. My initial foray into academia was in food science and microbiology. I was going to return as a nutritionist and make healthier people. It was not until my senior year in college that I made the switch to Sociology, having discovered at least two years earlier that it was what actually flipped my intellectual switch. The puzzles a sociological approach to the world revealed were exactly what I was looking for, yet at the end of the day I could not figure out how I could make something in Sociology that I could "kick." How does one convince oneself and others that s/he has been sociologically productive? Despite convincing myself that I had turned my back on my blue-collar, hand- and power-tool background, I still felt a need to show productivity, something that had "application."

While completing an MA in Sociology at Utah State University, I looked for Ph.D. programs that allowed a good mixture of sociology and application beyond the confines of the academy. I stumbled upon Rural Sociology, not knowing much about it, as a potential avenue to my need to apply tools to fix or solve things. I applied to the University of Missouri as they had a joint program in both Sociology and Rural Sociology. When I got there, the Department Chair of the Rural Sociology Department asked me if I was going to be a sociologist or a rural sociologist. I replied "both." He informed me that it would be "like walking on razor-blades." I responded that I was "willing to get cut." It had never occurred to me that to many, the sociology and rural sociology had to be seen and treated as separate things. I quickly learned that some faculty members in the Sociology Department referred to themselves as "real" sociologists and the rural sociologists as "pig counters," representing somebody's idea of status differences between approaches within a single discipline.

The fact that some people found differences did get me thinking very early on about the disciplinary status of Rural Sociology. What is at our core? To some observers, rural sociologists are noted for our heavy reliance, at least historically, on quantification that often precludes theory building. Do we have a theory (or theories) of rural social organization; a sociology of the rural that recognizes unique sociological properties embedded in the rural by the mere fact it is rural, or are we a "we" by name simply because we come together through membership in an institutional association? Do rural sociologists build theories? What is it about the social organization of rural life that is sociologically different from other forms of social organization? Has our development and use of sophisticated survey and quantification techniques to document the empirical "facts" of rural social life distracted us from developing a theory of rural social organization, a "sociology" of the rural? And if there are unique sociological principles/attributes to social organization in rural space, are these different from those already articulated in geography or a sociology of place?

It occurs to me that Rural Sociology as a *discipline* and as an institution both stem from two distinct "crises" experienced in the late 1800s and early 1900s. Its claim to disciplinary status originates from the post-Civil War period when the US was experiencing much social and economic disruption and dislocation. It was during this time that American social scientists established survey research and sampling methodologies to establish social needs and act on resolving them (Turner and Turner 1990). Rural Sociology as a discipline in large measure originates from the farm crisis at the end of the 19th century (Ford 1985). Rural areas were economically depressed compared to the emerging urban social landscape, creating conditions for an exodus from the Southern states due to existing land-tenure systems offering few opportunities beyond sharecropping to landless farmers. President Roosevelt's 1908–1909 Country Life Commission identified many deficiencies in rural life and set a discussion of people left behind as society urbanized and modernized. Despite attention given these problems through the Country Life Commission, government attention itself tended to go elsewhere and farmers did not get the attention they wanted or felt they deserved. Despite this lack of government attention, farmers and rural people generally were accorded a particular cultural status as the backbone of moral society. This Agrarian Myth (see Hofstadter 1955) notwithstanding, the economic position of most farmers deteriorated during much of the 20th century. For some observers, rural life was the foundation of decent human living, of moral life, and as such was to be preserved. To other observers, modern rural life is oxymoronic, an anachronism, woefully falling behind modern *urban* life. As the discipline emerged in the early 20th century, some may have asked whether rural sociology was to be an applied science used to improve rural life and livelihood along lines charged by the Country Life Commission (1909) or should the focus be on preserving all things rural as the moral foundation of modern life?

There is a reason the term "false dichotomy" exists; in my opinion, most dichotomies are overly simplistic and blur the complexities of important real-world issues. Why can't we be both scientists and saviors? Rural Sociologists can be and often are scientists documenting factual differences found among social and economic variables and often are engaged in actively doing something to improve the quality of rural life. Rural sociologists were not merely trying to preserve a way of life but also to understand how the rural was being shaped by the increasingly urbanized society, of which it was an increasingly small part.

Recent personal experience has sharpened my understanding of the subjective nature of science. Soon after starting work on this chapter, I was diagnosed with pancreatic cancer. Decades of research and billions of dollars have gone into the scientific investigation of cancer, but after initial treatments failed to provide a cure, my oncologist admitted that I had "now entered the world of opinion-based medicine." My training helped me understand that I entered that realm as soon as I was diagnosed.

Just because I am not willing to buy into the claim that scientists (who are human) make about science (which is a human product) as objective, it certainly does not mean that I discount science as being impracticable, not useful, or non-predictable. A crescent wrench can be adapted to a variety of applications. It is not its precision, its unquestioned objectivity, which is of value, but its application, its unique ability to solve a variety of problems through its application.

An Example: Yalobusha River System, Mississippi

An example from my professional career illustrates how a more universal Rural Sociological crescent wrench has helped me in being both a scientist and a savior in my efforts to solve some rather complex issues.

In 1996, I received a grant from the Mississippi Wildlife, Fisheries, and Parks (MWFP) Department to study the "human interface with the fisheries resources of the Yalobusha River system." MWFP had been receiving multiple complaints from fishers in the Yalobusha area that there "were no fish in the reservoirs." The agency reported that they had stocked the reservoirs to their peak and they could not understand why they were receiving so many complaints on lack of fish. I asked if they could tell if the callers were predominantly Black or White, and if they were male or female. Their perception was that they were predominantly Black female fishers. We conducted inductive interviews with fishers, local fisheries authorities, and others in the area connected to fishing. From these interviews, we constructed an interviewer-administered questionnaire that was randomly distributed to residents in the area.

Preliminary interviews and fieldwork revealed that there were distinct differences between Black and White fishers (Brown and Toth 2001; Brown 2003). The survey reaffirmed these differences and further substantiated differences between what we termed "subsistence" fishers (see Brown, Xu, and Toth 1998) and "recreational fishers" (Toth and Brown 1997). Black subsistence fishers tended to be predominantly females who were fishing in the mornings with cane poles from the bank of streams or ponds for that day's meal, while White subsistence fishers tended to be males using commercial fishing gear (nets) from boats for three to four months in the spring and then freezing several hundreds of pounds of fish for future consumption in out-buildings on their lots.

Traditionally, Black female fishers walked in the morning hours to a nearby pond usually on a White landowner's lot to fish for today's meal. While a simple act in and of itself, it was symbolic of a much more complex social relationship between the White landowner and the Black fisher and their respective families. A Black fisher would have a negotiated relationship based on trust developed over time with repeated interactions between the various parties allowing the fisher to fish on the owner's private land. The element of trust acted as a sort of guarantee that if any damage was done to the owner's property, there was confidence it would be repaid. More importantly, there was a mutual understanding that the owner's land would be respected and the fisher often "paid back" the owner by giving him some of her catch. This was not a prefabricated relationship but one that was crafted over time across different families and actors. As for the technology, the cane pole is ideal for this type of fishing. It is not made for casting long distances. At best, it may cast 12 feet. There generally is no reel associated with a cane pole. The fisher pokes the end of the pole into nooks and corners in ponds and eddies, and jigs it to attract the fish. Cane poles are inexpensive. Often, they are constructed by the fisher him- or herself using cane rushes found locally. In every way, the technology and approach is about frugality. The fisher usually walks in the early morning hours to the fishing site and uses inexpensive technology to put food on the breakfast table that morning.

Beginning in the 1980s this relationship began to change due to larger shifts in the national economy. A surge in land being posted ("no trespassing") occurred. What had once been regulated as a social relationship became redefined into an economic one. Rural landowners have come to realize that there are people who will pay good money to lease their land for hunting and fishing. Over time, access to traditional fishing grounds became monetized, effectively excluding poor rural African American women fishing for the daily meal.

The result was that Black women, who had traditionally walked to their fishing sites, now had few free public access points to fish. Reservoirs operated by the MWFP became increasingly important to these women but they tended to be much further than walking distance. In our surveys, we found that women often car-pooled to get to these public reservoirs. By the time they reached the sites, however, the sun was already on the water, and as any savvy fisher will tell you, when the sun hits the water, the fishing is over. Additionally, they had inappropriate technology to exploit the resource. Cane poles don't cast an appropriate distance to be of much use in a reservoir.

The problem was not a shortage of fish in the reservoirs; there were plenty according to my fisheries biologist colleague. It was a sociological problem illuminated by an understanding of larger macro-level shifts in the economic and social structure of the US and race relations in the Mississippi Delta and beyond. A knowledge and understanding of the sociological issues was a necessary component in an attempt to "fix" this issue, but not a sufficient one. Wildlife agencies generally do not contact "real" sociologists (to borrow a term from my former Sociology Department colleagues at MU) to help them solve such problems. And judging from the bewildered looks on their faces as they read through my report, they were not certain that a rural sociologist associated with the Agricultural Experiment Station at Mississippi State University was someone they should have contacted either.

The older systems of resource access based on social relationships formulated on trust are not coming back. There is no way to turn back the clock and reestablish these types of relationships between Black female fishers in the Mississippi Delta and White landowners. However, by applying a broad social science perspective that recognizes larger structural shifts in economic and social arrangements, race relations, social class, subsistence orientations and activities, and natural resource access (look how many "literatures" have already been brought to bear in this project), a practical understanding of why Black female fishers were not catching fish in the public reservoirs of the Mississippi Delta actually leads to a better question—"why were they fishing there in the first place, when traditionally they rarely did?" My rural sociological crescent wrench allowed me to step back and examine the "problem" from a much wider view, trying it on different issues to see how much torque I could muster from turns of the potential conceptual bolts holding the problem together. Having a better understanding of the layers of the problem allows one to better conceive of a more practical solution to it. Recognizing that access to smaller water resources, streams, ponds, river banks, etc., most of which are on private lands, was a major issue for many residents of the Mississippi Delta, the MWFP began several programs to create more public access to such locations. Knowing that they would never turn the clock back per se to more social versus economic relationships, MWPF began exploring ways to compensate private landowners for more public access.

Discipline or Institution?

Is Rural Sociology a discipline or an institution? Does it do applied or basic research? Are rural sociologists scientists or saviors? In the grand tradition of a multiple-choice question on an Introduction to Sociology test, the correct answer is "all of the above." And because it is all of the above, it lends itself and the rural sociologists who wield it into a powerful multipurpose tool that has conceptual backing and practical application across an unlimited variety of problems, including fishing in the Mississippi Delta.

References

Brown, Ralph B. 2003. "Identity of Self and Others through Work in a Land of Extremes: A Life of Commercial Fishing in the Mississippi Delta," pp. 157–176 in *Communities of Work*, edited by W. Falk, M. Schulman, and A. Tickamyer. Athens, NY: University of Ohio Press.

Brown, Ralph B. and John F. Toth Jr. 2001. "Natural Resource Access and Interracial Associations: Black and White Subsistence Fishing in the Mississippi Delta." *Southern Rural Sociology*. 17:81–110.

Brown, Ralph B., Xiaohe Xu and John F. Toth Jr. 1998. "Lifestyle options and economic strategies: subsistence activities in the Mississippi Delta." *Rural Sociology* 63(4):599–623.

Country Life Commission. 1909. Report of the Country Life Commission, February 9, 1909. Washington, D.C.: Government Printing Office. Available at https://books.google.com/books?id=67AZAAAAYAAJ&printsec=frontcover#v=onepage&q&f=false. Accessed on 8 June 2015.

Ford, Thomas R. 1985. "Rural Sociology and the Passing of Social Scientific Chivalry." *Rural Sociology* 50:523–538.

Hofstadter, Richard. 1955. *The Age of Reform*. New York: Vintage Books, Random House.

Toth, John F. Jr. and Ralph B. Brown. 1997. "Racial and gender meanings of why people participate in recreational fishing." *Leisure Sciences* 19(2):129–146.

Turner, Stephen Park and Jonathan H. Turner. 1990. *The Impossible Science: An Institutional Analysis of American Sociology*. New York: Sage.

Weber, Max. [1905] 2002. *The Protestant Ethic and the Spirit of Capitalism*. New York: Penguin.

9

AVOIDING BURNOUT

ALL WHO WANDER ARE NOT LOST

CONNER BAILEY, *AUBURN UNIVERSITY*

To avoid burnout, I have adopted two strategies in my professional career: (1) work on diverse topics and (2) use of an explicit moral compass in deciding which topics to pursue. Diversity in topics has enabled me to grow intellectually, to work with a wide range of colleagues from different disciplines, and to keep me from feeling intellectually stale. Working on topics that engage my sense of social justice gets me out of bed each morning, with a sense of purpose, bringing passion to both research and teaching. Questions of social justice relate directly to issues of power. Such issues are found in the many topics on which I have worked, including agriculture, fisheries, aquaculture, hazardous wastes, forestry, resource dependency, wetlands restoration, bioenergy, genetic engineering, rural development, stratification, race relations, land loss, absentee land ownership, and even Southeast Asian history. I have applied an explicit social justice perspective when working on those diverse topics. If there has been one thing that has been a constant in my work since the mid-1970s has been primarily work on fisheries and coastal aquaculture. In this chapter, I touch on some of the topics to illustrate the general approach used to avoiding burnout.

A good friend and colleague of mine once referred to me as a "research slut." I have embraced this term not because I am interested in research on people who are sexually promiscuous but because my friend helped me recognize that I am indeed intellectually promiscuous and that this is one reason why, 35 years after receiving my Ph.D., I am still looking forward to the next research question. The second and equally important reason is that I have had the freedom to choose my research questions and have been able to base my choices on addressing problems of those who confront forms of institutional power that are difficult to overcome. I have found that the concepts of power and social justice link nearly everything I do. Using a moral compass to direct my selection of research topics has imposed no constraints on the breadth of topics available to me, and it is what gets me out of bed each morning. There are injustices in the world, people who have been marginalized by powerful institutional actors, and I have the privilege (and in my mind the responsibility) to address these issues, both as a scholar and (sometimes) as an activist, whether on a podium or a soapbox. Sadly, injustices are all too easy to find. I did not start out as a researcher seeking out injustice, but rather have found it virtually everywhere I have looked. Whether that speaks volumes about me or the state of the world I will leave others to determine.

I am writing this chapter in hopes of encouraging others to find their own pathways toward prolonged intellectual engagement as researchers and teachers. My pathway is not for everyone, and there are merits in focusing on one topic, one theory, and one methodology, and becoming the expert within a particular domain. That has not been my course. I have worked on agriculture, fisheries, aquaculture, hazardous wastes, environmental justice, forestry, resource dependency, wetlands restoration, bioenergy, genetic engineering, rural development, stratification, race relations, land loss, absentee land ownership, and Southeast Asian history. For myself, after working on a topic over a period of years (for example, hazardous waste management), I reached the point where I felt I had nothing new to say. I could keep writing about the topic, keeping up on the literature and the technology, but I had passed the steep part of the "S-curve" of learning and looked for the next challenge.

There are costs to such restlessness, continually finding myself on the steep end of learning curves, but there is also excitement in mastering (at least to some extent) new material and interacting with new colleagues. My work with hazardous wastes led me to interact with geologists and civil engineers as well as community activists and scholars working on topics such as environmental justice and social movements. My work in forestry required that I learn something about land use patterns, land ownership, harvesting technologies, logistics, and the operation of sawmills, and pulp and paper mills. My work with aquaculture has made it necessary to understand issues of water quality, disease, different production technologies for different species and levels of intensity, as well as the social and ecological consequences of aquaculture production. Each of these endeavors, and the others listed above, have their own literatures and considerable time is required to become sufficiently familiar with the technical material in order to interact with, and be considered credible by experts in these particular fields.

Discovering Rural Sociology

This, to me, is the strength of my training and experience as a rural sociologist and it is what attracted me to the field in the first place. I was working on an interdisciplinary Master's degree in Southeast Asian Studies at Ohio University when I began applying for Ph.D. programs. I had been interested in that region since my first year as a history student at Southern Oregon College and spent three years in Malaysia with the Peace Corps doing rural health work. I was very focused on Southeast Asia and applied to Ph.D. programs in history and anthropology at universities with strong programs in that region. My interests were very much applied in nature, focused on questions of development. The anthropology program at Cornell had turned away from any applied work and my application was forwarded to the Department of Rural Sociology. I subsequently received a letter of admission to the Ph.D. program in Rural Sociology, a discipline I had never heard of. For that matter, I had never even taken an introduction to sociology course. Undaunted, I drove up to Cornell to see what this discipline was about and realized that this was the discipline—with a unique blend of applied and basic research—that fit what I was looking for. I received full rides at Australian National University and the University of Hawai'i in Southeast Asian history, and initially no offer from Cornell, but I was sufficiently excited by my discovery of a discipline that seemed to have been invented for me that I rolled the dice and committed to Cornell and rural sociology.

What I found in rural sociology was both a focus on the discipline of sociology and a conscious engagement with the practical worlds of rural life. It was possible just to study sociology, but it was also possible to study irrigation as a sociological phenomenon or study the impact of the green revolution on small farms in Mexico. In addition, when I designed a doctoral dissertation project that looked at how differences in the organization of labor and capital among rice farmers, rubber tappers, and fishers in Malaysia affected non-economic organization at the community level, this seemed to fit quite nicely into my adoptive discipline (Bailey 1983, 1991).

On my way to the field, I stopped at the International Rice Research Institute for a training program in rice production. Again, it was something that seemed perfectly natural for a rural sociologist to do. I had spent three years in the Peace Corps in a rubber-producing area and had gone back to that same area for my MS thesis research, so I had a pretty good sense of what was involved in that commodity. But I had no background in fishing. It turned out that this was to become the part of my dissertation that interested me the most and, if there has been one thing that has been a constant in my work since the mid-1970s, it has been work on fisheries and coastal aquaculture.

Marine Fishing and Coastal Aquaculture

I began my dissertation research by spending a year in a rice-farming community on the East coast of Peninsular Malaysia before moving about 30 miles away to a fishing community on the South China Sea. I often went out at night on small boats with men in the village where

I was living. We used drifting gill nets that would ensnare fish that were unable to see the net at night. As we were waiting to haul the nets, we often would hear engines of large trawlers operating nearby in violation of regulations. The trawlers would operate without lights at night in inshore waters because that is where the shrimp were concentrated. There was the ever-present danger of trawlers tearing up nets or traps, or smashing into the small boats ending their nets. This was a problem not only where I was working but throughout Southeast Asia, resulting in violence and bloodshed.

The appearance of trawlers throughout the region was the product of what Phillip McMichael (2008) calls "the development project." National governments and international donor agencies promoted not only the Green Revolution but a parallel "Blue Revolution" (Bailey 1985) involving investment in bigger boats, bigger engines, and bigger nets. Governments were motivated by the foreign exchange earnings they saw in expanded fisheries production and actively encouraged marine stock assessment experts to inflate harvest potentials. Donor agencies were all too eager to pour money into boats and harbors in a production-oriented strategy promoting export-oriented development. International trade in seafood in 2010 was valued at $109 billion a year and most of this trade moves from the global South to the global North (FAO 2012). During the 1970s and 1980s, international donor assistance overwhelmingly sponsored expanded production capacity but invested little in resource management (Bailey, Cycon, and Morris 1986; Bailey 1988). The end result was over-exploitation of marine resources and impoverishment of fishing households in coastal communities whose small boats and simple fishing gear were no match for the trawlers and purse seiners introduced by international donors. Here to me was the big guy pushing around the little guy, national governments and international development agencies making decisions without consideration for the interests of those whose lives were dependent upon the resource. Power and social justice issues were to me obvious and I wrote a series of articles cited above (see also Bailey 1997; Bailey and Jentoft 1990) using a political economy framework to identify the motive forces and the key actors that I thought were responsible.

I observed similar processes unfolding during the early 1980s when shrimp farming exploded onto the scene in Southeast Asia. Coastal fishing communities where I had been working often were located adjacent to mangrove forests. These forests provided sources of building material, firewood, wood for making charcoal, places for subsistence hunting and fishing activities, and served as important nursery grounds for fish and shrimp that support wild fisheries. Mangrove were open-access resources available to anyone until the shrimp boom hit, and then there was a closing of the commons as wealthy well-connected outsiders claimed ownership, tore up the mangrove, and built shrimp ponds. Often the ponds were only productive for a year or two because of acid-sulfate soil conditions or because disease outbreaks occurred due to poor management. As a result, the process was repeated and new mangrove was destroyed. The coastal zone of Southeast Asia was under serious assault, but governments applauded development of shrimp farming because shrimp earned foreign exchange. Again, international donors poured money into the effort, confident that their loans would be repaid because they were promoting export-led development. Once again, the interests of coastal residents were ignored, once again the nature of institutional and state power was on display, and once again the powerlessness of rural people was obvious.

I wrote about these issues (Bailey 1988; Bailey and Skladany 1991; Stonich and Bailey 2000) but I do not know what impact my writing may have had. I do know that the international fisheries research center where I did my postdoctoral research (now known as The WorldFish Center, part of the network of research centers under the Consultative Group for International Agricultural Research) has done work that I would be proud to think was influenced by my early work. I do know that many other researchers have built on the work I did on aquaculture and that major consumer group-led efforts have campaigned to change the way that shrimp are farmed. Donor assistance geared toward expanding the productive capacity of marine fishing fleets has declined dramatically as the realization that oceans are being overexploited finally seems to have sunk in. I was far from the only voice on these matters but initially, at least, I was one of the few social scientists to enter the fray.

Whether or not my work had an impact, I felt compelled to write and speak at conferences and in classrooms. I have been known to pound podiums or use other means to convey what I have regarded as the seriousness of my concerns. My work has rarely been dispassionate, and while I consciously adopt a reflexive approach in my research, questioning my observations, looking for evidence that challenges my thinking, I have never been seriously constrained by the myth of the purely objective researcher. I saw the marginalization of coastal residents in a region—Southeast Asia—where coastal and marine issues are central to the lives of millions of people, and I wrote about it to the best of my ability.

My work has not always been well received. In 1997, I was invited to be the plenary speaker at the 1997 meetings of the World Aquaculture Society in Seattle and had an audience of almost 2,000 people. I expressed appreciation for the rhetoric of aquaculturists—"we feed the world"—but I also pointed out that most of the research, development, and investment has gone into shrimp and salmon, which was doing nothing to serve the nutritional needs of people suffering from protein malnutrition. The message was not universally popular and there were those at my own university—a major center for aquaculture research—who loudly and in close quarters proclaimed me a "traitor."

This may have been not only for what I said during the plenary address (Bailey 1997) but also for my help in mobilizing the presence of non-governmental activists from 20 different countries who descended upon Seattle to protest shrimp farming during the WAS meetings. The Mangrove Action Project, with whom I have worked since their founding in 1992, and the Industrial Shrimp Action Network, organized a counter conference at the University of Washington and paid to have a billboard with an anti-shrimp farming message on display outside the Pike Place fish market in Seattle. There were many in the aquaculture industry who were surprised by the sudden appearance of critical voices in their midst.

Toxics and Environmental Justice

My work on marine fisheries and coastal aquaculture work continued when I moved from Southeast Asia to the Marine Policy Center at

Woods Hole Oceanographic Institution, where I worked from 1983 to 1985. I used this period to do some writing and thinking about what I had learned in Southeast Asia, and to examine critically the role of international donors in fisheries policy. In 1985 I accepted a position as Assistant Professor of Rural Sociology at Auburn University and moved to Alabama in the middle of that year.

To that point, my entire research career had been focused on Southeast Asia, but I realized there were good reasons to start doing research within my same time zone. I was by this time married and had two children, and I had learned that international work imposed disruption on family life. As I was thinking about research ideas in Alabama, I read a news article about the ocean-going hazardous waste incinerator ship *Volcanus* that was operating out of Mobile, Alabama. The ship was designed to carry 330,000 gallons of liquid hazardous wastes out into the middle of the Gulf of Mexico. There were three rotary kilns at the back of the ship, which sailed around in circles for 19 days until the load was completely combusted. I thought to myself that here was a "marine policy" issue of possible interest. I drove down to Mobile to meet with people who were concerned about this program.

I learned that the company operating the ship was pulling out of Mobile because of opposition but that they also operated the nation's largest hazardous waste landfill in Sumter County, Alabama. I drove up the road to Sumter County, a rural county on the border with Mississippi and half way between the Gulf of Mexico and the Tennessee line and met with some of the citizens concerned with the presence of this facility in their midst.

Two things stand out in my memory from that meeting. The first is them saying to me something to the effect that "since I was a sociologist, perhaps I could help them figure out how to get the local African American population involved in their anti-hazardous waste campaign." The people I was meeting with were all white and Sumter County was 70 percent African American. Here I was a white outsider and I was supposed to help them understand their African American neighbors? (This might be a good point to mention that, while I grew up in California, my mother was from Alabama and her mother was from Sumter County, and so I had some familiarity with the territory and local social conditions. It turned out that one of the leading activists lived in the home previously owned by my family. I also discovered that a second cousin of mine had established a small art museum in the little town of York, where the family home was located.)

The second thing they asked was who would be funding my research. These people were skeptical of outsiders coming in and doing research, and wanted to know where I stood on matters. The fact that I had local ties may have smoothed relations a little, but they were still skeptical. I answered that any work I would do would be funded by the Alabama Agricultural Experiment Station at Auburn University. That did not completely assure them, my first inkling that university researchers might be regarded with suspicion (a view I have increasingly come to realize is a rational viewpoint).

As I was about to begin work in Sumter County, I met a sociologist at Auburn who would become a good friend and colleague. Chuck Faupel had no experience with hazardous wastes but had worked on issues of natural disasters and expressed interest in working with me. Chuck and I had a very productive relationship, but our approaches were very different, something that became obvious when, about a year into our work, we were invited to appear on a public television show, "For the Record." Chuck, coming from a traditional sociology background, felt that we should not do the show because we were in the middle of field research and anything we might say could affect our ability to do our work. We did not have all the answers we needed, we had not yet talked to everyone we needed to talk with, and therefore to Chuck we should not go public with our preliminary findings. My view was different. The state legislature was in session and was considering bills that would affect management of the hazardous waste landfill in Sumter County operated by Chemical Waste Management, Inc. (CWM). Even though we were still in the middle of data collection, I felt we knew more than most people about the issues involved, and because we worked at a public university, we should share what we knew. Chuck and I both had good arguments to make and this was probably the first time I had a real appreciation of how different my professional socialization as a rural sociologist had been compared to people who had gone through mainstream sociology.

I realize I am painting with a broad brush here, and that there are rural sociologists who would have agreed with Chuck and sociologists who would have sided with me. In any event, we did the show and managed to keep doors from being slammed in our face.

Like most issues, even the burying of hazardous wastes in a poor rural area populated primarily by African Americans, there were more than two sides to the issue. CWM was a good employer, hiring as many as 450 people in a part of the country where there were few jobs. Workers were well paid and this was one of the few places where women and African Americans could find good paying jobs. CWM contributed significantly to the tax rolls and supported local civic organizations. Their Public Relations man was a solid professional and never lied to us; he did his best to convince us that CWM was a good corporate neighbor. I even visited the CWM corporate headquarters in Oak Ridge, Illinois. I wish I had taken a photo of the corporate marquee when I rode up in the taxi: "Welcome Dr. Conner Bailey."

As we delved deeper into the history of Sumter County and the opening of the CWM landfill, we became increasingly convinced that this was an obvious case of environmental injustice. The U.S. Environmental Protection Agency had identified Sumter County as a potential hazardous waste landfill site because of the combination of geology, transportation, sparse population, and the absence of endangered species. But in practice it was a process that involved a cold calculation of opportunity that led to Sumter County becoming home to what became the CWM landfill. The landfill was established in 1977 without public comment or news coverage, and even the engineer working for Alabama Power did not know what business was coming in when he hooked them up to the power lines. (In this state, Alabama Power knows everything that is going on.) The main focus of public attention in Sumter County was on local politics. Despite passage in 1965 of the Voting Rights Act, the first African American in Sumter County was elected to office in 1982. There were claims of ballot-box stuffing that resulted in the defeat of African American candidates before that date, and claims of voting irregularities ever since, for that matter. Even after local residents realized there was a landfill in their midst, local concerns for the most part remained elsewhere (Bailey and Faupel 1992; Alley, Faupel, and Bailey 1995).

Over time, the environmental activists in Sumter County came to trust Chuck and me, even as we tried to maintain enough balance in our approach to hear all sides to the issue. But things changed in 1990. I was invited to give a talk to the Auburn Rotary Club about hazardous waste issues, at that time a hot topic in the state. Again, the legislature was considering new regulations. I described the setting and the possible risks associated with geology of the area, citing work by geologists. In the audience was the Director of Public Relations for Auburn University, who called me up and asked if they could put out a press release addressing these concerns. I said that would be fine as long as they also included the Auburn geologist whose work I had cited, and this was done. The release led to a smattering of local and state papers picking up the story that said there were issues with the geology that CWM was ignoring while assuring everyone the chalk formation known as the Selma Group would provide 10,000 years of safety.

The original public relations man for CWM had left and the new person decided the best way to deal with this issue was to take out a full-page newspaper advertisement attacking me by name and discipline, in the meantime ignoring the fact that half the press release dealt with the concerns of a Ph.D. geologist. Of course the media, sensing a story, asked my opinion. The Montgomery Advertiser the next day carried the story under "Chem Waste Ad Angers Professor." Rather than letting the matter drop, CWM's public relations manager fired off another salvo, and that got the TV news interested in the story. The CWM spokesperson was quoted as saying "There has not been a single issue raised that has had as widespread an impact on the public perception of the safety of our facility as those made by the Auburn instructors" (Lewis 1990, C1). CWM declined my request for clarification and apology. I think the local citizen group opposing CWM finally concluded that I was not on the CWM payroll.

The work Chuck and I were doing in Sumter County expanded across the state as we found other environmental controversies, most of which involved environmental justice issues. Good friends and colleagues as we were (and remain), our paths increasingly diverged, and I became much more invested in the study of local environmental struggles. My view was that if we were going to study grassroots environmental groups, we had to be willing to give and not just take information. In other words, if we were asking groups what they were doing, what resources they had, who they were interacting with, we could expect them to ask us what we knew and for information about other groups engaged in similar struggles. Responding to such requests makes for a somewhat messy research design, perhaps, but not sharing such information is hardly the way to build rapport. Ultimately, in my view, rapport was far more necessary to gain the level of trust and detail of information necessary for good research. In the 1990s, I became increasingly involved not only as a researcher but as an activist scholar, marching in streets and speaking at environmental justice rallies. In 1994 I created a website, the "Alabama Grassroots Clearinghouse" as a web-based directory of citizen organizations in the state formed out of concern for natural resource and environmental issues, and regularly updated the site every year. New groups come and some old groups fold their tents. Who knew that there were between 160 and 180 groups active in the state at any given time?

Forestry and Natural Resources

Living and working in Alabama, one can only be impressed by the abundance of forestland. Over 70 percent of Alabama is forested and the forest products industry has long played a central role in the state's rural economy. I began delving into this topic in the early 1990s and this work too has been something that has continued and evolved.

Working with colleagues John Bliss, Larry Teeter, and Glenn Howze, we put together a successful national grant proposal to USDA's rural development program. We included in our proposal some data that showed that the greater the degree of dependency on forestry (as measured by employment), the greater the poverty and other social ills. We proposed to examine why this was the case. We also, after winning the grant, put together a small article for a magazine put out by the Alabama Agricultural Experiment Station. The article included these data and was approved by the editorial board. Before publication, however, the Director of the Station stepped in and pulled the article, explaining that it would embarrass the industry and—besides, he said—

you could say the same thing about the beef cattle industry. We thanked him for an idea for a new research project.

We proceeded with our work, supported by a series of six USDA grants, doing what I think is some pretty good research on resource dependency and uncovering, layer by layer, some of the causes of persistent poverty in rural Alabama (Bailey et al. 1996; Bliss and Bailey 2005). This research has attracted the attention not only of our professional peers in academia but also activists in the South who see industrial forestry as a threat to ecosystems and communities. New opportunities for scholarly activism arose.

In the mid-1990s, I worked with the Dogwood Alliance on what they called "the paper campaign," a two-year effort to convince Staples to carry on average at least 30 percent post-consumer recycled paper products in their stores and not to source paper products from certain designated ecologically sensitive regions of the world. My role in this campaign primarily involved attending a Staples Board of Directors meeting, and pointing out that the pulp and paper industry was responsible for serious chemical pollution and other environmental costs while operating in areas where poverty was the norm, and that Staples could benefit from adopting a different set of allies, including the Dogwood Alliance. I was not the only one who spoke that day to the Directors, and shortly thereafter Staples agreed with the Dogwood Alliance proposal. Office Max and Office Depot quickly agreed to follow suit. As a result, the market for post-consumer recycled paper in the U.S. dramatically increased, which in turn led to a decline in the cost of post-consumer recycled paper so that it is now competitive with virgin paper.

In addition to work on the industrial side of forestry, and in particular the pulp and paper industry, my colleagues and I worked on small-scale woods harvesting and processing technologies, and with architects of Auburn's Rural Studio (www.ruralstudio.org/) to design low-cost housing. In the process of looking into constraints to improved rural housing, graduate students working with me uncovered a topic of what I came to realize as being of major importance: heir property. Heir property refers to land and buildings passed from one generation to the next without a will. For a variety of reasons, many African Americans have not written wills and as a consequence ownership in a particular piece of property has been inherited by upwards of 80 people, each of whom owns some share in the property. The economic and legal result is that title to the property is "clouded" and owners are unable to access government housing programs, obtain conventional mortgages, or even cut timber on the land unless every owner signs an agreement (Dyer and Bailey 2008). Worse, heir property is a major source of land loss to African American farmers and landowners. Our research has shown that unscrupulous people will buy the share of one family member and then use legal means to force a sale of the property at auction on the courthouse steps. If the family does not have enough money to retain ownership, the land is lost. Imagine, an African American family in the late 19th or early 20th century being able to pull together enough money to buy a piece of property and pass it down to their heirs across multiple generations, only to have the land stolen out from under them. These are the kinds of injustices that exist where I live and work, and the kinds of issues that I will be working on in the years to come.

Concluding Comments

Being an activist and an academic is a natural combination of roles, and I would argue is no more incongruous than a chemical engineer consulting for the pulp and paper industry. To put this another way, why would a professor of business or engineering or political science working with a corporation or a government agency be considered legitimate and a professor of rural sociology working with citizen groups who may be opposed to actions of the same corporation or government agency be looked at differently? Is it because corporations and government agencies are formal institutional actors with political and economic resources, and community-based groups are marginal actors in society? I have thrown my lot in with those who are vulnerable to the actions of powerful institutions, but I have come to understand that these vulnerable populations are now powerless. They are, however, often ignored by university researchers. There is no reason in a democracy why this should be so (Bailey et al. 1995; McSpirit, Faltraco, and Bailey 2012).

My continued enthusiasm at age 68 for the work at hand is partly the diversity in topics and partly the focus on social justice, the combination of moral imperative and intellectual curiosity. I started out focused on Southeast Asia, a region to which I have a continuing affinity, with continued work in that region. I have branched out to work in Newfoundland, Canada, in Norway, and most recently in Brazil. The discipline of rural sociology has allowed me to explore a wide range of topics, different parts of the world, using a variety of methods. Had I not applied to the anthropology program at Cornell and then been accepted into the rural sociology program instead, my career trajectory would probably have been quite different. However, like others who accidentally stumbled into the diversity of topics and interests that constitute rural sociology, I am glad I made the choices that I did. I have never suffered from any sense of "burn out." Of course, there are also rural sociologists who have "plowed one furrow" and have become known specifically for their contribution to one theory or one methodology, but for me rural sociology has provided a base camp to explore many mountains.

References

Alley, Kelly D., Charles E. Faupel, and Conner Bailey. 1995. "The Historical Transformation of a Grassroots Environmental Group." *Human Organization* 54(4):410–416.

Bailey, Conner. 1983. *The Sociology of Production in Rural Malay Society*. New York: Oxford University Press.

Bailey, Conner. 1985. "Blue Revolution: the Impact of Technological Innovation on Third World Fisheries." *The Rural Sociologist* 5(4):259–66.

Bailey, Conner. 1988. "The Political Economy of Fisheries Development in the Third World." *Agriculture & Human Values* V (1&2):35–48.

Bailey, Conner. 1991. "Class Differentiation and Erosion of a Moral Economy in Rural Malaysia." *Research in Economic Anthropology* 13:119–142.

Bailey, Conner. 1997. "Aquaculture and Basic Human Needs." *World Aquaculture* 28(3):28–31.

Bailey, Conner and Svein Jentoft. 1990. Hard Choices in Fisheries Development. *Marine Policy* 14(4):333–344.

Bailey, Conner and Mike Skladany. 1991. Aquaculture Development in Tropical Asia: A Re-Evaluation. *Natural Resources Forum* 15(1):66–73.

Bailey, Conner, and Charles E. Faupel. 1992. "Movers and Shakers and PCB Takers: Hazardous Waste and Community Power." *Sociological Spectrum* 13:89–115.

Bailey, Conner, Dean Cycon, and Michael Morris. 1986. "Fisheries Development in the Third World: The Role of International Agencies." *World Development* 14(10/11):1269–1276.

Bailey, Conner, Kelly Alley, Charles E. Faupel, and Cathy Solheim. 1995. "Environmental Justice and the Professional," pp. 35–44 in *Environmental Justice: Issues, Policies, and Solutions*, edited by B. Bryant. Washington, DC: Island Press.

Bailey, Conner, Peter Sinclair, John Bliss, and Karni Perez. 1996. "Segmented Labor Markets in Alabama's Pulp and Paper Industry." *Rural Sociology* 61(3):474–495.

Bliss, John, and Conner Bailey. 2005. "Pulp, Paper, and Poverty: Forest-based Rural Development in Alabama, 1950–2000," pp. 138–158 in *Communities and Forests: Where People Meet the Land*, edited by R. Lee and D. Field. Corvallis: Oregon State University Press.

Dyer, Janice, and Conner Bailey. 2008. "A Place to Call Home: Cultural Understandings of Heir Property among Rural African Americans." *Rural Sociology* 73(3):317–338.

FAO (Food and Agriculture Organization of the United Nations). 2012. The State of World Fisheries and Aquaculture 2012. Rome: FAO. Available at www.fao.org/docrep/016/i2727e/i2727e.pdf. Accessed August 15, 2014.

Lewis, Pat. 1990. "Chem Waste Ad Angers Professor." *Montgomery Advertiser*, February 14, 1990, page C1. Montgomery, Alabama.

McMichael, Philip. 2008. *Development and Social Change; A Global Perspective*. Los Angeles, CA and London: Pine Forge Press.

McSpirit, Stephanie, Lynne Faltraco, and Conner Bailey, (Eds.) 2012. *Confronting Ecological Crisis: University and Community Partnerships in Appalachia and the South*. Lexington, KY: University Press of Kentucky.

Stonich, Susan and Conner Bailey. 2000. Resisting the Blue Revolution: Contending Coalitions Surrounding Industrial Shrimp Farming. *Human Organization* 59(1):23-36.

10
THE ACCIDENTAL RURAL SOCIOLOGIST

BILL REIMER, *CONCORDIA UNIVERSITY*

I have never considered myself to be a rural sociologist. I have never lived in a rural setting for more than a year, never taken a rural sociology course, and never taught under this banner. Looking back on my career, however, the label seems appropriate. This begs the related questions about how I got here and what does it mean, if anything, for rural sociology? This chapter provides some material to answer the first and a few speculations about the second. In the process, it identifies a few of the things I have learned along the way—particularly with respect to my experience as Director of the 11-year national New Rural Economy project in Canada.

Early Years

I grew up as the son of a machinist, fix-it master, and would-be inventor. I had plenty of encouragement to design, build, fix, and dismantle anything from cars to radios (most often the tube variety). We also had a basement full of the tools and space to do it. If something didn't work, it was never thrown out. Instead, it was dismantled, investigated, and repaired—or if that was not possible—a work-around was constructed. If we couldn't get it back together again, the exercise was applauded as a learning experience.

My parents were also avid explorers. Much of the year was spent planning the next two-week vacation my father was granted each year. Most often it meant piling our tent and sleeping bags on the roof of the car and climbing into the car with my two brothers to head out to investigate some logging road, remote town, lake, or stream somewhere in British Columbia. It gave me my first taste of rural places and the joys of visiting small towns.

My undergraduate transcript reflects a student without a goal—or perhaps one with many goals. My approach to university was more like a diversion until I had to get a "real job." Born in 1944, I also had the advantage of being at the leading edge of the baby boom and was able to enjoy the expansion of education and social services, employment opportunities, and consumer attention without the challenges of competition that were to come to those born only a few years later. By the time I entered university it was the early 60s, the enrollment options were expanding, and the first trickle of draft dodgers was finding its way on to the campus of the University of British Columbia (UBC). I started out in math, physics, and chemistry, but my curiosity and moral inclinations drove me to student groups, social action, and academic studies that eventually resulted in a first degree with Religious Studies and English literature as my majors. By that time, I had also learned the rudiments of organizing a club, symposium, or conference with associated skills of silk-screening and Roberts Rules of Order. Little did I know how useful these would eventually become.

Fifty years later, several of my students who participated in protests on the streets of Montréal characterize the 60s as one when the "issues were more clear" and the student responses were "more cohesive" than tuitions in Québec. I don't remember it so. For me, it was a time of uncertainty and ambivalence—where even if a position were clear, the appropriate course of action was not. Each discussion required a balance of conflicting concerns and each action carried the possibility of subversion or misinterpretation. We were learning how to live in a world of uncertainty (if not yet chaos) and to manage our own ambivalence without paralysis. We had plenty of material to work with, and considerable time and opportunity to do so.

As my attention was drawn from the facts and figures of the natural sciences to the debates of the humanities, so was my course selection. It was only in my final year, however, that I took a course in sociology and found a combination of topic, perspective, and methodology that fit my inclinations. With only one sociology undergraduate course under my belt, I applied to the MA program. My grades, the expansion of the discipline, and the imagination of the admission committee were in my favour. They admitted me with the proviso that I take some more sociology undergraduate courses at the same time. This was a minor price to pay since I had the time and the enthusiasm for the topics that would carry me through many years to come.

As a graduate student, I remained preoccupied with social organization. In a world where war, racism, sexism, and inequality were hotly debated, and sit-ins, teach-ins, demonstrations, and arrests were the order of the day, it was unclear why we didn't degenerate into Hobbes's "war of all against all." For a young person who grew up in an environment that was extraordinarily congenial, the news reports and most of the campus activities threatened an imminent collapse of our social relations. Each instance of successful collaboration, therefore, came as a surprise and the relative tranquility of Canadian politics threatened to be a massive delusion. It was no wonder that I was attracted to sociology—and its longstanding preoccupation with the "problem of order."

These issues remained throughout my graduate work—even if their resolutions evaded me. Once transformed into sociological jargon, my interests lay in social exclusion, social organization, and the impacts of technology on social relations. The UBC Department of Anthropology and Sociology was fertile ground for exposure to a wide variety of perspectives and approaches—from formal experimental design and approaches to large-scale survey research, and the newly minted approach of ethnomethodology. The attraction of Vancouver to West

Coast draft dodgers meant that the department became a haven for California-style sociology and its challenges to more traditional perspectives. These different approaches were manifested in deep theoretical and interpersonal divisions, in some cases so nasty that engagement across those divisions was missing. Students like me who were interested in the full range of options were left to self-organize events so that we could explore material from Popper, Mills, Merton, Schütz, Garfinkel, Parsons, Bateson, Simon, Lazarsfeld, Goffman, Selznick, and even the young upstarts Berger and Luckman.

Looking back, I can see how fortunate it was that a small group of graduate students remained outside the divisions within the department, and the myopic visions and experiences they engendered. In my case, there were four experiences I remember as particularly important for my eclectic understanding of theory and methodology.

The first comes from the extensive time I spent in the small groups lab established by Dr. Reg Robson. I felt comfortable with the clarity and precision this style of research demanded in theoretical formulations and the relative simplicity of the methodology and analysis. The logic and advice of Popper became a point of reference for both my research and activist activities. My concerns for social organization and exclusion found expression in experiments in the interactions of small groups, people with machines, and the manipulation of statuses, resources, or information. I remember the delight I felt when my fellow graduate student discovered how a small group of people trading trinkets would consistently stratify into two depending on the initial distribution of those trinkets (Foddy 1972). It became a compelling illustration of the rudiments of social stratification and its link to the conditions that maintain it.

My introduction to survey research and the promise of computers occurred via a class project in which a small group of students attempted to replicate Stinchcombe's research on Rebellion in a High School (Stinchcombe 1965). Our instructor, Dr. Landauer, suggested we find a local high school and when we approached the principal for access to a classroom of students, he invited us to survey the whole school of 1,500. These were in the days before ethics forms and committees. Not wanting to forgo such an opportunity, we went ahead with the task of designing an instrument, organizing its distribution and collection, and conducting the analysis of 1,500 rather than 25 forms. This was before photocopying machines existed, so we had to rely on Gestetner and Spirit Duplicators (Ditto) machines for the production of documents. It was also in the days before desktop computers, so constructing one 2 × 2 table required us to sort twice through 1,500 returns. We quickly began to search for a more efficient method once the stacks of completed forms were returned. That was when I was introduced to the benefits of IBM punch-cards—the primary way of preparing data for the mainframe computers that were just becoming available on university campuses. Our analysis of the survey, therefore, became a sequence of preparing a few thousand punch-cards from the survey forms (one card could only contain 80 responses), then repeatedly feeding them through a counter-sorter machine to construct each table. As I looked at the photos of computer punch-cards falling like tickertape into the streets of Montréal during the student occupation of 1969, I cringed at the thought of the disaster this would be if they were like mine—the repository of data, programs, and even my thesis. Little did I imagine that in a few years I would be on the faculty of that university conducting research in a totally new domain.

Our high school research was also the occasion where I first learned FORTRAN—one of the early computer programming languages—in order to facilitate our analysis using the UBC mainframe computer. The process itself was a challenge. It meant taking the few thousand cards containing our data, along with the 100 or so cards with the program for analysis, to the computing center across campus. The full stack of cards would be submitted to the center personnel for an overnight run. The results could be picked up in the morning, often containing an error that would mean searching for the right card, repunching it, then resubmitting the full stack once again for the evening run. Needless to say, we thought carefully about which tables were necessary each time we would submit a request.

A third formative experience came via Dr. Martin Meissner and his work regarding the influence of working conditions on the relationships among laborers and their leisure activities (Meissner 1971). Much of his work was conducted in a mill town in BC—one that I had visited as a youth since my aunt and uncle lived nearby. It was the first occasion where I could see the possibility of blending my long-term interest in more remote places with scholarly pursuits.

Into this mix of formal theory, survey research, computer analysis, and fieldwork was added the phenomenological perspectives of Schütz, Berger, Luckman, and Garfinkel. Unlike many of my peers, I was not put off by this mix and felt that the separations into "empirical" and "phenomenological," "quantitative" and "qualitative," or "positivist" and "antipositivism" were not terrains to be occupied and defended, but alternative approaches that were to be explored for their relative value in answering the many questions we face and informing the choices to be made. It is for this reason that I found Dr. Dorothy Smith's early explorations of institutional ethnography, the experiments of my colleague, and the survey results of our class project to provide valuable insights on the nature and explanation of social order.

By 1972 I was married (to another sociologist, Dr. Frances Shaver) and in the final stages of my Ph.D., sociology had become my discipline "of choice" if for no other reason than we had a three-year-old child and were expecting our second later that year. My moratorium period was finished and I had finally to transform my diversions into a career. I sent off applications to our two first choices: the University of California at Santa Barbara and Sir George Williams University in Montréal. Once again, our good fortune at being born just before the baby boom meant that we were moving into an expanding market, so were faced with the pleasant task of deciding between two attractive alternatives. It was Fran's good judgment that made the decision—she wanted the advantage of a bilingual milieu and a very different culture.

Bringing the Rural to Sociology

Montréal had a great deal to offer. Once the initial demands of preparing courses, finding a home, doctor, daycare, and grocery store were met, we turned to the potpourri of language, music, arts, and climate of our new location. Where we may have lost the easy access to mountains and oceans of Vancouver, it was made up for by the shops, restaurants, and local neighborhoods of Montréal. We set about learning the language and in the process set the stage for my transformation to a rural sociologist.

After several years of attending French classes, we had gained a functional level of capacity. This meant we were quite able to understand and converse with classmates in the "baby French" of new language learners and had become accustomed to the particularities of each instructor, but when we engaged with those on the street they quickly switched to English—either out of sympathy for our struggles or to better understand us. Fran suggested we move where we wouldn't have the option of English—and neither would our neighbors.

This suggestion fitted well with my newly established research focus. Following the approach of Meissner, I had begun exploring the impact of industrial technology on labor. As a means to familiarize myself with our new province, I chose agriculture as a domain for investigation and I focused on the impacts of changes in agricultural technology on the organization of the family farms that had been such an important feature of Québec society. I could combine my interests if we were to focus on one of the many francophone villages where family farms were undergoing the transformation in which I was interested.

Following my sociological inclinations, I turned to the census tools at my disposal and identified all the counties in Québec where there were a high proportion of family farms and unilingual French speakers. In anticipation of my upcoming sabbatical, we all piled into our van and began a tour of the province using my list as a guide. When we found a note on a dépanneur's bulletin board for a rental in the local village of Cap-St-Ignace, we paid it a visit and phoned the owner. It set us up for a year of field work in this town—one that would change all our lives.

We moved to Cap-St-Ignace in August 1978, enrolled our children in the local school, and joined several of the local clubs. With two children and a dog, it was not hard to become known—and we were helped by the local community in some surprising ways. About a month after we moved in, we were greeted by a couple at our door who introduced themselves as our godparents. We invited them in and learned they had been selected by the community to meet with us, help us if needed, and invite us to the monthly community dinner. Before they left, our godparents offered to pick us up on the date of the event and take us to the dinner. True to their word, they accompanied us to the dinner, made sure we were settled at our table, and introduced us to several of the people nearby. Part-way through the evening, the music and dancing stopped when the mayor came to the microphone and invited us to come to the front of the room with our godparents. The godparents introduced us to the village and the mayor provided us with a certificate. We were, of course, thrilled by the welcome we received and it was only later—as I visited other communities where strangers were viewed with suspicion and unease—that I realized what a brilliant response this was to the integration of newcomers. It is no wonder that we remain friends with several of our neighbors from that year.

It was also during that year that my research focus became clearer and broader. The introduction of machines in farming significantly changed the organization of agricultural production, families, and communities, but not always in the simple manner suggested by aggregated data. An analysis at the level of the household provides a different picture—one where machines may have a short-term benefit, but in the longer term can increase the labor demands (Reimer 1984). My research during that year also shifted my focus from the impacts that technology might have on the organization of farming, to the community itself. I began to read more of the literature on communities, starting with the many case studies in Québec, then expanding to the general literature on community structure, development, and change. I had started on the path to rural sociology.

A natural extension of this shift in my attention was the transformation of my professional network from BC and the Canadian Sociology and Anthropology Association to the RSS, and a newly formed network of Canadian researchers concerned with conditions in rural areas (the Agriculture and Rural Restructuring Group—ARRG). I was introduced to this latter group by my wife who had used our year in Cap-St-Ignace as a springboard for her Ph.D. work on women in agriculture (Shaver 1982, 1987). By the time that ARRG had changed its name to the Canadian Rural Restructuring Foundation (and later the Canadian Rural Revitalization Foundation—CRRF) I was a core member of the group—having served as fellow, president, and board member over the years.

The Canadian Rural Revitalization Foundation (CRRF)

CRRF (and ARRG before it) arose from the frustration of declining attention to rural issues in Canada and the narrowing of government attention to sectoral concerns. In 1988, Ray Bollman and Tony Fuller called a meeting with a small group of researchers and policy-makers to discuss issues such as the dependency of rural Canadians on urban taxpayers, underfunding of science applied to rural issues, and the persistent dominance of political criteria for government-sponsored research and programs in rural Canada. This group decided to meet the following year for a national seminar in Saskatoon—and the first annual event of ARRG was born. Since that time, ARRG—and its later incarnation as CRRF—has been the central network for rural, remote, and northern research and education in Canada. It has held more than 25 conferences and 25 workshops over its 25 years of existence, attracting around 200 participants in the conferences and 40 for the workshops. Early in its history we discovered the value of holding our events in collaboration with rural communities, so have now collectively visited more than 40 small towns and villages in all parts of Canada. In addition to the conferences and workshops, this national network of researchers, policy-makers, practitioners, and citizens has encouraged research, supported publications, and advocated on behalf of rural communities and people in both provincial and national venues (http://crrf.ca/). It has survived on a patchwork of funding from foundations, federal agencies, and rural community organizations.

Although the plethora of small contracts and short-term funding allowed CRRF to contribute significantly to the understanding and policy framework of rural Canada, during our first ten years we grew increasingly dissatisfied with the way these conditions detracted from a strategic and focused research agenda. Coming out of a series of highly successful international conferences and workshops, and with our policy document (Apedaile and Reimer 1996) featuring prominently in the "Think Rural" report of the House of Commons Standing Committee on Natural Resources (Mitchell 1997) we prodded each other to be more ambitious in our vision for CRRF.

The New Rural Economy Project (NRE)[1]

The NRE project did not emerge as a clearly articulated plan. It was more like a series of outrageous suggestions, followed by more cautious but supportive questions in a cycle of collective encouragement over many months. We were like a flock of geese: each one taking the leadership for a while until the loss of courage or energy became too much. The leader would then drop back for another to take the lead—always drawn on by the support of the flock. We dreamt of a national project, in spite of the formidable challenges that distance and diversity created. We dreamt of a collaborative project, in spite of the wide range of disciplines and experiences represented. We dreamt of a comprehensive project, in spite of the legion of issues affecting rural communities and people. In addition, we dreamt of a long-term project, in spite of the short-term funding we had come to expect. It was no wonder that our first working names for the project were "Ambitious I" and "Ambitious II".

We were fortunate because CRRF had provided the years of collaboration that made the negotiations and compromises of our ambitious projects to be successful. Over the years of working together we learned a considerable amount about the demands each of us faced from our institutional contexts, the skills and general perspectives that we brought to the table (or kitchen or bar), and many of the personal preferences we held in our professional and personal lives. We also knew many of the common concerns we shared—especially our commitment to logical and critical analysis, respect for empirical evidence, desire for seeking the practical and tractable implications of our research, and open engagement with rural people, communities, and policy-makers. When we were ready to put our ambitions into practice, therefore, we were able to tackle some of the thorny methodological and administrative challenges of the task.

Ambitious I was a program of research to prepare a proposal for Ambitious II (Reimer 1997). This included a macro-level analysis of existing data to identify some of the major factors driving the rural economy and society, then the use of these insights as a basis for constructing a "Rural Observatory" of communities for the more focused work of Ambitious II. Our inventory of existing case-work research in Canada had revealed a rather ad hoc selection of rural sites, so our plan was to design a national sample frame that was more strategic for investigating the impacts of the key drivers of rural changes (Reimer 2002).

Our statistical analysis of macro-level data along with numerous discussions identified four likely drivers of rural change and one outcome of interest to policy-makers. These formed the basis for a 32-cell sampling matrix that would allow us to compare the impacts of differences on each of the five dimensions (Reimer 1995). We located all the rural census subdivisions (CSD) in Canada within an appropriate cell and randomly selected 32 research sites from within each cell. Some changes were made to this original assignment in order to accommodate the availability of willing researchers but only under the condition where substitutions of sites were made from within the CSDs in the same cell. By selecting the sites on the basis of strategic comparisons we were able to link them to general processes affecting rural places. The framework also allowed us to integrate other study sites in our analysis, providing a useful point of comparison for any research with a geographic component. The value of this approach was recognized by our colleagues in Japan and they identified two sites in that country which were integrated into our research program (Apedaile and Tsuboi 2008).

We were not initially aware of the many other benefits provided by the Rural Observatory that emerged over time. First, it provided a common point of reference for all the people involved in the project. As our understandings of each location increased, they were shared among the team and immensely improved our individual research. Second, it served to build cohesion among a rather disparate number of people—researchers, policy-makers, and rural citizens alike. It reduced the isolation that comes with the size of the rural space in Canada. Researchers got to visit places far from their geographical field of inquiry—and to do so with a depth of integration that reflected the many years of collaboration with local people. Third, it served to provide a rich source of information that enhanced our research, education, and policy agendas. Since we met each year in one of our field sites, it meant that we collectively visited more than 22 small rural communities, heard from them regarding their concerns and accomplishments, and discussed in depth the details of their situations. Fourth, the Rural Observatory provided a framework for intersite exchanges among local citizens and leaders. Each year we held an event where they met with one another for comparison, analysis, and learning. These events led to considerable cross-fertilization and inspiration of ideas—from new visions for local communities to significant changes in personal action among site citizens.

For the first three years of the NRE we continued to function on the basis of short-term contracts (mostly from government departments), many volunteer hours, and risky promises. We were faced with the dilemma of establishing long-term commitments with rural people in spite of the fact that most of our funding was short-term. We were also forced to focus on specific objectives dictated by the contracts signed. We chose them in such a manner that fulfilling the contracts would contribute to our long-term objectives either directly or indirectly. In the end we were able to conduct the macro level analysis that provided the basis for the Rural Observatory and advance our site-level analysis that serves as the basis for our Site Profiles. We also established relations with most of the field sites.

This early period of the NRE was fraught with administrative challenges, as we worked out our commitments to each other, the field sites, and the range of research and operating styles of the team. This diversity was crystallized as we came to the allocation of funds. The economists typically asked for a clear research question to answer, $40,000 to hire a graduate assistant, and promised to produce a report on a clearly specified timeline in return. The historians asked for $5,000 to produce a report—presumably after hours of work in a library. The geographers asked for $10,000 to hire an assistant or two plus expenses for travel in the field, and the sociologists would ask either for the same, or for $25,000 to design and conduct a survey, depending on their methodological inclinations. Managing these different approaches and associated expectations while maintaining collegial working relations became one of my major preoccupations. Our final agreements emerged as the result of a complex combination of compromises, changes in team members, and only the occasional default on the commitments made.

We also explored a number of models for the administration of the project. We began with an administrative team of graduate students supporting the Director and Steering Committee. We were fortunate to find a manager who was a very competent administrator, but she did not have the formal credentials expected by some of the team members and our contract partners. We felt consistent pressure from those funders (especially government) to move to a business model of organization, complete with business and strategic plans. When we received a relatively lucrative contract in 1997, we hired a post-graduate director in an attempt to structure the project in this more formal manner. The approach soon failed, however, since our funders did not provide the consistent and adequate funding required. It was during this time that government policy shifted to exclude "core funding" support while the general resources for rural research declined. We moved back to a model in which the manager was hired for her administrative skills rather than research experience and interest.

In spite of these challenges, we were able to identify most of the key changes that occurred within rural Canada and to direct our attention to the important role of local social services for the revitalization of rural communities within those changes. Our study on voluntary associations, for example, revealed the way in which these associations were often stressed as state services withdrew and populations declined (Bruce, Jordan, and Halseth 1999). It also highlighted the key role of social cohesion for rural communities. This served as the basis for our next cycle of funding.

In 1999 we applied for and received three-year funding from the Social Sciences and Humanities Research Council (SSHRC) to study social cohesion in rural Canada (http://nre.concordia.ca/__ftp2004/reports/SoCoFinalProposal2SSHRC.pdf). This was a significant change in our situation since it meant that more of our effort could be directed to the research agenda rather than fund-raising and administration. It was during this period that we were able to design and conduct our household survey in about 2,000 households from 20 of our field sites. This face-to-face survey provided us with information regarding the organization of the household, employment, social support, social cohesion, community integration, informal economy activities, and a number of perceptions regarding the community and local governance. We also developed and updated the Site Profile study originally conducted in 1998.

Our study of social cohesion in rural Canada reinforced our view of the importance of social relations and laid the basis for a dynamic model of the process by which local assets are reorganized into valued outcomes (Reimer and Tachikawa 2008). A central feature of this model was the identification of four types of normative structures that are likely to guide that process (Reimer et al. 2008). Our attention, therefore, turned to examine the ways in which the local assets, the social processes, and the community context affected the capacity of rural communities to successfully meet the changing conditions.

It was also during this period that I learned three important lessons regarding the administration of large-scale projects such as the NRE. The first was the value of a liaison officer. This person's primary role was to make regular, informal, and pleasant contact with all the members of the team. A phone call a month, a short e-mail, or a visit at one of our events were the most common ways in which the liaison officer created opportunities to learn about project collaborators' progress, the challenges they faced (both with respect to the research and other aspects of their lives), the insights they had gained, and their plans for the next few months. This information allowed us to anticipate problems, identify opportunities, and reorganize the workloads among participants to manage the surprises and competing demands that are part of any such project.

The second lesson emerged as the result of our attempts to implement a business model for the project. I began to realize that a more appropriate vision for the NRE was that of a voluntary organization. Except for the few staff members, most of the participants were volunteers, and their commitment, therefore, was contingent upon their personal values and goals, the support we could offer for the achievement of those goals, the nature of competing demands in their lives, and the personal commitments they built up among the network itself. Each of the core researchers, for example, was paid by their institutions for activities that often competed with ours. Finding and supporting ways in which the activities of the NRE could contribute to their institutional obligations, therefore, became a necessary element of the project administration. We were fortunate because we had a sufficiently large critical mass, so could manage informal arrangements to facilitate this. Since most of the liaison work with the field sites, preparing popular media materials, and policy deliberations were not recognized by our universities, the more senior members of the team (those with tenure) made an informal agreement with the junior members. Senior researchers agreed to manage the liaison work if the junior researchers would concentrate on publishing more academic materials.

The third lesson developed when I adjusted my framework to see the NRE as a volunteer organization. This extended to the staff as well, since most of them were students, with their own set of competing demands. In order to accommodate those demands—as well as manage the continual requirement for training—I instituted a buddy system for each task. Under this system, we identified a "point person" for the task along with a "backup person." The backup person's job was to keep informed about the nature of the task and the progress of the point person, helping them along the way, and stepping in when a paper, exam, ski trip, or sickness drew them away. Each backup person was in turn a point person for some other task with backup support as well.

This system had a number of surprising advantages. It meant that the level of communication among the team increased considerably. Each team member became more familiar with the work of others and was able to make useful contributions to the task. It also meant that the level of innovation and problem-solving ability increased since at least two people were engaged with the challenges involved. Most surprising, it also meant that the demands on me and my time as director significantly decreased. With only one person responsible for a task, they would come to me when issues arose—even relatively insignificant ones since they were often in an early stage of their own learning. With two, however, they would work out the issues between them, building their confidence along the way and generally coming to a reasonable decision. I soon made it a practice to split any funds I had among two or more students rather than hire one alone.

In 2002 the fortune of the NRE changed significantly. We applied for and received $3 million, four-year funding under the Initiative on the New Economy established by SSHRC and Industry Canada. Entitled Building Rural Capacity in the New Economy, this project allowed us to expand our investigation in capacity-building processes and opportunities in the rural context. Continuing our focus on the social dynamics of rural places, this research investigated the special role of social capital for rural revitalization. One feature of this work was the identification and analysis of innovations in service delivery, governance, communications, and resource management (Reimer 2006). The project also allowed us to continue the Site Profile data collection, conduct a number of specific projects relating to the topic, and gather national data regarding environmental values among all Canadians (Beckley et al. 2005; Teitelbaum and Beckley 2006; Huddart-Kennedy et al. 2009).

As the INE money ran out we began to consider our options for the future of the NRE. Do we begin another round of applications for funds, do we look for contracts, or do we close down the project and move to other objectives? We had largely achieved the dreams of Ambitious I and II. Not only had we contributed significantly to the description, analysis, and policy context of rural Canada, but we had built the capacity of a number of rural and northern research centers in the country. We felt we were in a position where these centers could continue on their own so long as we remained connected. The CRRF network and activities would ensure this communication would last. We archived our website (http://nre.concordia.ca) and prepared our data for more public use.

The relationships and network we built over the 11 years of the NRE project have not disappeared. We have continued exchanges with our Japanese partners when opportunities permit, we continue to use the data and materials for ongoing research, and we maintain our relationships with the field sites in new and sometimes surprising ways. When the Fukushima nuclear power plant disaster shut down one of the towns with which we collaborated, Canadian community members who had visited the site offered assistance and sought information at each stage of the process (http://crrf-japan.blogspot.ca/). When my Australian colleague planned a cross-Canada bicycle trip to investigate community capacity I was able to include several of our sites on his voyage—allowing him to interview and record his visits with mayors and councillors along the way (http://canadothis.com/; http://visual journeyacrosscanada.com/).

This last cycle of the NRE project also led us to realize the importance of rural and urban relations for the revitalization of rural Canada (Reimer 2010). The urbanization of Canada has meant the dominance of urban concerns. This will most likely continue into the future. The future of rural Canada, therefore, will depend on establishing strong alliances with urban places. To this end, our research agenda should consider the extent and nature of interdependencies between rural and urban places. Food quality, water, environmental amenities, and energy are four of the obvious issues around which rural and urban alliances may form. Additional research needs to be conducted that would make visible the many ways in which rural resources and activities contribute to the sustenance of urban places. This would include an expansion of our work regarding the values held by both rural and urban people. The details of this research direction are only now being developed within our network. The direction we take depends to a large extent on the opportunities that emerge.

Rural Sociology

With the increasing urbanization of Canadian society, the visibility of rural sociology is likely to decline (Reimer and Bollman 2010). This is especially the case in Canada since we do not have the institutional legacy of the Land Grant University system or the policies that target rural places (often with funds attached). Canadian rural studies are usually found in Extension Schools, Agricultural Colleges, and Agricultural-Economics, Regional Planning, or Geography Departments (Hay and Basran 1992). Except for Québec, most of our rural-related policies are sectoral, social, and municipal. Federally, the focus on rural issues and associated multi-departmental deliberations has disappeared with the demise of the Rural Secretariat of Agriculture and Agri-Food Canada. The rural objects of study, however, will continue to be important. Food, water, resource extraction, transformation, and trade, the natural environment, recreation, energy, climate change, and community change will remain important, not only for rural and remote places, but for urban sustenance and sustainability as well. We will continue to need the sociologists, geographers, economists, engineers, and other researchers who investigate these issues, but considerable challenges remain for encouraging and facilitating the collaboration among them (Reimer 2010; Reimer and Brett 2013).

Rural Sociology will continue to play an important and useful role in the academic and policy spheres, I expect, but most likely in modified forms. It has the advantage of a tradition in place-based visions and analyses of social and economic life that remain salient in the age of globalization (Halseth, Markey, and Bruce 2010). It provides valuable insights regarding the way in which identity, distance, and density interact to make local places more than the conjuncture of specific characteristics and it has contributed an important set of tools to better understand the dynamics of communities (Flora, Flora, and Fey 2003). The shifting demography of rural and urban places is unlikely to undermine this legacy since places continue to provide the venues and infrastructure for important political action, and in many cases remain the objects of our economic and social policy (Bradford 2005).

Rural Sociologists will be well advised to move outside their comfort zone, however. The usual focus on rural society and economy as relatively distinct is unlikely to survive as either a question or an answer. Just as agriculture, forestry, or aquaculture curriculums have had to expand into health, engineering, management, and trade, so too must we learn about climate change, political science, communication technology, and health to adequately understand the dynamics of rural society. It may mean learning the basics of these topics ourselves or it may mean recruiting students with the background in these disciplines in our teaching and research endeavours. In any case, it means redefining the nature of Rural Sociology to make the case for its relevance to others. It means, for example, demonstrating to a student concerned with food quality how the social or economic conditions of rural producers and processors are relevant to those concerns. It is not necessary to make Rural Sociologists of them, but it is necessary to facilitate the exchange of insights in both directions.

As I enter my retirement years I have fewer opportunities to write "Rural Sociologist" beside my name. I have become more comfortable with the label, however, since I realize the many ways in which my interests in the natural sciences, humanities, methodologies, communities, and inequality have merged in my analysis of rural places and spaces. I have also enjoyed the sustained and inspiring support of those who have flown with me on this rural flight. In some cases I have taken the lead, but most of my time has been spent enjoying the upwash of those flying alongside, whether they be Rural Sociologists, Economists, Geographers, Health Scientists, policy-makers, or rural citizens. We still don't know where we are going, but I am convinced that the path is right. Rural matters, urban matters, and, most of all, the interdependence among rural and urban places matters. Understanding the dynamics of that interdependence, therefore, is a worthwhile preoccupation for research, analysis, insights, and ambitious dreams.

Note

1. I wish to thank Lisa Roy and Anna Woodrow who assembled many of the background documents and descriptions that have served to remind me of the NRE project details.

Reference

Apedaile, Leonard P., and Bill Reimer. 1996. *Towards a Whole Rural Policy for Canada*, edited by Agriculture and Rural Restructuring Group. Ottawa: Senate and House Committee on Natural Resources.

Apedaile, Leonard P. and Nobuhiro Tsuboi, Eds. 2008. *Revitalization: Fate and Choice*. Brandon University: Rural Development Institute.

Beckley, Thomas M., Emily Huddart, Solange Nadeau, and Bonita MacFarlane. 2005. *Environmental Attitudes and Behaviour in Canada: Common Ground or a Rural–Urban Divide?* Montreal: New Rural Economy Project, Concordia University.

Bradford, Neil. 2005. *Place-Based Public Policy: Towards a New Urban and Community Agenda for Canada*. Ottawa: CPRN.

Bruce, David, Paul Jordan, and Greg Halseth. 1999. *Voluntary Organizations in Rural Canada: Impacts of changing availability of operational and program funding*. Montreal: New Rural Economy Project, Concordia University.

Flora, Cornelia Bulter, Jan Flora, and Susan Fey. 2003. *Rural Communities: Legacy and Change*. Vol. 2. Boulder, CO: Westview Press.

Foddy, William Henry. 1972. The Formation of Cliques in Collectivities as a Consequence of Initial Distributions of Dimensions of Wealth. https://circle.ubc.ca/handle/2429/41221. Accessed July 15, 2014.

Halseth, Greg, Sean Markey, and David Bruce. 2010. *The Next Rural Economies: Constructing Rural Place in Global Economies*. Cambridge, MA: CAB International.

Hay, David, and Gurcham S. Basran. 1992. *Rural Sociology in Canada*. Toronto: Oxford University Press.

Huddart-Kennedy, Emily, Thomas M. Beckley, Bonita L. McFarlane, and Solange Nadeau. 2009. "Rural-Urban Differences in Environmental Concern in Canada." *Rural Sociology* 74 (3):309–329.

Meissner, Martin. 1971. "The Long Arm of the Job: A Study of Work and Leisure." *Industrial Relations: A Journal of Economy and Society* 10 (3):239–260.

Mitchell, Andy. 1997. "Think Rural!" Ottawa: House of Commons.

Reimer, Bill. 1984. "Farm Mechanization: The Impact on Labour at the Level of the Household." *The Canadian Journal of Sociology* 9 (4):429–443.

Reimer, Bill. 1995. *A Sampling Frame for Non-Metropolitan Communities in Canada*. The Canadian Rural Restructuring Foundation, available at http://nre.concordia.ca. Accessed August 15, 2014.

Reimer, Bill. 1997. "Understanding The New Rural Economy: Choices and Options." Montreal: New Rural Economy Project, Concordia University.

Reimer, Bill. 2002. "A Sample Frame for Rural Canada: Design and Evaluation." *Regional Studies* 36 (8):845–859.

Reimer, Bill. 2006. "The New Rural Economy." *Journal of Rural and Community Development* 1 (2):50–185.

Reimer, Bill. 2010. "Rural–Urban Interdependence as an Opportunity for Rural Revitalization," pp.10–21 in *The Rural-Urban Fringe in Canada: Conflict and Controversy*, edited by K. B. Beesley. Brandon University: Rural Development Institute.

Reimer, Bill and Ray D. Bollman. 2010. "Understanding Rural Canada: Implications for Rural Development Policy and Rural Planning Policy," pp. 10–52 in *Rural Planning and Development in Canada*, edited by D. J. A. Douglas. Toronto: Nelson Education.

Reimer, Bill and Matthew Brett. 2013. "Scientific Knowledge and Rural Policy: A Long Distance Relationship." *Sociologia Ruralis* 53 (3):272–290.

Reimer, Bill and Masashi Tachikawa. 2008. "Capacity and Social Capital in Rural Communities," p. 15 in *Revitalization: Fate and Choice*, edited by P. Apedaile and N. Tsuboi. Brandon: Rural Development Institute.

Reimer, Bill, Tara Lyons, Nelson Ferguson, and Geraldina Polanco. 2008. "Social Capital as Social Relations: The Contribution of Normative Structures." *The Sociological Review* 56 (2):256–274

Shaver, Frances M. 1982. "Social Science Research on Women in Agriculture: The State of the Art." *Resources for Feminist Research* XI (1):3–4.

Shaver, Frances M. 1987. *Le Travail Des Femmes À La Suite Des Transformations de La Production Agricole: 1940–1980*. These de Philosophiae Doctor, Département de Sociologie, Université de Montréal.

Stinchcombe, Arthur L. 1965. *Rebellion in a High School*. Edited by Quadrangle. Chicago.
Teitelbaum, Sara, and Thomas M. Beckley. 2006. "Harvested, Hunted, and Home Grown: A National Overview of Self-Provisioning in Rural Canada." *Journal of Rural and Community Development* 1 (2; Special Issue: The New Rural Economy).

Contributors

Johannes Iemke (Hans) Bakker
Department of Sociology and Anthropology
University of Guelph
Guelph, Ontario N1G 2W1
Canada

Conner Bailey
Department of Agricultural Economics and Rural Sociology
Auburn University
Auburn, AL 36849
USA

Ralph B. Brown
Department of Sociology
Brigham Young University
Provo, UT 84602
USA

Lawrence (Larry) Busch
Department of Sociology
Michigan State University
East Lansing, MI 48824
USA

Cornelia Butler Flora
Department of Sociology
Iowa State University
Ames, IA 50010
USA

Jan L. Flora
Department of Sociology
Iowa State University
Ames, IA 50010
USA

Linda Lobao
School of Environment and Natural Resources
The Ohio State University
Columbus, OH 43210
USA

William (Bill) Reimer
Department of Sociology and Anthropology
Concordia University
Montréal, Quebec H3G 1M8
Canada

Michael D. Schulman
Department of Youth, Family, and Community Sciences
North Carolina State University
Raleigh, NC 27695
USA

Stephen Turner
Department of Philosophy
University of South Florida
Tampa, FL 33620
USA

Anthony (Tony) Winson
Department of Sociology and Anthropology
University of Guelph
Guelph, Ontario N1G 2W1
Canada

Julie N. Zimmerman
Department of Community and Leadership Development
University of Kentucky
Lexington, KY 40546
USA

INDEX

academic research value to sociology 114
access to fisheries 150–152
activist environmental groups 112, 161, 166, 167
administration of research projects 183, 184
advocacy coalitions 129
Africa 81–82
Agrarian Myth 148
agrarian reform 49, 87, 91; *see also* social reform movements
agricultural technology impacts 178
Agriculture and Rural Restructuring Group (ARRG), Canada 178–179
agro-industrial complexes 97–99
AI *see* Appreciative Inquiry
Alabama, USA 162–167
Alexander, Frank, D. 23, 40–41
Ambitious I/II research programs 180–181, 186
American Sociological Association (ASA) 36, 43–48
anti-war activity 120–121, 130
Appreciative Inquiry (AI) 133–134

aquaculture 160, 161
Archibald, Peter 83–84
ARRG *see* Agriculture and Rural Restructuring Group
ASA *see* American Sociological Association
asset-based approach to community development 133–134

BAE *see* Bureau of Agricultural Engineering
Bernard, Luther Lee 46–47
buddy system for research projects 185–186
Building Rural Capacity in the New Economy project, Canada 186
built capital 132
Bureau of Agricultural Engineering (BAE) 41–42
burnout avoidance 155–170
Busch, Lawrence 3–7

Canada 81–103, 171–189
Canadian Rural Revitalization Foundation (CRRF) 178–180

INDEX

capitalism 88, 92–93, 105, 109, 110–111, 115
CCF *see* Community Capitals Framework
charitable organizations 11–13
chemical pollution 162–165, 167
Chemical Waste Management Inc. (CWM) 163–165
church surveys 21, 121
churches 12, 14–15, 21, 121, 145
cities: migration from rural areas 4, 14–15; urban–rural relationships 3–5, 187, 189
Clarksdale, Mississippi 23–24
class issues 82, 92, 105, 106–107, 110
Coahoma County, Mississippi 23–24, 39–41, 42
collective agency concept 130
College of Agriculture, Missouri 19, 26–30
communication 21, 185
Community Capitals Framework (CCF) 128–134
community, ideas and research 20, 22, 24–25
community development 9, 128–134
computer technology 174–175
Contingent Work, Disrupted Lives; Labour and the Community in the New Rural Economy (Winson/Leach 2002) 101
Cornell University 16–17, 23, 36, 120–123, 157–158
Costa Rica 88–89, 93, 126–127
Country Life Commission 10, 12, 147–148
court cases 111–112, 114
CRRF *see* Canadian Rural Revitalization Foundation
Cuba 95
cultural capital 131
Cultural Reconnaissance surveys, USA 23–24, 40–41
CWM *see* Chemical Waste Management Inc.

diet and nutrition 101–102
Division of Farm Population and Rural Life, USDA/BAE 36–42

Dogwood Alliance 167
Duncan, O.D. 43, 44–45, 50

economist–rural sociologist relationships 114
Entrepreneurial Social Infrastructure (ESI) 127–129
environmental issues 4, 30, 95, 131, 135, 161–167
epidemiology–sociology relationship 74
ESI *see* Entrepreneurial Social Infrastructure
estate economies 88, 93
ethnic issues 83; *see also* racial issues
expert witnesses 111–112, 114
export-led development effects on local communities 159, 160
extension programs 21

Faupal, Chuck 163–165
financial capital 132, 133
first generation rural sociologists, USA 15–16
fisheries: Mississippi waterways 149–152; Southeast Asia coasts 158–161
Flora, Cornelia Butler and Jan L. 117–142
"folk depletion" *see* migration to cities
food and nutrition 101–102
food-processing–farming complex, Canada 97–99
Ford Foundation 123–127
Forest Service of USDA 129, 134
forestry 166–167
future of Rural Sociology 188

Galpin, Charles J. 13, 15, 20, 24–25, 29
gender issues: Latin America 124–126, 128; Mississippi fisheries 149–152; occupational hazards and injuries 73–74; Pentecostalism 121–122; RSS 39; Women's studies 122–123
geography of inequality 112–113
Goldschmidt, Walter/hypothesis 42, 110, 113, 130

INDEX

Gomillion, Charles 38–39
government influences 113, 134–135

Halifax, Canada 93–94
hazardous wastes 162–165
hazards and injuries at work 72–74
health and safety 72–74
healthy eating 101–102
heir property 167–168
household survey 71, 184
human capital 131
Human Community (Hassinger and Pinkerton 1986) 24–25

The Industrial Diet; The Degradation of Food and the Struggle for Healthy Eating (Winson 2013) 102
industrial relations/unions 70–71, 76
industrial scale fishing versus small scale fishing 159
industrialization of agriculture 109, 110, 111–112
industry: deskilling 106; political economics of food 101–102; relationship with rural communities 3–4, 97–101
injuries, occupational health and safety 72–74
input producers' influence 3
insurgencies 88, 89–90, 126–127
integration of newcomers 177–178
international donor effects on local communities 159, 160
The Intimate Commodity; Food and the Development of the Agro-Industrial Complex in Canada (Winson 1993) 99

justice: court cases 111–112, 114; environmental justice 161–167; social justice 117, 122, 155–156, 159, 168, 169

Kannapolis, North Carolina 70–71
Kansas rural communities 127

landfill dumping of chemicals 162–165
land ownership: access to fisheries 150–151; inequality in Latin America 87–88, 89, 92–93, 126–127; inheritance 167–168
Larson, Olaf F. 36–37, 42, 45
Latin America 85–96, 107, 119, 121, 123–127
Lenin, Vladimir 88, 93
Lively, C. E. 18, 28, 29

Malaysia 158–159
mangrove forests 160
marine fisheries in Southeast Asia 158–161
market forces 22–23, 134–135
Marxist influences 83, 84, 93, 109, 115
migration to cities 4, 14–15
Mississippi 149–152
Mississippi Wildlife, Fisheries and Parks (MWFP) 149, 150–152
Missouri 17–29
moral foundations of life 148
Morgan E. L. 17–18
Mormonism 143, 145
Murmis, Miguel 85–87
MWFP *see* Mississippi Wildlife, Fisheries and Parks

natural capital 130, 131
natural resource over-exploitation 159, 160, 167
New Rural Economy (NRE) project, Canada 180–187
Nicaragua 88, 89–93, 94–95, 100, 102, 126
North Carolina State University 68–72
NRE *see* New Rural Economy
nutrition 101–102

occupational hazards and injuries 72–74
Ogburn, William F. 46–47
output processing industry influence 3–4, 97–101

paternalism 71
Pentecostalism 121–122

Phelan, John 13–14
policy-orientated sociology 114
political activism 117–135, 155–169
political capital 132
political economics: agriculture and industry 110–111; development 93; food 101–102
political sociology 67–68
pond fishing 150, 152
poverty: agrarian change 88; forestry relationship 166–167
productivity of work 145, 146
progressivism/progressive movement 12, 14
Protestant work ethic 143, 145
Prussian path of agrarian development 93
public access fisheries 150–152
public health 72–74
pulp and paper industry 167

quantification in rural sociology 147
Quebec 176–177

racial issues: Africa 82; Alabama 162–168; Coahoma County, Mississippi 23–24, 39–41; hazardous waste dumping 162–165; land inheritance 167–168; Mississippi fisheries 149–152; North Carolina 69–70; occupational hazards and injuries 73–74; RSS conferences 38–39; segregation of rural sociologists 38–39
Readings in Rural Sociology (Phelan, J 1920) 13–14
recreational fishers versus subsistence fishers 149–150
recycled paper 167
reform 10, 11–15, 21, 49, 87, 91
research funding 30
reservoir fisheries 149, 150–152
Rhodesia *see* Zimbabwe
Roanoke Rapids, North Carolina 70
RSS *see* Rural Sociological Society
Runyan, Carol 72–73
Rural Observatory, Canada 181–182

Rural Sociological Society (RSS): origins 43–45, 47; presidents 36, 45, 75–76, 113, 123; *Rural Sociology* journal 74–75; segregation at conferences 38–39

safety at work 72–74
Sanderson, Dwight 16
school surveys 174–175
Schulman, Michael D. 65–79
scientific application 12, 148–149
seafood industry 159–161
second generation rural sociologists, USA 17
segregation 23–24, 38–39, 82–83
social capital 70–71, 129, 132–133, 135, 186
social cohesion study 183–184
social justice 117, 122, 155–156, 159, 168, 169
social organization 173
social reform movements 10, 11–15, 21, *see also* agrarian reform
social relationships 150, 151
Social Sciences and Humanities Research Council (SSHRC), Canada 91, 94, 95, 96, 100, 102, 183, 186
Social Survey movement 9–10, 12–13, 147
sociology–rural sociology divide 11, 16, 26–28, 43–48, 146–147, 163–164
spatial inequality 112–113
SSHRC *see* Social Sciences and Humanities Research Council
standards 6
stories and biographies importance 35–61
subnational scale inequality 113
subsistence activities 149–152, 160
Sumter County, Alabama 162–165
surveys: churches 21, 121; computer use 175; Cultural Reconnaissance 23–24, 40–41; farm workplace hazards 73; prohibition 24, 41; rural life 71, 184; schools 174–175; Social Survey movement 9–10, 12–13, 147
sustainability 129, 130–131, 134

INDEX

Taylor, Carl 44, 45–46, 47, 68
technology: changing 4, 71, 177, 178; fishing 150–151, 157, 159; impacts on social relations 173
technology treadmill 4
teen occupational hazards and injuries 72–74
textile communities 70–71
theories in rural sociology 66, 109, 127, 129, 134, 147
tobacco farming 69, 70
tools 143–146, 152
tourism 95
trades unions 70–71, 76
trawlers 159
trust in social relationships 132, 150, 151
Turner, Stephen 9–33

unions 70–71, 76
United States Department of Agriculture (USDA): Bureau of Agricultural Engineering 41–42; Division of Farm Population and Rural Life 36–42; Forest Service 129, 134; relationship with rural sociology 16, 22, 24; restrictions on research 24, 41–42; Rural Development program 166–167
Universities, US history 16–29
urban–rural relationships 3–5, 187, 189
USDA *see* United States Department of Agriculture

value conflicts 22–23

war 89–95, 120, 126
Weber, Max 10, 15, 93, 145
Wimberley, Ron 108–109, 110, 111
Winson, Anthony 81–103
Wisconsin, USA 66–67
witnesses in court cases 111–112, 114

Yalobusha River system, Mississippi 149–152
young people, occupational hazards and injuries 72–74

Zimbabwe 81–82
Zimmerman, Julie N. 35–61

eBooks from Taylor & Francis

Helping you to choose the right eBooks for your Library

Add to your library's digital collection today with Taylor & Francis eBooks. We have over 50,000 eBooks in the Humanities, Social Sciences, Behavioural Sciences, Built Environment and Law, from leading imprints, including Routledge, Focal Press and Psychology Press.

Choose from a range of subject packages or create your own!

Benefits for you
- Free MARC records
- COUNTER-compliant usage statistics
- Flexible purchase and pricing options
- All titles DRM-free.

Benefits for your user
- Off-site, anytime access via Athens or referring URL
- Print or copy pages or chapters
- Full content search
- Bookmark, highlight and annotate text
- Access to thousands of pages of quality research at the click of a button.

Free Trials Available
We offer free trials to qualifying academic, corporate and government customers.

eCollections

Choose from over 30 subject eCollections, including:

Archaeology	Language Learning
Architecture	Law
Asian Studies	Literature
Business & Management	Media & Communication
Classical Studies	Middle East Studies
Construction	Music
Creative & Media Arts	Philosophy
Criminology & Criminal Justice	Planning
Economics	Politics
Education	Psychology & Mental Health
Energy	Religion
Engineering	Security
English Language & Linguistics	Social Work
Environment & Sustainability	Sociology
Geography	Sport
Health Studies	Theatre & Performance
History	Tourism, Hospitality & Events

For more information, pricing enquiries or to order a free trial, please contact your local sales team:
www.tandfebooks.com/page/sales

www.tandfebooks.com